MICHIGAN'S UPPER PENINSULA

Life, Legends & Landmarks
~Sonny Longtine~

©2002 Sunnyside Publications

All rights reserved. No part of this publication
may be reproduced or transmitted in any form or
by any means, electronic, or mechanical, including
photocopying, recording or any information storage
and retrieval system without permission in
writing from the publisher.

First edition published by:
Sunnyside Publications
1201 N. Front Street
Marquette, MI 49855

Printed in the United States of America

ISBN 0-9718089-0-2

LCCN 2002091346

Research, writing, photography	Sonny Longtine
Cover Design and Book Layout	Bob Koski, M. Tavernini & Assoc.
Illustration	Dawn Reynolds
	Kelly Dorcy
	Patricia Gimse
Photography	(See Photography Credits)
Printing	Signature Press Inc.

TABLE OF CONTENTS

Life

Legends

Landmarks

Photography Credits

Bibliography

- Burt, John S. *They Left Their Mark*. Rancho Cordova, Calif.: Landmark Enterprises, 1985.
- Clarke, James W. *American Assassins*. Princeton, N.J.: Princeton University Press, 1982.
- Dodge, R. L. *Michigan Ghost Towns*. Sterling Heights, Michigan: Glendon Publications, 1970.
- Doyle, Earl L. *The History of Pequaming*. Ontonagon, Michigan: The Ontonagon Historical Society, 1999.
- Dunbar, Frederick Willis. *Michigan: A History of the Wolverine State*. Grand Rapids, Michigan: William B. Erdmans Publishing Company, 1985.
- Magnaghi, Russell M. *The Way It Happened*. Iron Mountain, Michigan: Mid Peninsula Library Cooperative, 1982.
- The Mid Peninsula Library Federation. *The Upper Peninsula: A Miscellany*. Iron Mountain, Michigan, 1974.
- Rich, Ben R. and Janos, Leo. *Skunk Works*. Boston, New York, Toronto, London: Little Brown and Company, 1994.
- Stanley, Jerry. *Big Annie of Calumet*. New York, New York: Crown Publishers, Inc., 1996.
- Thurner, Arthur W. *Rebels on the Range*. Hancock, Michigan: Book Concern Printers, 1984.
- Vinette, Dale. *Deep Water Man*. Milwaukee, Wisconsin: Network Printers, 1999.

To My Children:

Christopher, Shawn
& Heather

PREFACE

As I traveled the Upper Peninsula, I trod in the footsteps of the Ojibwa, the early French fur traders, miners, immigrants and their ancestors. This earth had sanctity; it was hallowed ground and I was following in their footsteps, telling some of their stories.

For three years I immersed myself in researching and writing about the Upper Peninsula; this experience expanded my awareness on the vastness and wealth of the land. Above all, it provided me with a deeper understanding of the humanity of its people.

This book is a tapestry, a book of many hues that draws its narrations from the history, culture, sites, people and events in the Upper Peninsula. It is not a finite document but a microcosm of the Peninsula. *Life, Legends and Landmarks* weaves a story through a series of vignettes that hopefully provide the reader with a more intimate connection to the Upper Peninsula.

The narration is laced with hyperbole, unabashed glowing commentary, unfettered accolades, and a host of dialogue praising and extolling the virtues of the Upper Peninsula. For this, I offer no apology. If this aggrandizement appears thickly layered – then so be it. I delighted in writing this book – on my terms.

It was a challenging task to write a book that would capture the essence and spirit of the Upper Peninsula. It felt, at times, an impossible task, there was just too much. It would take volumes to do what I was attempting to do in one book. As a result, I selected what I felt most readers would enjoy. The number of stories and tales that can be written about the Peninsula is limitless, the only constraint being that of the writer's vision.

If the reader finds these narratives informative, interesting and in some cases a bit playful, then I have succeeded.

Some may feel slighted because their community was not represented in this book; to include all was impossible. This unfinished task, I leave to others – to chronicle the rich history of the Upper Peninsula.

In October of 2001, my oldest sister Lois was diagnosed with a terminal illness; she had but a short time to live. During her last two months when she was often bed-ridden, I shared with her excerpts from my book. She delighted in the short pieces that I read to her every week; her eyes danced with curiosity whenever I read her a story that particularly piqued her interest. There was a connection we shared in those moments; a brief period of time when we wandered down a path together, gaining a deeper feeling for each other and the land we called home. I shall not forget her.

Above all, I hope you receive as much pleasure from reading this book as I did writing it. Friends and colleagues were surprised at my patience in rooting out obscure stories in remote places. They didn't realize how delightful I found it to uncover charming tales and interesting events. I always wondered what nugget I would find on my next excursion. Creating *Michigan's Upper Peninsula: Life, Legends and Landmarks* was not work – it was a journey of joy.

Sonny Longtine
May, 2002

ACKNOWLEDGEMENTS

For the most part, writing is a solitary task. There are however, those that you must enlist for their expertise.

Laverne Chappell, my good friend and writing colleague, was one that I enlisted to edit and proofread the manuscript. Her skills were most appreciated, as were Becky Tavernini's and Sarah Harnett's final proofing during the book layout.

Dawn Reynolds provided the delightful sketches that give the book an added richness. Her dedication to the task was most appreciated.

Again, Jack Deo at Superior View provided me with just the right historic photographs and, quite often, on a last-minute notice. He has my gratitude for his quick responses to my urgent calls.

I am most appreciative of the efforts of Bob Koski, of M. Tavernini and Associates, for his amazing skill in attractively formatting the book and designing the striking cover. I asked Bob to design a cover that was simple, yet elegant; the great cover stands in testimony to his achieving this goal.

A special thanks to all my friends who encouraged me and asked me how my book was progressing. They were pleased that their friend was writing a book about the Upper Peninsula, a land they love and call home.

The following people also made a contribution, be it small or large, to make this book become a reality.

Wayne Autio
Sheila Bondsteel
Duane and Joan Bennett
Ralph Bietila
Susan Burack
Joe Buys
Tina Erickson
Emerson and Linda Fleury
Linda Gamble
Tom and Maureen Gardner
Doug Hamer
Scott Holman
Bill Jornes
Laluri LaBumbard
Brenda Lindquist
Russ Magnaghi
Janet Ogden
Carmen Paris
Brian Roell
Dwight "Bucko" Teeple
Robert Ubberlhode

HOW THE UPPER PENINSULA
BECAME A PART Of Michigan

*Michigan lost the territorial war with Ohio
and was awarded the Upper Peninsula
as compensation – a piece of land
they deemed worthless.*

Ironically, the Upper Peninsula was the loser's prize in a war – the "Toledo War." From the early 1800s to 1837, Michigan and Ohio were involved in a protracted confrontation over where the border should be between the two states: a "war" was the end result. It wasn't really a war; in fact it wasn't even a good scrimmage – more like backyard neighbors squabbling over where the fence should be that separates their property. It is the only war on record that didn't have casualties. The Upper Peninsula, although not directly involved in the scrimmage, would eventually be awarded to the loser of the border dispute, even though neither state knew at the time that the Upper Peninsula would be the defeated party's laurel wreath.

The southeast corner of Michigan and the northwest corner of Ohio, land adjacent to the Maumee River, were coveted by both Ohio and Michigan in the early 1830s. Ohio believed the Ohio Constitution of 1802 gave them rights to the 468 square miles located just south of the present Ohio/Michigan border. The small sliver of land is eight miles wide on the east and five miles wide on the west end, a piece of land of no particular significance other than it had the prized Maumee River on its southern edge. Michigan claimed the Northwest Ordinance of 1786 set the boundary and that Michigan owned the land up to and including the mouth of the Maumee River. Ohio desperately wanted the river in their state. A recently developed canal system in Ohio had to have the river to gain access to Lake Ontario. To the Ohioans it was a matter of significant economic importance, while they viewed Michigan's desire to have the territory as nothing more than a territorial land grab.

The problem had been brewing since 1802 but did not come to a head until 1833 when Michigan applied for statehood. In 1834, the Michigan Territory Council passed a resolution imposing a fine of $1,000 or five years of imprisonment for anyone except Michigan officials or federal officials to exercise legal functions in the disputed area. Governor Mason of Michigan organized a militia and became the enforcing agent of the resolution. Mason was a man of action; he proceeded to the "strip" in question with his militia and arrested nine Ohio surveyors. Mason dispersed the rest of the surveying party by firing shots over their heads as they retreated to safety. Tales of the "bloodthirsty" Michigan militia panicked and aroused the ire of the Ohio citizenry. The conflict had come of age.

President Andrew Jackson was upset over the border dispute. Jackson, like most presidents, wanted to settle the dispute in a way that would cost him minimally in the next presidential election. He responded with a quintessential government move: when in a quandary, appoint a commission to solve the problem – this is exactly what he did.

The Jackson Congressional Commission recommendation was to give the disputed land (Toledo Strip) to Ohio, and as compensation, give Michigan the Upper Peninsula. This recommendation took the form of a federal Congressional act that established statehood for Michigan in 1836. The act required Michigan hold a convention for the sole purpose of giving their consent to the statehood. After considerable wrangling and dissent, a state convention finally ratified the Federal Congressional Act and Michigan was admitted to the Union. It was a bitter pill to swallow by the Michigan delegation. The Upper Peninsula was unwanted by the state and was characterized as, "the sterile region on the shore of Lake Superior, destined by soil and climate to remain forever a wilderness." The *Free Press* called it "the region of perpetual snows..."

The Michigan Convention reluctantly agreed to the terms recognizing they had to approve the Congressional act to gain statehood. Even though the Michigan delegates felt they had been "had" in the land swap, they proceeded with ratification. One convention delegate did see some merit in Michigan obtaining the Upper Peninsula when he wryly stated, "The whitefish of Lake Superior might be a fair offset for the lost bull-frog pastures of the Maumee." Michigan became a state on January 26th, 1837.

As it turned out, Michigan won the war. The state – unknowing at the time – obtained some of the richest mineral deposits in the continental United States. Shortly after Michigan's statehood, copper was discovered in the Keweenaw Peninsula (1843) and iron ore was unearthed in Negaunee (1844). This resulted in untold millions of dollars in revenue for the state of Michigan. For the next hundred years, Michigan laughed all the way to the bank as they harvested the iron and copper from the rugged Upper Peninsula. These resources propelled Michigan in becoming an industrial leader in the Midwest.

The Upper Peninsula is now the crown jewel of Michigan's vast territory. When Michigan obtained the Upper Peninsula by default, they received a land of pristine beauty, a region abundant in mineral and lumber wealth and a people that are proud, industrious and hearty. Not bad for being the loser in a war.

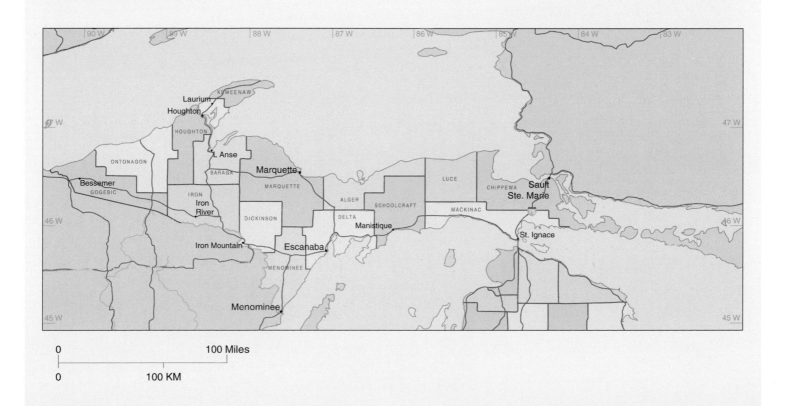

Life

THE YOOPERS' APOTHECARY

THE SAUNA

With firm thrusts, the willowy branches delivered their message with stinging accuracy, striking the tender flesh with relentless blows. Beading perspiration rolled off the crimson skin and fell in anguish to the floor, coagulating into a residue that bore witness to the beating.

Punishing blows came repeatedly – blow after blow – until the skin, sanguine from the repeated inflictions, glowed with an ominous foreboding. The whip-like action of the slender birch branches snapped unforgiving on the gelatinous torso, the mass of flesh jerking under the constant barrage of the battering boughs. The pulsating body sporadically emitted painful guttural sounds.

With the room temperature at an unbearable 200 degrees, the dehydrated, withering body, in a desperate act of self-preservation, jolted to the exit door of the inferno, only to enter another living hell – the outside in midwinter. Raw winter winds lashed at the unclad body, trudging shoeless, through mounds of hard-packed ice. Driving snow pierced the exposed skin with a biting exactness. Approaching the icy water of a nearby lake, the tortured soul plunged recklessly into the frigid waters, where the shock caused the frail frame to convulse and shudder.

Could this be an interrogation chamber of the KGB during the Cold War?

Or is it a depraved act of sadomasochism being played out in some dark sinister place?

None of the above!

This is life at the sauna (sow-naw), an ancient Finnish body cleansing practice, where birch boughs are applied to the

In Upper Michigan, with its rich Finnish heritage, nothing is more Yooper than a Saturday night sauna.

1

body (gently?) by you or a friend for the explicit purpose of encouraging blood circulation. In Finnish, this sauna act of pleasurable flagellation is known as "*vasta*," or "*vihta*." In addition to facilitating blood circulation, the sauna expels waste from the body.

The sauna, or steam bath, comes from Finland and was transported by early Finnish settlers to the Upper Peninsula. The Finnish sauna is not the only steam bath, though it is the most prevailing steam bath in the United States. The Turkish bath (*hamman*), and the Russian bath (*bania*), as well as the sweat lodge by Native Americans are other sauna-like experiences. Many cultures throughout the world have found the steam bath, or sauna, an efficient way to keep clean.

The first mention of a sauna appears in literature as early as 1113. At the time, it was little more than a primitive covered pit. Finnish literature bears witness to the importance of the sauna as an essential part of the culture: Fifteen of the fifty poems in the sweeping narrative, The *Kalevala*, address the sauna.

The sauna served as a maternity hospital for the Finnish people until the 19th century. It was a germ-free environment with plenty of water – ideal for a maternity setting. In addition, the sauna smoke contained tannic acid which sterilized the interior surfaces.

One of the many old-fashioned saunas located at camps across the Upper Peninsula.

The first recorded sauna in the United States was built by early settlers in the Delaware Valley in 1638. Finnish immigrants first erected saunas in Upper Michigan in the latter half of the 19th century as they settled in enclaves throughout the peninsula. The Finnish custom spread to other ethnic groups in the Upper Peninsula, and any "Yooper" considers the sauna native to the Upper Peninsula culture.

Today, saunas are found as outbuildings to camps as well as in the basements of ultra-modern homes. Many saunas have shed the image of the old cedar, free-standing dilapidated shanty, with a nearby cord of seasoned maple waiting patiently to stoke the sauna stove. In its place are elaborate, and spacious, buildings, replete with whirlpools, large changing rooms, and a state-of-the-art electric sauna stove.

For many, beer is a necessary additive to the camp sauna

experience. However, one should be cautious with alcohol in the sauna; it exacerbates dehydration that is already taking place in the 200-degree heat. To accompany the refreshments, sausages are put in aluminum bags and heated on top of the heater rocks.

The purists consider the smoke sauna the ultimate sauna. It is the most traditional and least-used type of sauna. Smoke from the stove is kept in the sauna until the last minute before the bathers enter; it is called "*savusauna*."

Many of today's Upper Peninsula city dwellers use electricity as the source of heat for the sauna. Purists scoff at these innovations as characterless and producing an unacceptable, dry heat. To the traditionalist, the old wood-fired stove is the only admissible heat source.

Char McDonnell brings firewood into her sauna on Deer Lake in Shelter Bay. The ultra-modern sauna is equipped with a hot-tub in the changing room.

The sauna has only a few basic procedures: first take a shower, and then enter the sauna with a sitting towel. Do not exceed a temperature of 200 degrees Fahrenheit. With a higher temperature, you run the risk of internally baking your organs, and becoming a hors d'ouevre for a hungry companion. Adjust the room temperature by throwing water on the heated rocks. This is not to be a competitive experience to see if one bather can "out-sauna" another by getting the room hotter than the earth's core. Finish the sauna by rinsing off. Put your clothes on only after you stop sweating.

It's a personal choice whether to bathe naked or partially (swimsuit) clothed. (There are probably some people you would choose not to bathe with naked.) However, clothed or unclothed, the sauna has an undeniable intimacy. The self-consciousness of sharing your most secret blemishes, and the extra 50 pounds of flesh wrapped around your waist will dissipate as you observe others in the sauna with physical infirmities that far exceed your minor flaws.

To many Upper Peninsulans, the sauna is the pre-eminent Finnish experience. It is the only Finnish word to have entered

Many sauna bathers claim the relaxation properties are equal to its health benefits. Enthusiasts also assert the olfactory delights of the sauna, claiming it permeates the air with the scent of fresh bread.

the world vocabulary. The sauna is not a luxury to the Finnish people; it is a part of life. Finland has more saunas than cars; over a million saunas dot the Nordic landscape – one sauna for every five citizens. The Finnish have transported their love of the sauna to the Upper Peninsula.

Russian Cosmonaut Gierman Titlor was the most famous person to ever die in a sauna. In September 2000, Gierman, the second man in space, departed for a loftier place in space when he perished in his sauna. Generally, it is safer in a sauna than circumnavigating the globe in a spacecraft.

In the United States, golf courses are used for negotiating business deals. In Finland, the sauna is the place where commercial negotiating often takes place. It may well be the Upper Peninsula is the only place where the sauna rivals the golf course as a place to consummate business. (A word of caution: it is not advisable to take your laptop to the sauna.)

The popularity of the sauna remains undiminished in the Upper Peninsula. An old Finnish proverb, "*Sauna on koha apteet,*" translated means, "The sauna is the poor man's apothecary." With the current price of prescription drugs, the advice given in this ancient aphorism should be given serious consideration. And, for a second opinion, just ask any Yooper Finn about the medical and health value of the sauna.

THE STAFF
Of Life

THE PASTY

A nutritional necessity.

Pasty – a Cornish meat, potato, and rutabaga pie.
Pastry – fancy baked goods, sweet rolls, cakes, etc.
Pastie – a small adhesive breast covering used by exotic dancers.

It is pronounced *pas-tee*, but non-natives (sometimes referred to as trolls) often confuse pastry or pastie with the edible pie. Upper Peninsulans find it amusing when an outsider orders a pasty. Frequently the unknowing visitor is perplexed by the chuckles he hears from those nearby. If ever there was a food that was considered native to the Upper Peninsula, it's the pasty. In the Upper Peninsula, the pasty – not bread – is the staff of life.

Forget the chateaubriand, the escargot and the caviar; all a native Upper Peninsulan needs for sustenance is a pasty. Throw in some cole slaw, a bread and butter pickle, a bottle of catsup and you have a meal fit for the discerning palate of any reigning king. (It is possible the king may not know this.)

This meat pie, long considered a staple in a "Yooper" diet, has its origin in the mining region of Cornwall, England, although the Finnish and other Upper Peninsula ethnic groups have proudly, but falsely, claimed it to be native to their ancestral country.

Contrary to popular pasty experts, the ingredients varied over the years.

In Cornwall there were mackerel, lammy (stillborn lambs) and leek pies; even one called the "starry-gazy" pie in which sardines were placed in a vertical position so the heads protruded through the top crust, thus able to watch their own immolation.

The variety of fillings were so varied that an old Cornish

> The devil is afraid of coming to Cornwall for fear of being baked in a pasty.

5

aphorism describes the concern about the ingredients of the pasty: "The Devil is afraid to come into Cornwall, for fear of being baked in a pasty."

The pasty was ideally suited for the Cornish miners; it was portable, easily reheatable, and a full course meal – all in one wrapping. The Cornish miners migrated to the Lake Superior region after the discovery of iron ore in the 1840s. The poor economic conditions in Cornwall compelled tens of thousands of its inhabitants to seek a better life in America. Known as "Cousin Jacks," the English transplants were experienced miners and fit in well with the burgeoning mining industry in the Upper Peninsula. With the miners came the pasty.

In the bleak dank of a Superior iron mine, 1,000 feet below the earth's surface, a pasty at lunch was a brief respite from the grueling labor in the black cavern that was the miner's home for 12 hours a day. The pasty was often wrapped in newspaper and kept in the miner's pocket until the lunch hour. The pie was then placed on his shovel and held over a lantern until warm; this provided the miner with enough sustenance to continue working for another six hours.

Frank Matthews, a Negaunee mining historian, (of Cornish ancestry, and now deceased) said there was only one way to eat a pasty: use no utensils; hold the pasty upright on end so the juices can drain down to the last bite. For Frank, this last bite was a delicacy.

Underground iron ore miners in the Marquette Range having a lunch break with the traditional pasty (circa 1950).

There does not appear to be any standard pasty recipe. Suet has largely given way to other shortenings while beef and pork are still the meat of choice; ground hamburger is a frequently used meat substitute.

Arguments still exist among purists whether the meat should be cubed or diced. Rutabagas or carrots? A personal choice, although purists insist on the rutabagas. Some chefs add parsley for additional flavor. The choice of the chef determines what the end product will be. Most "Yoopers" aren't that fussy, just give them a well-made pasty, regardless of the ingredients, and a large bottle of catsup – and they're ready for five-star dining.

THE CORNISH PASTY

CRUST RECIPE

3 cups of all purpose-flour
1 teaspoon of salt
1 cup minus one tablespoon of solid vegetable shortening

FILLING RECIPE

1/2 to 3/4 cup peeled, finely sliced potatoes
1/4 to 1/2 cup yellow turnips (rutabaga)
1/2 cup of flank steak/pork steak mixture,
cut into one inch strips
2 tablespoons of finely diced yellow onion
1 tablespoon of chopped fresh parsley
salt and pepper to taste
top with pat of butter

Mix the crust ingredients. Divide the crust dough into four balls. Roll out the crust into circles and fill each with 1/4 of the mixed filling. Moisten the edges of the pastry, lift the two sides to the top and pinch together. Using one hand to roll the pinched edges, use the other to twist and tuck the roll into a rope-like "Cornish Crimp." Cut off any excess dough from the ends, making sure the cut edges are sealed. Place the assembled pasties on an ungreased baking sheet.

Place in a pre-heated 425 degree Fahrenheit oven and bake for 10 minutes. Reduce the oven temperature to 375 degrees Fahrenheit and continue to bake for 45-50 minutes until golden brown. Remove from the oven and allow to sit for ten minutes before serving.

*yield: 4 pasties.

Other foods and food traditions are typically thought of as Upper Peninsulan: The Friday night fish fry is a U.P. custom and is evident in most communities on any given weekend. Local VFW posts and churches are the largest promoters of the Friday fish fry. Reaping Chassell strawberries in July and blueberry picking on the Sands Plains in August are a must for many U.P. families. Cinnamon toast, a Finnish product from the Trenary Home Bakery, and cudighi from Geno's Italian Delicatessen are other foods with a strong Upper Peninsula tie.

One of the many signs on Upper Peninsula highways that advertise the area's most famous food.

In spite of other U.P. foods and food traditions, the pasty still reigns supreme; the most noted and most consumed Upper Peninsulan ethnic food.

Pass the catsup, please.

Many folk tales have evolved around the pasty. One of the more delightful reminiscences about the pasty is the story about Jenny Philips, who tried to stretch her food budget by scrimping on the beef and the pork for her husband s pasties. His instant response upon returning home was, "Jenny, let s be having a little more mayt in me pasty and not so much turmit and tatey — me stummick s no bloody root cellar, y know."

SEVENTY-THREE DIE
In False Alarm Fire

THE ITALIAN HALL DISASTER

The local church was lined with white coffins – most of them children's coffins.

All that remains of the Italian Hall is this brick and sandstone archway that commemorates the great disaster.

Five hundred children gayfully pranced about, their eyes dancing with delight and reflecting a rainbow of colors from the lights on a nearby Christmas tree. The children on the second floor of the Italian Hall eagerly pressed forward toward the stage at one end of the room in anticipation of a gift from Santa, who was positioned prominently at the front of the stage. It was 1913, on a snowy Christmas Eve in Calumet, a thriving copper mining town in the Keweenaw Peninsula. For the children this was the best of times.

Then the unbelievable happened.
Someone yelled, "Fire!"

Within minutes, this gala Christmas celebration would turn deadly; seventy-three people would die, fifty-four of them children, crushed in a mass of humanity at the bottom of a staircase. Panic reigned in the Italian Hall as the alarmed adults and children quickly scurried to an exit that led down a staircase to the first floor. Once at the bottom of the staircase they could quickly exit to safety. When the frenzied crowd got to the bottom of the staircase, they discovered the doors opened inward. This not only prevented them from fleeing to safety, but also created an inescapable congestion at the bottom of the staircase.

As a result, this surging mass of humanity was pushed together at the bottom of the staircase without any outlet. In the ensuing melee, the terrified victims became stacked like cordwood – one on top of the other – at the bottom of the staircase, until the bodies bloated the entryway and the only sounds being heard were the crying and weeping of dying children.

The white caskets of the children, most between the ages of six to ten, who died in the catastrophe. Over half of the 73 deaths were children.

The catastrophe was for naught – there was no fire. No one knows for sure who falsely yelled "fire" that tragic Christmas Eve, but speculative blame placed the responsibility for the calamity on "strike breakers" from the local mining company. The miners had been on strike for five months with no end in sight. They felt this tragedy was the result of the mining company's attempt to coerce them back to work. This was never proven and the responsible party was never found out.

The gathering that evening was supposed to be a joyous celebration in the otherwise bleak and impoverished world of the local miners. The strike was finally settled on Easter Sunday 1914, some four months after the Italian Hall disaster. By then, it was too late for many of the hard working miners; over 2,000 left the Copper Country for Henry Ford's burgeoning car factories in the Detroit area. They were not only making

$2 an hour more, but also leaving behind the horrific memories of the fateful Christmas Eve.

The Italian Hall as it appeared prior to the 1913 calamity.

The day — December 24th, 1913 — will long be remembered as the time the rugged Keweenaw landscape wept.

The interior of the Italian Hall after the disaster in 1913.

DEATH IN A WATERY GRAVE

BARNES-HECKER MINE DISASTER

It hath often been said that it is not death but dying that is terrible.

Henry Fielding, Amelia

Fear rushed in and filled the empty, dark space around me. Eerily, I felt death was near, but didn t know why. I shouted to Jack Hanna and Joseph Mankee, "I think we better get out of here!"

A sudden strong rush of air startled me; it's force blew out my carbide lamp and sent me tumbling to the ground. The lights on the drift wall slowly dimmed, flickering briefly and then slowly gave into the pressing darkness. Within a few fleeting seconds my world went black – an intense black – not the slightest emission of light was to be seen. I could hear a low ominous rumble in the distance, the threatening sound reverberating off the cold iron walls. It scared the hell out of me. I was in the bowels of the earth, 800 feet below the surface surrounded by pitch black and feeling something was dreadfully wrong. My senses screamed at me – get out!

My heart began to race; a cold sweat enveloped me and sent chills throughout my body. I knew we had to immediately get out of this dank, entombing black hole. For whatever reason, I began to kick the train rails, knowing the track would lead me to the elevator shaft. This could be our only way out. Each tap of the boot on the steel rail faintly echoed in the dark chamber. Hanna and Mankee joined me in the blackened trek down the horizontal drift. We cautiously stumbled forward in the dark. In what seemed like an eternity, we finally made it to a ladder that descended to a pump-house below. My first thought was the pump-house could provide us refuge from whatever was happening. However, the tremendous air pressure and the din of the incessant rumbling compelled me to proceed to the main shaft that exited to the surface.

Finally reaching the shaft, where mud and rock were descending from above, I could see a small patch of light – barely visible – 800 feet straight up. The tiny speck of light was unable to penetrate the remote black hole. It seemed so far off. The only way to safety was to climb a ladder attached to the wall of the vertical shaft. In total blackness, we scurried to the ladder and began the long ascent up the precarious funnel, Hanna and Mankee right behind me.

While ascending the ladder, I heard a deafening roar far below in the belly of the shaft; this alarmed me even further, and with increased determination and fright, I climbed even faster. The cacophony increased with each passing second, until all I could hear was a deafening rumble inside of my head. An intolerable feeling of infinite terror swept through me. Continuing to move up the ladder at a furious pace, my gloved hands began slipping on the slimy rungs. With panicked ferocity, I tore at the gloves with my teeth, never stopping my ascent, finally extracting my hands from the gloves. Gripping the rungs was now somewhat easier.

Wilfred Wills, the lone survivor of the 1926 Barnes-Hecker Mine disaster. After the tragedy, Wills moved out of the area. He died in 1973.

Hanna and Mankee begin to lag behind. Thomas Kirby, one level up from where we started, unaware that something awful was occurring, joined our ascent. There were now four of us – trying to out-race what I thought was sure death.

The deep rumble emanating from somewhere in the cavity became louder and louder, until finally I could make out what the sound was – water, rushing water, surging up the shaft just below us. The turbulent swell of water spiraled up the shaft below threatening to sallow everything in its path. The cauldron of seething water was a message of terror and death. The thought of drowning in this hellhole was more than I could bear. Death was about to swallow us in a torrent of water. As we frantically made our way up the shaft, it became apparent that Hanna, Mankee and Kirby were losing the battle with the faster rising water. Quickly, the surging water caught up to them; their desperate cries for help echoed up the shaft, but nobody – least of all me – could do anything to help them. Their pathetic wailing went unanswered and soon the fading sound of their desperate pleas dissipated into the icy surging water and mud. I could now feel the cold, icy water swirl about my feet. Without breaking stride I climbed even faster. My lungs felt like they were going to burst with each movement upward.

Suddenly, in what seemed to be only seconds, the water was waist high. Rivulets of sweat eked down every crevice of my shuddering body, but somehow I kept going. The only thing propelling me upward was the thought of imminent death.

As suddenly as the water had surged upward, it began to retreat; unbelievably, I was soon out of the water. Fearing I would lose my grip, I squeezed the ladder rungs tighter, not looking down for a moment; I knew below me was the throat of eternity – a black abyss with nothingness at the end. The small patch of light at the top of the shaft was getting larger. I felt at any moment that my body would explode.

Miners and friends gathered at the Barnes-Hecker site immediately after the accident. Fifty-one men perished in the mine.

Nearing the surface, I met Edward Hillman and Albert Tippett who were descending the shaft to find out what was happening. Hillman searched the shaft below with his flashlight and yelled into the black chasm. There were no voice responses, only a petrifying roar spewing a threatening rebuttal. With death on our heels, Hillman, Tippett and myself made the last desperate thrust to the top.

Before I knew it, a pair of hands grabbed my jacket and pulled me the remaining way out of the shaft. Dimly conscious, I collapsed on the surface totally exhausted. I looked up with relief only to see it was my brother who pulled me to safety.

I didn't know it at the time, but of the 51 men trapped in the mine below me, I was the only one to cheat death.

This is what Wilfred Wills, the lone survivor of the mine disaster at the Barnes-Hecker mine shaft in Ishpeming; the worst mine disaster in the history of Michigan, must have felt when he climbed to safety over 70 years ago.

The year was 1926 and Wilfred was a strong, lean 23 year-old at the time of the tragedy. He would move to Flint in 1937 and remain there until his death in 1973. Years after the tragedy, Wills was haunted by nightmares; he refused to talk about the incident, even after 26 years. One year before his death, in 1972, he came to terms with the mine trauma and attended a memorial dedication at the site of the cave-in in 1972. A memorial plaque placed at the site (near the old Evergreen Drive-in Theater) was later moved to the Michigan Iron Ore Museum.

What had created the great mine disaster was a cave-in that sucked an entire swamp into a gaping hole; filling the mine

The Barnes-Hecker Memorial rests on the perimeter of the Michigan Iron Ore Museum, located on Marquette County Road 492.

shaft and all the drifts with water up to 185 feet from the surface. A clog of swamp debris in the Morris drift prevented the disaster from being worse. Ten bodies were recovered. The remaining 41 are entombed forever in an iron ore mausoleum.

Today the site is overgrown with shrub brush and small trees; a rectangular plastic orange fencing marks off the capped shaft that stands as a lone reminder of the great tragedy that occurred on this site seventy-four years ago.

THE BABY CARRIAGE
Colossus

LLOYD LOOM

In the 1920s and 1930s Lloyd's was the largest baby carriage manufacturer in the world.

Paper furniture?

That's precisely what Lloyd's finely hand-crafted furniture was made of – hygienic, warp free, woven paper. The genius of Marshall Lloyd (1858-1927), a Menominee inventor and industrial tycoon, devised a new way to make wicker furniture.

The use of paper was an ingenious improvement on wicker furniture that previously depended on either rattan or cane. Not only was the new tightly-wrapped paper superior in strength to the old cane or rattan, but it was also impervious to dampness and dirt. While cane and rattan came in specified limited lengths, paper could be used in any length and finished with fewer seams; this made the furniture less likely to snag clothing. Lloyd furniture was smooth to the touch and known for its durability.

Two of Lloyd's more popular baby carriages. The buggy on the left is a 1930s model while the one on the right is a 1920s model.

The Lloyd factory was built in 1907 in a prominent location on the north side of Menominee, just south of the U.S. 41 – M 35 intersection. The plant expanded in 1920 and again in 1932, eventually the monolith would be over a quarter-of-a-million square feet. From the plant's inception in the early 1900s, it provided much needed jobs to a city where lumbering once was king, but declining in importance by the second decade of the 20th century.

Many U.P. residents heading south from points north of Menominee have driven by the old Lloyd factory giving little thought as to what the aging factory was about. Few knew it housed the production facilities of Lloyd's world famous wicker furniture.

The Lloyd Flanders factory, built in 1927, was over one-million square feet. The huge building is on U.S. 41 on the north side of Menominee.

Wicker furniture was popular in the 1920s; right up to World War I, it was often found in private clubs, up-scale homes and even airships. Wicker furniture during the 1920s and 1930s was considered stylish and functional. It fell out of favor after the war and production declined. Menominee continued to produce wicker furniture for the next three decades, but the heydays of the popular furniture were long gone.

In the 1980s, wicker furnishing experienced a resurgence, it slowly came back into favor, and not only as durable, comfortable and stylish furniture, but earlier manufactured pieces as collector items; museums began to search for Lloyd originals.

What made Lloyd's furniture superior to other wicker furniture was the construction design, and the material used to make the wicker. Previously all wicker furniture was made out of either cane or rattan; Lloyd's was made out of tightly-wound paper. The paper construction proved to be superior to either cane or rattan. Lloyd, a genius at simplicity, separated the frame construction

The Lloyd people didn t dare refer to it as paper furniture, this would have given it a ring of being cheap — flimsy; instead it was called woven fiber, thus encouraging the impression that it was a new, exotic material.

from the woven fiber. This made the furniture easier to build and of considerably greater strength. Prior to this, the frame and woven fabric were all one unit. In addition, Lloyd inserted metal rods down the center of the wicker; this not only gave it additional strength but also maintained the shape of the furniture. One of Lloyd's ads in 1938 demonstrated this by showing four men weighing nearly 600 pounds standing on a piece of Lloyd's fabric. Lloyd's major design and fabric changes revolutionized wicker furniture.

Lloyd's marquee product was the baby carriage; it was the company's signature creation. The Menominee plant in the 1920s and 1930s was the largest producer of baby carriages in the world; at the company's zenith it produced 1,000 baby carriages a day.

Lloyd, although possessing no formal engineering training, was an innovative whiz, creating over 200 inventions in his lifetime. He had a couch (wicker of course) in his office on which he frequently reclined when meditating on company concerns. Not many of today's CEOs are afforded this luxury, but when you own your own company you may recline – when so inclined.

Marshall Lloyd died at the age of 69. The prolific inventor was buried in 1927 in this grand mausoleum in the Menominee cemetery.

Lloyd was active in Menominee's community affairs, twice being mayor and providing funding for a local theater and department store. In addition, he was instrumental in building a hospital with an estate bequest. Lloyd died at the age of 69 in 1927, leaving a fortune of over $2-million. He was buried in an impressive mausoleum in the Menominee cemetery.

The Menominee factory that produced the wicker furniture since 1907, closed its doors in 1982 after several decades of decline, but was reinvigorated by Don Flanders later that year. Flanders resurrected the old wicker furniture line with the same design construction and time-honored craftsmanship that were used in the 1920s, but added a weather coating that made the new Lloyd wicker furniture ideal for patios.

If you want to know if you have an original Lloyd furniture piece, look at the underside of the piece for the manufacturer's name, or use a magnet to detect (remember the steel bar inserts) if it's a Lloyd original.

Lloyd's legacy is 10 million pieces of furniture – some still in use, others in private collections, and very rare pieces in museums. Perhaps his greatest legacy though, is the smile he put on a content mother's face when she proudly strolled down Main Street with a slumbering baby riding in the classiest baby carriage in the world.

THE BIRTHPLACE Of THE Woody

KINGSFORD FORD PLANT

By 1928, the plant employed 8,000.

Two huge, 190-foot smokestacks in Kingsford puncture the heavens in an ethereal thrust. They are Kingsford's "Twin Towers," aging, dormant sentinels, eerily standing vigil over decayed and sprawling buildings that were once a thriving industry. This enterprise once gave life and hope to the people of the community and was the heart of Kingsford's economy.

From the 1920s through the early 1950s, this huge plant made wood parts for Ford's Model T, Model A, and the classic "Woody" station wagons.

One of several delapitated buildings located at the Kingsford Ford plant.

Today, all that remains of what used to be a great local industry are ramshackle buildings spread over Kingsford's west side. Tall spindly weeds eke out a meager existence in the crumbling cement cracks of the deteriorating buildings. Twisted, rusted steel that once was the bone of the buildings now lies lifeless. Interspersed in the ruin, a few small industries have set up shop and given some life to the old plant site. But for the most part, it remains a desolate, unsightly blight on the Kingsford landscape.

In the early 1900s, Henry Ford was interested in the iron and lumber resources in the Upper Peninsula. He needed these resources to supply his burgeoning automobile industry in Detroit. With this expansion in mind, Ford contacted Edward G. Kingsford, a local land-looker and real estate agent in Iron Mountain who was married to one of Ford's cousins. In 1919, Ford obtained 400,000 acres in the Upper Peninsula, most of which were valuable hardwood forests. With the land secured, Ford was ready to build. In 1920, he unveiled a plan to build a sawmill and then a factory to manufacture Model T body parts.

These 190-foot towers belched out smoke during Kingsford's prosperous car manufacturing days. (circa 1920).

Land was purchased west of Iron Mountain and work began immediately on the sawmill. It was the first of many buildings Ford built on the site. This was a phenomenal time for Iron Mountain's economy.

By the end of 1920, over 3,000 men were busily engaged in constructing the huge plant. Iron Mountain became a boomtown; real estate sales mushroomed. New streets were constructed and local merchants' businesses expanded. During this prosperity, delighted shopkeepers derived great solace in the sweet sound of ringing cash registers. By 1925, the Ford plant reached its peak labor force of over 8,000 workers.

The sawmill was completed one year after construction began and was touted as the most modern in the world. This fact, however, did not impress one group of Rotarians who were present at the plant's christening in July of 1921. During a ceremony marking the special occasion, all went well until a rogue maple log became untracked and sought out a group of dignified Rotarians. The errant log did little other than frighten the esteemed visitors and let them know that "high tech" equipment often determines its own course of action. (Anyone who owns a computer can verify the preceding statement.)

The sawmill's primary supplier was a logging company 60 miles away at Sidnaw. The busy Sidnaw company shipped over a quarter-of-a-million board feet to the Kingsford plant one weekend in 1922.

Greg Lindstrom of Marquette proudly displays his 1935 "Woody." Greg restored the Ford wagon to showroom condition.

The nucleus of the Kingsford factory was the body plants. These plants manufactured wooden body parts (pillars, sills, door frames, floor boards, top ribs) for Ford sedans and touring cars.

Eventually there were three body factories built on the site; the largest, built in 1923, was 640 feet long. The completed wood parts were sent to Detroit for assembly.

Fifty-two dry kilns constructed on the site extracted moisture from the hardwood used to make parts for the body plants. This was no small operation. If all the piping in the plant were laid end to end, it would have stretched from Kingsford to Chicago and back again.

Waste slashings (scraps of wood including sawdust) from the sawmill were used to make by-products. Ford constructed two chemical buildings for this purpose, a carbonization building and a distillations building. Acetate of lime, methyl alcohol, charcoal, tar, light oils, creosote and fuel gas were the useful by-products that were developed from the wood slashings. Some of these by-products Ford sold (briquettes), and others were used at the plant (fuel oil). Nothing was wasted at the Kingsford Plant.

The power plant, with its distinctive twin smoke stack towers, stands as the greatest reminder of Ford's presence in Kingsford. The towers expelled waste from four behemoth boilers that cranked out 12,000 horsepower, enough energy to run the entire plant. The boilers could burn most anything to create energy, but relied primarily on oil, wood and refuse.

Ford did more than building factories for making car parts. He built a self-sustainable city that included a commissary, hospital, clubhouse and homes. Kingsford was the classic company town.

The commissary, built in 1923, was for the explicit purpose of providing lower prices to Ford employees; however, he allowed the general public to also use the facility. Frugal Henry Ford operated his commissary on a cash-only basis. The store had a complete line of work clothes, shoes, fresh and salted meats, and fresh fruits and vegetables that were kept in the cool basement.

Ford recognized the need for medical attention for his

employees. If you were injured or became ill at work, you received medical treatment for a nominal fee (assessed $1.10 a month) at Ford's five-bed hospital. The hospital, a Ford house on Woodward Avenue, was a replica (but much smaller) of the famed Henry Ford Hospital in Detroit.

The rapid expansion of the Kingsford plant presented a pressing concern for adequate housing for company employees and their families. The housing shortage was critical, often resulting in employees living in other cities. Bunkhouses and camp buildings were pressed into service to meet the critical housing shortage. This camp-like living was not a desirable alternative for many of the men who had wives and children. Because of these living conditions (or lack of), the attrition rate was high and became a serious concern for Ford.

An assembly line in the Kingsford Ford plant. Pictured here is a classic "Woody" nearing completion. (circa 1940s)

As a result of the housing problem, Ford reluctantly got into building homes for his employees. He built the first 50 houses in the Crystal Lake District, each selling for between $4,000 and $8,000. Uniquely, this was not the uniform "cookie cutter" housing that is so common today, as each house was architecturally different.

In a continued expansion, Ford built another 160 homes, with prices ranging from $3,500 to $5,000, in what became known as the Ford Addition. These homes had all the contemporary amenities of electricity, indoor plumbing and telephone capability.

Left to right, Thomas Edison, Henry Ford and Ed Kingsford ham it up in this 1926 photo at Cowboy Lake in Kingsford.

In addressing family concerns in the subdivision, Ford created a family park. It was equipped with benches, picnic tables, tennis courts and even a bandstand. The social-minded Ford arranged for concerts every Wednesday evening during the summer months. The Kingsford complex was more than a place of employment; it became a community.

In the late 1930s, production of the station wagons was declining and by early 1942, all production of the wagons ceased. In joining the war effort, the plant was converted into a facility for building gliders for World War II. Glider production was discontinued after the war and car parts production returned, but on a minimal scale. By the late 1940s, the plant no longer generated enough revenue to be sustainable. Closing the operation was just a matter of time.

Finally, in 1951, the death knell rang a sad refrain for the Kingsford residents when the Ford plant closed for good. Ford sold the chemical plant and deactivated the body plants. Close to 2,000 workers lost their jobs and the Kingsford economy suffered a severe blow. During the late 1940s, city officials, with foresight, saw the writing on the wall and, with wisdom, petitioned the voters to make Kingsford a city. In August of 1947, with voter approval, Kingsford became a city.

In spite of Ford's withdrawal, many of the old buildings are still in use. The sawmill building and all three of the body plants are occupied by local businesses. The chemical plant was torn down. Only the smoke stacks remain from the power plant. The old Ford Commissary is now a tire company, and the hospital and clubhouses are private residences on Woodward Avenue. Many of the homes Ford built are still in use and

provide residents with comfortable housing.

The Ford plant in Kingsford was Kingsford. Though only remnants of the once prosperous enterprise remain, it started a community that 80 years later is thriving and proudly producing some of the best high school football teams in the Upper Peninsula.

This elegant home, built in 1925, was once the clubhouse for visiting officials. The beautiful gambrel-roofed home is located on Woodward Avenue in Kingsford.

CATCH
Of The Day

NAUBINWAY FISHING

Although the Watchers no longer fish, four fishing vessels still operate out of Naubinway.

Sinewy, weather-hardened hands exhaustingly pull the nets out of the icy waters on bone-chilling November mornings.

Delicate, hand-carved, miniature fishing boats carefully placed on small shelves dominate the living room of the Watcher residence in the small lakeshore village of Naubinway. Each boat is a replica of one that plied the vast waters of Lake Michigan over the past century. The craftsman who made these models, Don Watcher, a retired fisherman and educator, painstakingly toiled over each piece, knowing they represented the Watcher fishing legacy in Naubinway.

Don Watcher and his three brothers earned their living each day by taking a two-and-a-half-hour boat ride to the deep waters in Lake Michigan that teemed with whitefish. Once there, nets were cast and left to trap the unsuspecting denizens of the deep – hoping on the return voyage the nets would be brimming with silvery whitefish. The income from fishing provided the Watcher brothers enough money to pursue a college education. The Watchers last fished out of Naubinway in 1972.

The Watcher brothers learned from their father who fished the shores of Lake Michigan for over 44 years. In the early spring and late fall, the biting cold on their fishing voyages could be unbearable. Fishermen like the Watchers were hardy men who could withstand the penetrating November chill that blew off Lake Michigan. Their lean bodies were used to the harsh conditions that were part of a fisherman's life.

Fishing has changed significantly over the years. Gill nets are fast becoming a relic of another age. These nets trapped all species of fish, catching some that were either illegal or undesirable. This was a waste of the fish resource. The newer trap nets not

Expensive automated machinery processes whitefish at the King Wholesale Fish Market in Naubinway. The fish is shipped to New York and Chicago while the caviar is sent to Japan.

only catch the desired species, but allow the others to swim away for another day. In Naubinway, three of the four boats in operation are trap net boats and one is a gill net boat. The trap net boats are easily distinguished by a wide-open stern area. Gill net boats are larger in appearance and have a housing on the rear deck of the boat.

The only catchable fish off Naubinway is whitefish. Lake trout are a legal catch only for Native Americans in both Lake Michigan and Lake Superior.

Don Watcher of Naubinway stands alongside an old family boat the Watchers used on Lake Michigan until 1972.

The Chippewa Tribe controls the licensing of commercial fishermen. In an attempt to preserve the fish stock, the tribe issues only a set number of licenses each year.

Fishing in Naubinway, as well as other U.P. communities, had its productive years as well as lean ones. In the 1930s, fishing was so poor that often not even a single trawler left the harbor; their holds were barren. The early to mid-1940s saw an upswing, only to decline again in the late 1940s. The '60s were a prosperous time, only to fall again on hard times in the '70s. Over-fishing and the sea lamprey affected the quantity of fish taken during some of the lean cycles.

Today, the fish market is thriving in Naubinway. The King Wholesale Fish Market, located adjacent to the fishing docks, processes fish and prepares them for market. Years ago, the catch was filleted and packaged by hand. Today, expensive machinery arranged in an automated assembly line expediently processes the day's net. The seafood catch is then shipped to New York, Chicago and Detroit while the caviar (fish eggs) is sent to Japan.

The *Ernie C.*, one of the few active fishing vessels in Naubinway that cruise Lake Michigan for Whitefish.

Other communities, in addition to Naubinway, along the Lake Michigan shoreline, still have small fishing fleets that ply the waters in search of whitefish. Manistique, Fairport, Cedarville and Detour all have trawlers that go out seven months a year to provide their communities with a fresh take. Although commercial fishing is no longer a major employer or economic force in the Upper Peninsula, it is an activity that is closely allied with nature – an alliance with the earth's resources and something sacred to those who call the Upper Peninsula home.

THE COMPANY
ON THE
CUTTING EDGE

MARBLE ARMS CORPORATION

Teddy Roosevelt, Charles Lindbergh, Admiral Byrd, and Admiral Peary – all users of Marble Arms products.

What business could be more representative of the Upper Peninsula than a corporation that makes products for outdoor sportsmen? Marble Arms is that corporation. The company, located in Gladstone, Michigan, has an international reputation for producing the finest quality hunting knives, gun sights and compasses.

Marble Arms and the Upper Peninsula are a natural fit. The Upper Peninsula, a mecca for hunting and fishing enthusiasts, has more truck gun racks per capita than any Third World nation in the midst of a revolution. Bumper stickers that proclaim the sanctity of the Second Amendment are as common on U.P. highways as Volvos are on the Kennedy Expressway in Chicago.

Webster L. Marble, founder of the Marble Arms Corporation, was the prototype woodsman and represents, in the best tradition, what most Upper Peninsulans feel about hunting and fishing. He was an inquisitive man who served as a landcruiser in the Gladstone area in the latter part of the 19th century.

Landcruisers surveyed a given area, determined whether it was suitable for logging, and how many board feet could be harvested from the area. This information was then transferred to Marble's employer, who made a determination based on Marble's data as to the advisability of purchasing and logging an area of land assessed by Marble. Webster Marble was a hearty woodsman who could trek the isolated wilderness with ease; he was a true pioneer at home with the natural inhabitants of the wilds.

As a landcruiser, he carried a short-handled ax that was used to blaze trails and mark boundaries. Chipping small chips

In 1918, a grateful soldier, Cliff Murker, wrote a letter to his dad expressing his gratitude for a Marble matchbox that saved his life. Murker wrote, "Thanks to my field belt and the Marble matchbox that I had in my coat pocket, the force of the bullet was spent on the matchbox and merely went into my hip, not at all serious, but darn sore..."

of wood from the bark of a tree was done with a razor-sharp ax. A series of trees with removed chips delineated a given boundary line in a specific region. The finely honed ax created a safety problem for Marble. He frequently cut himself or sliced up valuable supplies that were housed in the same backpack as the ax.

To solve this problem, Marble created the "safety axe." A protective guard folded over the blade when the ax was not in use. Marble got a patent (the first of over 70) on his safety axe in 1898, and with typical Upper Peninsula entrepreneurial drive, began to manufacture the ax in a shed behind his home. As business increased, Marble sought out a larger site for a production building, and for a partner to assist in the expanded operation. Frank Van Cleve joined Marble in the venture, and the new co-owners named the enterprise The Marble Arms and Manufacturing Company. Van Cleve had invested in other businesses prior to Marble Arms, many of them unsuccessful. The Marble investment, however, was one of Van Cleve's more successful financial ventures. Van Cleve was a partner in Marble Arms until his death in 1920.

The Marble Arms Company in Gladstone is located near Little Bay de Noc. The Corporation caters to the needs of the sportsman.

Webster Marble was not content to just produce the safety axe; he augmented his outdoor line to include: a waterproof matchbox, a pin-on-your-coat compass, gun sights, and gun cleaning equipment. In addition, he manufactured the Ideal Hunting Knife, a clincher gaff for fishermen, and an "over and under" rifle.

The most controversial and interesting product that Marble manufactured was a small-bore, foldable shotgun that could be transported in one's sleeve. Needless to say, gangsters found this gun to be most useful in their pursuit of earning a living. The federal government noted that nefarious characters were enamored with the weapon and soon had the gun outlawed.

The famous have used Marble Arms products in worldly adventures. Polar explorer Robert E. Peary carried Marble knives and safety axes on two of his Arctic explorations. Teddy Roosevelt used Marble products on his African safaris, while Marble products accompanied Admiral Byrd on many of his Antarctic journeys. The first solo transatlantic flight by Charles Lindbergh in *The Spirit of St. Louis* had a Marble Arms compass, matchsafe and knife in the cockpit. Marble Arms products have faithfully served in every major American conflict from World War I to the Persian Gulf War.

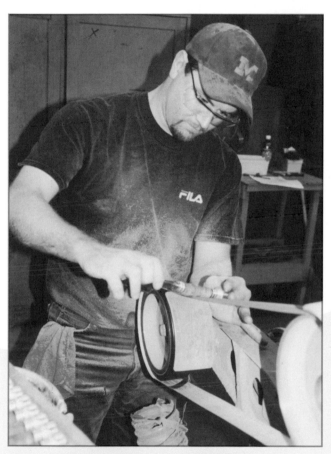

One of Marble's 40 – 45 employees grinds a knife with precision and care. It takes six months of training to become a skilled knife craftsman.

The Marble Arms Corporation has undergone a series of changes. Its ownership went from the Marble family to corporations, both big and small, including, IT&T, and Bell & Gosset. In 1994, Craig and Jim Lauerman, a local Gladstone family, purchased the business. Craig Lauerman's wife Tracy said, "My husband bought the business because of his love for the outdoors." That love for the company compelled the Lauermans in 1997 to resume the full-time manufacturing of the Marble signature product – hunting knives.

Today, the prospering company with 40-45 employees is an economic anchor for the community of Gladstone. Many of the jobs in Marble Arms require highly skilled workers. It takes six months of on-the-job training to become skilled enough to make a precision, hand-ground Marble Arms knife. Skilled craftsmen operate the delicate computer-driven machines that create exacting gun scopes that are sold to major gun manufacturers Remington and Marlin. In addition to distributing the hunting knives to all 50 states, Marble has shipped their premier product to Canada, Japan and France.

Tracy Lauerman said, "Christmastime is a busy time for us; the hunting knife is a great seller as a Christmas gift." With deer hunting as the national sport in the Upper Peninsula, there is probably not a deer hunter that does not either own or want a Marble Arms knife. Most Upper Peninsula hunters who purchase a Marble Arms knife consider the $75-$125 price of a handmade quality knife a hunting necessity – and money well spent.

THE HARDCOURT KING

HORNER FLOORING

Michigan State coach and Iron Mountain native Tom Izzo won the national college basketball title on a Horner floor.

Not far from Lake Superior, on the outskirts of Dollar Bay (this is a stretch), is a long, rambling, aging building which appears unused, as though time had passed it by. There are no signs, markers, or anything to give an indication as to what the antiquated structure is about. This building, however, is the property of one of the leading hardwood floor manufacturers in the nation – Horner.

Surprisingly, directly behind the timeworn, unused building is an ultra-modern, streamlined, computer-driven plant that produces tens-of-millions of board feet of hardwood flooring yearly. Within the past four years, Horner has heavily invested in state-of-the-art milling machinery, making it one of the most efficient hardwood flooring factories in the nation.

In 1871, Bill Horner, a lumbering entrepreneur and founder of the Horner Flooring Company, established his first sawmill in Reed City, Michigan. He was a legend. The colorful and charismatic lumberman never drank or smoked for five decades, and then at the age of 50, he thought they were worth a try – and so he did. He never looked back. Deriving such great satisfaction from his newfound recreations, he continued to indulge in the questionable behavior for the rest of his life. Bill Horner lived each day with gusto; he lived in the moment long before it became the rhetoric and lifestyle of the pop culture.

He was an innovator in the lumbering business. He found a way to mill and mass-produce hardwood such as maple and oak. Until that time, many lumbermen considered hardwood too difficult to work with; they used it only as a secondary source of

Doug said of his lineage, "We have sawdust in our veins."

lumber. Before Horner introduced mass production of hardwood, it was custom made; this was a slow and expensive process.

The main office of Horner Flooring in Dollar Bay. The company's glamour product is the premier hardwood basketball floor.

A catastrophic fire at the turn of the century destroyed the Horner plant at Reed City. After the ruinous disaster, Horner figured it was a good time to move his sawmill. He realized that the Lower Peninsula was rapidly being depleted of the stately white pine and soon there would be little left to log. In 1926 he decided to move his sawmill to Newberry, in Michigan's Upper Peninsula.

It was a prosperous plant, turning out 17 million board feet a month. Horner became the largest hardwood flooring sawmill in the world. Fires, however, continued to plague the Horner sawmills; in the second decade of the century, two more fires swept through the Horner Newberry Plant.

These disasters, plus an economic downturn in the early 1920s, jeopardized Horner's solvency. However, the sawmill did manage to somehow survive, and remained in business in Newberry until 1932.

Bill Horner died in 1925, leaving the sawmill to his son Sam, who moved the mill to Dollar Bay in 1926. Sam continued to run the plant and the hardwood empire until the 1950s when his two sons, Jack and Dave, took over the operation of the family business.

The Hamar family acquired the sawmill from the Horners in the 1960s. Today, the Chief Executive Officer of Horner is third-generation flooring entrepreneur Doug Hamar. After Doug's grandfather acquired the company from the Horner family in the 1960s, Doug's father, and then Doug, continued to operate the mill, keeping the tradition of producing fine quality, maple wood flooring.

Horner is a small company with a big reputation – and a company that relies on Upper Peninsula forests for its existence. Horner obtains most of its lumber for its hardwood floors in a 400-mile radius of the plant in Dollar Bay. Mom and pop sawmills are a primary and dependable source of raw lumber for Horner, supplying them with the grade of maple they need for hardwood flooring. Ninety-five percent of the lumber Horner uses is maple, with small amounts of oak, birch, beech and cherry as the other five percent of usable hardwood.

Doug Hamar, C.E.O. of Horner Flooring, scans a basketball court nearing completion.

Although most of the flooring that Horner ships out ends up in the hands of large-scale flooring contractors, they have a glamour floor product – the world famous Horner basketball floors. These floors dress the elite gymnasiums and athletic centers around the nation with the finest basketball floors available – all made with Upper Peninsula resources and workers. The basketball floors are not cheap ($80,000), but then, quality never is.

For the past 14 years, Horner has made the floor for the prestigious final four NCAA basketball tournaments. Horner floors are sold worldwide, with the most recent floor shipped to Australia for the Goodwill Games.

Doug is most proud of his Upper Peninsula work force. He said, "They have a work ethic you just can't find in other places." Doug knows this only too well; he employs workers in other operations in different parts of the country and noted that one of his business associates said, "Why can't you send me a truckload of Yoopers to work at my plant?" The strong work ethic – instilled in today's Upper Peninsulans may well date back to a time when their fathers and grandfathers toiled pridefully in the iron ore mines and the forests, knowing they owed a good day's work for a decent day's pay.

Doug Horner describes himself as a conservationist. He said, "We (Horner) cannot exist without harvesting the hardwoods on a sustained yield basis." He continued, "Selective cutting of the harvestable 75 year-old maples is good forest management." Maples need adequate light filtering through the leafy canopy to the forest floor (which selective cutting encourages) so seedlings are able to take root and propagate the species.

Horner Corporation is a natural fit for the Upper Peninsula: the availability of a quality tree resource and a work force that is both efficient and loyal.

Karl Malone, John Stockton, and David Robinson, all world-class athletes, ply their phenomenal skill on a Horner Floor. They don't know this, but any Yooper will tell you, they play better because their talented feet are rhythmically weaving down a floor that was made from U.P. forests with U.P. hands.

Currently, eight National Basketball Association (NBA) teams are playing on Horner floors and a countless number of Division 1 National Collegiate Athletic Association (NCAA) schools dribble away on Horner hardwood.

Horner has a tremendous impact on the Dollar Bay economy with its 75 employees contributing one-and-a-half to two million dollars yearly to the local, hard-pressed economy.

THE MECHANICAL MARVEL

PETTIBONE MICHIGAN CORPORATION

*Mechanical genius Phillip LaTendresse
of Baraga invents the world famous "Cary Lift."*

NEEDED: A VERSATILE, RUBBER-WHEELED PIECE OF EQUIPMENT THAT LIFTS, CARRIES AND REACHES – ALL IN ONE UNIT. This was what the Northwood Timber Company in L'Anse needed for their sawmill operation when Highway U.S. 41 cut a swath through the middle of the mill in the late 1940s. It became apparent that the slow and cumbersome horses used to transport the lumber would no longer be useful. (To say the least, crossing busy U.S. 41 traffic would be a health hazard for the beasts of burden.) A rubber-tired vehicle that would not damage the road, be considerably faster than the horse – and have lift and reach capability – would nicely fit the company's need. But, that machine didn't exist – it was just a whimsical fantasy of the Northwood Timber Company, that is, until inventive genius Phillip LaTendresse of Baraga came along.

LaTendresse, owner of a small welding shop in Baraga, thought he could solve Northwood's problem. He set out to design and make a machine that would do all the things that the Northwood Timber Company needed – and then some. With his mission clear, LaTendresse and the six men in his employ began the project of creating the world's first "Cary-Lift."

Like many inventors, LaTendresse relied on his facile mechanical mind, and used spare parts, to create his mechanical wonder. He labored in anonymity; shaping, pounding, and fitting odds and ends of unused war surplus materials into useable parts. Anything he could strip, reshape, or contort into a serviceable piece went into his creative project. By 1949, the long-tinkering

LaTendresse's small shop began to manufacture and commercially sell his Cary-Lifts to local loggers and lumber-yards. The fledgling company was on its way.

process bore success; an embryonic machine was created. It was the first practical machine that had a lift capacity. This inauspicious beginning evolved into what would become a landmark logging machine.

Later models would add the all-important reach dimension; a machine that operates much like an arm reaching up to a shelf to retrieve an object. It was designed and built specifically with the loggers in mind, but its wide range of application soon became very apparent to the builders.

The first Cary-Lift was primitive in performance, compared to sophisticated machines of a later date; it nonetheless "filled the bill," as one satisfied lumberyard owner stated.

A 1958 Pettibone Cary-Lift on display at the Baraga Historical Museum on Keweenaw Bay.

The Cary-Lift was built on the principle of a parallelogram with pivoting hinge points. The forward reach was the linchpin of the device. The machine was ideal for loading pulpwood or freight on the far side of a railroad car.

As the demand for his new Cary-Lift increased, LaTendresse needed – and sought, financial support from larger corporations that could assist in the expansion. In 1951, Pettibone Mulliken Corporation of Chicago, recognizing the Cary-Lift's potential, eagerly jumped in with financial support and became an integral part of the company.

The machines were also becoming larger and more

complex, and a growing market necessitated moves to larger facilities. In one instance, their manufacturing plant had such low ceilings that it was necessary to deflate the air in the tires just to get the completed vehicle out of its incubator.

The burgeoning company compelled LaTendresse to make four moves, always to a bigger plant. One move, in 1956, required the company to travel across Keweenaw Bay to Baraga. Pettibone was no longer a cottage industry, but a powerful economic force in the L'Anse/Baraga area.

LaTendresse and Pettibone relied heavily on subcontractors to make Cary-Lift parts; castings and specialty pieces were manufactured in small shops scattered throughout the Baraga and L'Anse area. The parts were then transported to the main plant on U.S. 41 in Baraga where they were assembled into a Cary-Lift.

The fork was the principal front unit on the Cary-Lift; it was extensively used in logging. However, the inventors realized that by removing the fork and replacing it with another unit, the Cary-Lift became even more valuable as an industrial work machine. Buckets, bailers, clams and snow removal equipment were some of the units that were adapted for use by the basic Cary-Lift machine. The apparatuses were the arsenal of "add-ons" that made the Cary-Lift an even more useful machine, not only for loggers, but other industries as well.

The main plant of the Pettibone Corporation in Baraga. The company distributes the world famous Cary-Lift world wide.

In 1966, the Pettibone Cary-Lift became the Michigan Product of the year. It was the third time the Upper Peninsula walked away with the coveted honor. Engstrom Helicopter Corporation of Menominee won the previous year, and John Voelker's famed novel, *Anatomy of a Murder*, won it a decade earlier. All were clear confirmations of the immeasurable talent residing in the Upper Peninsula.

In a free-market economy, prosperity is not guaranteed to perpetuity. Pettibone became painfully aware of this in the 1970s, when the corporation fell on financial hard times and was forced into Chapter 11 bankruptcy. The Chapter 11 declaration allowed the company time to reorganize while still being in operation.

They survived the financial downturn and once again are economically healthy. Pettibone, one of the major employers in the L'Anse/Baraga area, provides 100 jobs at the main plant for the hard-pressed region. The 12 sub-contractors provide work for an additional 100-plus employees. The company produced 300 Cary-Lifts in the year 2000, distributing them all over the world. New Zealand, Russia, Germany and Sweden are a few of the many foreign countries that found the Cary-Lift an essential work machine in an industrial economy.

The Cary-Lift's primary outlet to loggers is still active, but an increasing number of machines are sold to construction companies for new construction projects. Expanding the basic Cary-Lift's design to new machines has made the unit adaptable to other applications that are not logging related.

Today, the Pettibone Corporation, nestled in the cradle of Keweenaw Bay, serves as a reminder of what can be done when the creative energies of one man are applied to solving a local problem. The seeds of genius reside just as easily in the northern hardwoods of Upper Michigan as they do on Wall Street. Phillip LaTendresse personified that genius. His Cary-Lift legacy is not only a testimony to his mechanical creativity, but reflects the perseverance and spirit that characterizes the people of the Upper Peninsula.

The 1970s were the most prosperous for the Pettibone Cary-Lift with 150 employed in the main plant and another 100 employees scattered in sub-contractor shops throughout the community.

THE PRINCELY PINE

And The Majestic Maple

LOGGING IN THE UPPER PENINSULA

It is hard to believe – and probably not well known – that 10 million cords of wood are growing in Michigan's forests and only 4.5 million cords are being removed.

At the beginning of time, God gently passed his arm over the Upper Peninsula. Blossoming in the wake of his stroke was a lush green canopy of towering white pines and emerald-crowned maples. Soaring into infinity, the pines pierced the billowing white clouds that clung delicately to the clear blue sky, while the expansive maples, leafing out in their finest fall plumage, greeted the early morning sun. For thousands of years, this was what the Upper Peninsula looked like, a dense forest of choice timber that provided food and shelter for the wildlife of the isolated region.

Then came man.

Until 1830, Upper Michigan's forests were relatively untouched, but soon civilization came with a voracious appetite for the prized timber that was needed to feed the expansive building needs of a burgeoning Midwest population. Logging companies had never heard of "selective cutting" or maintaining a "sustained yield." They looked at the vast untouched forests in Upper Michigan believing they could last forever; the supply looked limitless. An early lumber baron emphatically stated, "There's enough lumber here for the next 500 years."

This assessment, however, was grossly inaccurate, and very quickly the Upper Peninsula forests were decimated by the loggers' saws. Near the turn of the century the handwriting was on the wall: the prized white pine and sugar maple were rapidly being depleted. By 1920, the white pine was close to extinction.

The logging industry made millionaires in the Upper Peninsula; Bill Bonifas of Escanaba was one of those millionaires who reaped a financial harvest from the Upper Peninsula's virgin timber.

Prior to the use of machinery in logging, this huge two-wheeled device transported logs with horses supplying the power.

Bonifas emigrated to the Upper Peninsula from the small European Duchy of Luxembourg. He had little money and was living on the edge of poverty when he got to the Upper Peninsula. However, he did have two assets that served him well: his ambition and his strength. Bonifas was a powerful man, standing six feet two inches and weighing 250 pounds; he backed down from no one. In a rough and tumble logging camp his power and tenacity were his biggest allies.

His first job in the Upper Peninsula was piecework in the Garden Peninsula. With his strapping build, Bonifas could do the work of two men as he cut railroad ties and fence posts for just pennies apiece. He led an exemplary life, abstaining from the rugged weekend carousing that was common to most loggers. For Bonifas, there were no Saturday night forays of hard drinking and cavorting with loose women. The squeaky clean Bonifas managed to save enough money to send for his four brothers and three sisters who were still living in Luxembourg.

When the new family members arrived, they quickly set up a logging camp in Garden. The industrious family had Bill's sisters do the cooking and washing for the loggers, while his brothers joined him in the woods. Bonifas knew a well-fed logger is a happy logger – and much less likely to cause trouble in camp. His sisters saw to it that they were well-fed. He soon employed 40 men and the logging operation flourished making railroad ties and fence posts. The rugged loggers (shanty boys) called the no-nonsense Bonifas, "Big Bill." This was the beginning of his logging empire.

Bonifas hired an Irish immigrant as a maid for the family clan, who would eventually become Bill's wife. She was a quiet, unassuming lady and performed the daily household chores for Bill until his death.

Within a short period of time the prosperous logging baron had saved $125,000. Now, with a solid financial base, Bonifas expanded his operation into the Watersmeet and Marenesco area. His success in cutting timber at a profit continued in his western Upper Peninsula operation. Soon, he had several hundred men working for him and he proudly wore the moniker of "The Timber King."

Bonifas was a frugal man – to be more exact, miserly –

better yet, just plain cheap. In an attempt to save money, he had his dutiful wife pack his lunch whenever he traveled. No swank restaurants for Bonifas. On one occasion at an employee's wedding, those in attendance were throwing silver dollar pieces for the children. For some time, Bonifas shrewdly observed others pitch the dollar pieces to the kids. He finally retrieved a silver coin from his pocket – and then reluctantly cast it in the direction of the children, mumbling, "Oh, hell." Making charitable contributions was never his long suit.

Lumberjacks in Garden, Michigan pose with the largest load of cedar posts ever pulled by two horses. (circa 1910)

Bonifas was a sports enthusiast. One time he and his brother attended a boxing match in Escanaba when one of the boxers failed to make his appearance. Rather than have fans go home disappointed, Bonifas jumped into the ring and took on the seasoned Milwaukee pugilist. He stripped to the waist and exposed his well-chiseled torso to the delighted fans. In the second round of the impromptu match, Bonifas leveled his opponent and walked away an easy victor. It was just another day at the office for Big Bill, who was used to subduing cantankerous loggers in his camps.

The normally tight-fisted Bonifas out-did himself when he built an extravagant lodge at the west end of the Upper Peninsula on Lake Gogebic. The lodge was close to his logging operations and provided a place where he entertained other logging magnates and entrepreneurs. The famed novelist Edna Ferber visited Bonifas's grand lodge where she gathered information for her next book on the early lumbering days.

"The Timber King," Big Bill Bonifas of Escanaba, became a millionaire logging Upper Peninsula forests.

She didn't do Bonifas any favors. When the book *Come and Get It* was released, it was not kind to lumber barons. Whether Bonifas knew this would be in her book when he entertained her at the lodge is uncertain.

Big Bill Bonifas died in 1932 at the age of 67, leaving his entire fortune, estimated at $20 million, to his wife. Mrs. Bonifas's life was one of cooking, scrubbing and cleaning house. She had little idea what the wealth she inherited was worth. Escanaba, however, benefited from her charitable nature when she bequeathed money for a fine arts building.

The Bonifases are buried in the only mausoleum in the Escanaba Cemetery.

The wealthy lumber entrepreneurs however, were the exception. The vast majority employed in the lumber industry worked long hours for little pay. A typical lumberjack made between $20 and $26 dollars a month and toiled dawn to dusk six days a week in the cold, tundra-like winters of Michigan's Upper Peninsula. Lumberjacks were renowned for their toughness and strength, and a Saturday night brawl in a rough local saloon could mean death. In testimony to this life, a headstone in the infamous Boot Hill Cemetery in Seney, an early lumber town, reads, "Died fighten."

The decline of logging in the 1920s was catastrophic for some small communities in Upper Michigan; towns like Seney and Covington, formerly thriving small villages, faded into obscurity.

Log marks were important in the early years of lumbering. These insignias were hammered into the end of each log to signify who owned the log. First used in Muskegon in 1842, they soon became the ideal way for owners to keep track of their logs as they floated down a river to the nearest sawmill. Log piracy was common when disreputable loggers hijacked competitor's logs and cut the end off that had a mark on it and replaced it with their mark. Log piracy was one of the earliest industrial crimes in Michigan.

Today in Upper Michigan, thanks to sound forest management practices, the logging and lumbering industry is again thriving. Eighty years ago it appeared the depleted forests would never recover, but forests are one of a few renewable resources, and decades of wise management and hard work paid off. The Upper Peninsula forests are once again productive, and yielding lumber that enhances the citizens' quality of life.

The rebirth of the forest is the result of natural seed regeneration and tree plantation farming. Thirty million trees are planted each year in Michigan.

Christmas tree plantations are big business in Michigan. Upper Michigan Christmas trees are highly prized; as a result, Michigan has become one of the nation's leading Christmas tree producers. Because of their abundance and beauty, the Capitol holiday tree (74-foot white spruce), called the "Tree of Hope" was

Bonifas expanded his financial empire by acquiring stock in General Motors, oil wells in Texas and a bank in Seattle. When asked why he worked so hard, he replied, "I just enjoy making money."

In 2001, the nation's holiday tree (Tree of Hope) was selected from the Ottawa National Forest. Here, Marquette residents sign the greeting scroll bound for the White House.

selected in 2001 from Upper Michigan's Ottawa National Forest. On the White House lawn it was imbedded with a rainbow of colored lights that not only embellished the tree's beauty, but also proudly reflected Upper Michigan's contribution to the national holiday.

Just how do you get a prize tree to the nation's capital? Very carefully wrap the tree in a protective layer, then place it on a special cradle and load it on an International truck. Next, provide a police escort and cautiously caravan the "Tree of Hope" to its final destination, the White House.

The amount of timber harvested in Michigan each year is unbelievable – enough to stretch a cord (8 feet wide, 8 feet long, and 4 feet high) from Ironwood, in the western Upper Peninsula, to Monroe in the southeast corner of Michigan. It is comforting to know however, that twice that amount of timber is being grown in the state.

Who owns the timberland in Michigan? Forty-five percent is privately owned; twenty percent is state forest land; fourteen percent is in the national forests, and eleven percent is corporate (Mead, Louisiana Pacific, Champion International). It takes a coordinated effort from all these entities to ensure the Upper Peninsula forests are sustained and healthy. Numerous agencies, industries, and the private sector coordinate management efforts on public, corporate, and non-industrial private forestlands.

The sugar maple is the most harvested tree in Upper Michigan. Red and white pine are still harvested, but are secondary to the sugar maple and other hardwoods. Horner Flooring in Dollar Bay and Robbins Flooring in Ishpeming are two of the primary lumbering manufacturers that depend on a reliable supply of quality hardwood. The U.P. hardwood forests have a nice fit with Horner and Robbins.

The largest white pine in the United States, in its entire regal splendor, resides in the Porcupine Mountains in western Upper Michigan. Discovered in 1998, the behemoth tree has a 200 inch circumference at 4 feet above the ground and stretches 150 feet skyward. The previous largest pine tree was located in the Huron Mountain Club, but that grand pine recently expired, and a replacement tree had to be designated by the Michigan Big Tree Project. Not content to be just a state champion, the geriatric pine was nominated for the National Register of Big Trees, sponsored by the American Forests of Washington, D.C.

There is a positive side to the rape of the landscape by early loggers; conservation programs are now firmly in place that guarantee a sustained yield of timber from Upper Michigan's valuable forest land. The logging era left a rich legacy of songs and stories about the Upper Peninsula. These ditties and tales are now a part of the rich folklore of the Upper Michigan tapestry.

WEALTH
IN THE
EARTH

IRON ORE MINING

"Gold is for the mistress – silver for the maid – copper for the crafts-man cunning at its trade." "Good!" Cried the baron sitting in his hall, "but iron – cold – is the master of them all."

Rudyard Kipling, 1910

When the Upper Peninsula was awarded to Michigan as a result of the Toledo War, little did anyone know that the Lower Peninsula had just inherited one of the richest iron ore producing areas in the world. Had the Michigan authorities known of the great wealth they came by, their volatile protest over the U.P. annexation would not have been one of angst, but one of jubilant approval, at just having engineered a territorial coup.

Mining began in the Marquette Range in the mid 1840s, making it the oldest iron mining range in the United States. The Menominee Range in the southwest region of the U.P. didn't get underway until the 1870s, while the Gogebic Range in the western Upper Peninsula was the last to develop and began shipping ore in the 1880s. Of the three iron ranges, only the Marquette range is still producing iron ore.

All three mining regions thrived on deep shaft mining where the higher-grade ore was located. However, the cost of extracting the ore from depths of over 1,000 feet became prohibitive, and deep shaft mining was abandoned. Now only open pit mining on the Marquette Range remains. The lower quality surface ore (jasper) can be processed into iron ore pellets at a profit.

The discovery of iron ore in 1841 by William Burt in the Marquette Range was an accident. Burt was surveying the territory with his new solar compass for the U.S. government when his surveying party ran into a mountain of iron near what is now Negaunee. Burt could have cared less that they discovered iron ore, as he was ecstatic that his new solar compass worked. The older magnetic compasses gave Burt grief with suspicious readings

Three great iron ore bodies were discovered after the Upper Peninsula became a part of Michigan: the Marquette Range, the Menominee Range and the Gogebic Range.

– if not totally inaccurate data – while his new solar compass provided him with precise surveying data.

Philo Everett followed up Burt's discovery in 1844 with a small mining party that eventually set up a mining operation on the Carp River just south of Negaunee. Everett's mine was known as the Jackson mine and was located at the site of the present Michigan Iron Industry Museum.

"Double Jacking" at the Jackson iron mine in Negaunee. Notice the relative youth of the miner on the right. (circa 1870)

Iron ore was transported from the Negaunee area to the port city of Marquette. In the 1840s to mid 1850s, moving the ore to Marquette was a slow process. Mules hauling the ore fought nearly impassable terrain while pulling small carts to Marquette, just 12 miles away. By 1855, a crude plank road made of 2x8 timbers was built from the Jackson Mine to Marquette's south harbor. This was an improvement, but still time-consuming. A transportation breakthrough came in 1855 when a crude iron strap railway was built from Marquette to Negaunee. The strap railway was nothing more than a piece of metal attached to wood that provided a base for train wheels to run on. In 1867 this culminated in the first authentic, all-steel rail line with a steam powered "iron horse" that catapulted iron mining into the industrial age.

Two other significant developments occurred in the mid to late 1850s that made Upper Peninsula mining profitable. Opening of the Soo locks in 1855 facilitated the speed of shipping ore to the markets in the southern Great Lakes. The other development was the 1857 invention of the "pocket dock." The pocket dock was a system where ore was dropped from the bottom of rail cars into holding bins in the top of the dock; then gravity fed the ore to a chute that deposited it into the hull of a boat. The mules and the plank road were now just a footnote in history.

While the Jackson Mine was in full swing, iron ore was discovered in the 1870s in the Iron Mountain area by H. A. Chapin of Niles, Michigan; this would become the Menominee Range. The Chapin Mine in Iron Mountain became one of the richest ore strikes in the United States. The size and quality of the ore produced in the Chapin were unequaled anywhere else in the world. Eventually it would have three shafts, extending as deep as 1,880 feet below the earth's surface. Ten miles of drifts, or tunnel corridors, were created by 600 miners unearthing the ore, which was shipped to the port city of Escanaba.

The Chapin mine had a serious water problem and required the service of the largest dewatering pump in the world (see Cornish Pump) to keep it dry enough for the miners to extract the ore. There were other small mines in the Menominee Range, but none equaled the Chapin Mine. The Menominee Range ceased ore production in the 1960s. The cost of extracting the ore from the phenomenally deep shafts proved to be too expensive to continue.

Iron ore on the Gogebic Iron Range was discovered in 1871 by Harvard Professor Raphael Pumpelly (the name sounds Harvardish) in the Newport Hill area of Ironwood. This was the beginning of the Gogebic iron ore exploration era. Pumpelly, a trained geologist, was on a woods excursion when he spotted smoke on a distant horizon. Fearing for his wife's safety, he left his wife behind and ventured forward to check out the smoke. In the process, Pumpelly climbed a rock outcropping to evaluate his location and check on the smoke. Fortuitously, the rock he scaled was a quartzite ledge. The skilled geologist noticed a number of yellow spots in the rock. Pumpelly thought he was perched upon a concentration of iron oxides. He was. With great wisdom, he purchased two miles of the range around the rock outcropping. Pumpelly did little with the land after his discovery in 1871. However, within a short time this land would be worth a small fortune.

Richard Langford, a local trapper and hunter and noted hermit, was the first to see iron ore on Colby Hill. But, it was not until 1873 that N. D. Moore, looking for pine timber, discovered a rock in the roots of a tree that he suspected might be iron ore. An analysis of the rock proved correct; it was a high-quality iron ore. Moore then obtained financing to purchase the land and began mining the Colby Hill area that Langford had earlier explored.

Mining now began in earnest in the Gogebic Range. Moore's Colby Hill development in 1884 became the first mine to ship iron ore out of the area. From then on, the area became a prospector's bonanza. The word quickly spread throughout the mining community that the Ironwood area was to become the richest iron ore site in the United States. The "Gogebic Boom" was on, and investors, both rich and poor, sought capital – be it beg, borrow or steal – to invest in what they thought would soon be a lucrative ore mine.

Within two short years, the bottom fell out, and of the 184 companies selling stock, only 15 were left. Racine, Wisconsin had many residents investing in the Gogebic mines; most lost every dollar that they spent.

The Gogebic iron ore range was the smallest ore producer of the three ranges, even though the range stretched 54 miles in an east-west direction. The iron ore corridor roughly paralleled Highway U.S. 2. Wakefield was the eastern-most end of the ore body and Mellen, Wisconsin was the western terminal point. The cities of Wakefield, Ramsay, Bessemer and Ironwood are on the Gogebic iron ore corridor. In the early years, the prosperous mines saw an influx of eager miners, and by 1885 there were over 2,000 miners in a nine-mile stretch.

The Cliff's "A" headframe located near Lake Bancroft in Ishpeming. The headframe housed the pulley system that transported men and ore to the surface. The hoist engine was housed in a nearby building.

Ethnic enclaves sprouted up around the area. The Italians, Finns, Cousin Jacks, and other nationalities nestled into neighborhood or "location" areas. The Gogebic mining communities, like other mining areas, were rough places to live in the early years. Raising a family in communities that had whole streets dedicated to pleasuring the miners on the weekends was not always the best place for family activities.

Across the river from Ironwood was the notorious frontier town of Hurley that sponsored more than its share of drinking and gambling establishments. Prostitutes and liquor were comforting companions for men who toiled all week long in a dark hole in the

In 1884, there were 184 mining companies in the Gogebic Range, all floating stock certificates that promised investors a rich return.

earth. The Gogebic Range, like the Menominee Range, would flourish for a half century, but then it too would fall victim to hard economic times, and by the 1950s ore production died in the Gogebic Range.

Only the Marquette Range still actively mines iron ore, but it too is facing difficult times. The dumping of cheap foreign steel on the U.S. market has threatened the viability of the Marquette Range. The year 2001 saw a major effort by the Cleveland Cliffs Iron Company, along with local and state officials, to prevent the foreign dumping of iron in the United States. The success of these political efforts would determine the fate of the Marquette Iron Range.

The variety of ethnic groups that immigrated and emigrated to the Upper Peninsula in the heydays of mining left lasting contributions. They transported their cultures to the Upper Peninsula, making it a most unique land: a collage of ethnic fragments that blended into a rich cultural ensemble.

Today, remnants of the iron ore mines speckle the Upper Peninsula landscape. Faded cement obelisk headframes in Ishpeming punctuate the skyline, while a water-filled crater in Iron Mountain ripples in the wind, both reminders of the role that iron ore mining played in the development of the Upper Peninsula.

LORD OF THE Wilderness

MOOSE

In the mid 1980s, fifty-nine moose were transported to central Upper Michigan.

They stand alone: lords of the land, masters of the deep forest. Distinctive with their large heads, overhanging upper lips, and humps that slope to the rear, they are a physical oddity, and yet blend in with their rugged Upper Peninsula surroundings. Intimidating and immense, with powerful front quarters, they effortlessly surge through the thick undergrowth of the peninsula's timberland.

This is the moose, the largest animal that roams the wild, solitary forests of Michigan's Upper Peninsula.

Moose are not new to the Upper Peninsula. In 1652 a French explorer, Radisson, recorded in his journals that he saw moose in Michigan. The thriving moose population, however, was short-lived with the arrival of man. The human encroachment into the moose habitat through logging, farming, and unrestricted hunting eventually depleted the moose population, and by the mid 1800s they were practically non-existent in Michigan. Michigan passed a law protecting moose in 1889, but by then it was too late: there was nothing left to protect.

The re-introduction of moose in the mid 1980s was not the first attempt to re-establish moose in the Upper Peninsula. In the mid 1930s sixty-nine moose were taken from Isle Royale's overpopulated herd and transported to Keweenaw, Marquette and Schoolcraft counties. This early moose relocation had success in the beginning as the herd steadily increased in numbers. During the early 1940s however, the moose population began to decline and by the mid 1940s, there were few left. Biologists attributed the decline of the moose herd on wartime meat rationing and

Weighing more than 1,000 pounds and graced with massive palm antlers up to five feet in width, they are rulers of the woodland.

what later became known as brainworm. The moose had become a dinner menu item for the meat-depleted Upper Peninsula families. The brainworm parasite is hosted by white-tailed deer and transmitted to moose; it is harmless to deer but deadly for moose. (At the time it was called "moose sickness" and biologists had not yet discovered it.)

Emerson and Linda Fluery, Big Bay photographers, captured a moose taking a leisurely stroll through the village of Big Bay. He was refused service at the Thunder Bay Inn.

In the 1970s, the Department of Natural Resources (DNR) made the decision to re-establish a moose population in Michigan's Upper Peninsula. The DNR sighted the moose as an indigenous species and felt it only fitting to re-establish them in the wilderness of the Upper Peninsula. The DNR noted a small moose herd of 30 or so animals already existed in the eastern U.P. and decided it was time to expand the population. The small number of moose in the Sault area had migrated across the St. Mary's River from Canada. They were too few and too geographically scattered to reproduce at any significant level.

With the planned introduction of a larger herd in the central U.P., the chances of bulls and cows finding each other for mating would increase significantly and hopefully result in a more sustainable moose population.

Good habitat exists in Upper Michigan for moose. Moose range widely and can avail themselves to food even by traveling though deep snow to feeding areas. In addition, moose browse on balms and fir; food sources that are not palatable for deer. Moose also have the ability to browse higher in the trees than deer, thus increasing their food supply.

In the late 1970s, the planners were busy with the logistics of re-establishing moose to Upper Michigan. The actual moving of moose did not take place until 1985 and again in 1987.

The Michigan Department of Natural Resources obtained the moose (25 bulls and 36 cows) from the Algonquin Provincial Park in Ontario, Canada. In return, the DNR agreed to provide the Canadian Park with 150 turkeys over a three-year period.

The lord of the wilderness caught in the wilds by the Fleurys' camera.

Getting the moose from Ontario, Canada, to the Upper Peninsula was a challenging operation. The moose were first located in the Canadian park by two helicopters; the first would sight the moose, and from the air, a DNR rifleman would shoot an immobilizing tranquilizer into the animal. After the animal was narcotized, the second, or chase helicopter, would land and prepare the animal for transport. At this critical time, the animal was blindfolded and kept calm. Checking the animal's breathing and body temperature were extremely important at this point. Minimizing stress was the most important consideration at this juncture. With the moose resting upright on its chest it was loaded into a sling and transported to a base station 15 minutes away.

The base station crew's responsibility was to ear-tag each moose, weigh it, and attach a radio collar. A veterinarian who completed an international health certificate for each animal carefully examined each moose.

With the preliminary work completed, the moose was now ready for its 18-hour drive to the heartland of the Upper Peninsula. Each moose was carefully loaded into a transport crate and injected with a drug to reverse the narcotic affect. In five to ten minutes, the moose would again be active.

After many years of planning, the moose were finally released in Western Marquette County near Michigamme. A veterinarian completed a last examination before the final release. The bulk of the moose they released roamed an area dominated by northern hardwoods that included western Marquette County, eastern and northern Baraga County and northern Iron County. The average moose range is 16 miles.

In the early years of release, the primary method of keeping track of the moose was by a sophisticated radio collar. The collar

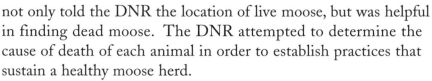

They continue to delight tourists who are fortunate enough to catch a glimpse of one ranging the Upper Peninsula woodlands. Moose may not be as sleek appearing as white-tails, or as fast as wolves, but they are the most imposing — and rightfully hold their place as sovereigns of Upper Michigan s wilderness.

not only told the DNR the location of live moose, but was helpful in finding dead moose. The DNR attempted to determine the cause of death of each animal in order to establish practices that sustain a healthy moose herd.

In 1995, ten years after the initial moose relocation, a study was done on the moose mortality. Necropsies (examinations of dead bodies) were performed on 59 moose. Brainworm or liver flukes caused the death of 48%, while 17% were attributed to vehicle collisions; reproductive and natural deaths were connected to 18% while in the remaining 16%, the cause of death was undetermined.

Law protects the moose, and anyone found guilty of killing one may suffer severe penalties. In 1991, a Flint man was convicted of shooting a moose and was ordered to pay $3,500 in fines and restitution. In addition, he was electronically tethered for six months, lost his hunting privilege for four years, and his 308 Veldt (weapon) was seized. There have been other prosecutions resulting in similar stiff penalties. The severity of the punishment handed down by the courts has kept the killing of moose to a minimum.

The present status of the moose population is encouraging, even though the exact number that roams the central U.P. is unknown. A survey in 1997, using two different counting systems, resulted in wildly disparate numbers; one survey had the population at 120 while another had it at 400. The DNR was not satisfied with either count and are now in the process of doing a more sophisticated analysis that will hopefully yield a more accurate number. Of the initial 61 that were transplanted, none are left. Presently, 63 moose are collared and being tracked.

The DNR is optimistic that the population will increase to a number where a limited hunting season can be permitted. According to DNR wildlife research technician Brian Roell, there isn't a magic number that must be reached before a hunting season is permitted; it will depend upon what the public will allow. Roell said, "The moose has almost a cult following. I suspect it would take high numbers before the public would support a hunting season."

In the meantime, moose can leisurely stroll the forests, unconcerned about man as a predator.

MUSHING
MANIA

DOGSLEDDING

The "U.P. 200" gives the Upper Peninsula international status in competitive dogsled racing.

With an abundance of snow and breath-taking wooded trails, free-spirited mushers thrive on testing their courage and resilience against the majestic Upper Peninsula wilderness.

Lashing winter winds, deep snow drifts, below-zero temperatures, frozen hands and feet and miles to go for the comforting confines of a warm hearth. Not a very inviting environment in which to find oneself – unless, of course, you're an Alaskan husky or malamute pulling a sled across the frozen winter tundra of the Upper Peninsula. For a husky, this is as good as it gets. Sled dogs were born to pull loads through winter's nasty elements; they thrive in conditions that most humans would find unbearable.

Today, sled dog racing is a sport, but at one time it was an important transportation system for isolated U.P. residents. Mail from Milwaukee and Green Bay was transported by dogsled in the 1850s to the remote Upper Peninsula. Peter White, an early Marquette pioneer, was one of those responsible for getting the mail to Marquette in the early years. In 1856, White was offered $1,000 by the city fathers of Marquette to pick up the mail from the Green Bay route at a Michigamme drop point, and then deliver it to Marquette.

In the cold winter of '56, White, as he had promised, fulfilled his end of the agreement by retrieving the mail from Michigamme and delivering it to Marquette over a hazardous trail. The city fathers, however, did not honor their end of the agreement and didn't pay the young Peter White (21) the money he was owed. (This is where the phrase, "get it in writing," originated!)

Dogsledding always enjoyed some recreational popularity in the Upper Peninsula, even after its practical use as a conveyor of goods or people was no longer necessary. That is, until the "iron dog" (snowmobile) became pre-eminent in the 1960s, and replaced the cruising canine. But the sole love affair with the snowmobile was temporary, and by the 1980s, outdoor enthusiasts recognized the joy in dogsledding and a renewed interest began in the old sport. The resurrection came full circle when the Upper Peninsula hosted a world-class sled dog race – the "U.P. 200" – in 1996.

Presently, the Upper Peninsula snowmobiler and the musher (a French word meaning, "to walk") have a tenuous alliance, both recognizing they must share a precious resource – the pristine, forested Upper Peninsula wilderness; jointly they must wisely use this vast, unspoiled woodland.

Mike Rosario's Alaskan Huskies receive pre-race encouragement from a U.P. 200 volunteer.

The Upper Peninsula has the essential ingredients for a sled dog's nirvana – cold and snow – lots of snow.

A sled dog is a special animal – not a formal breed as you may think, they are a "mutt" or mixed breed. Breeding dogs with physiques for sled pulling is essential. Ideal sled dogs are rarely over 55 pounds and have a quick and efficient gait and remarkable strength. A dog team of 200 dogs has been known to pull vehicles and even help to move houses. Getting the dogs to pull together is one of the most difficult tasks of training sled dogs. Months of training in the off-season to develop a coordinated team is necessary. This means huskies are often hooked up to wheeled-carts for summer training.

Ironically, these tough, cold-hardened dogs have sensitive, tender feet. Caring mushers must double as podiatrists to provide protection for the feet of their canines. Their tender appendages are securely wrapped in polar-fleece booties. Booties last about a hundred miles and must be changed several times in more lengthy races.

The premiere dogsled race in the Upper Peninsula and in the continental United States is the world-class U.P. 200. Actually there are two races, the longer 200 begins in Marquette, takes a circuitous route through Marquette, Alger, Delta and Menominee Counties, and returns to Marquette after covering 244 miles in three days. The companion race is a six-dog, 68-mile race, known as the "Midnight Run," which begins in Marquette, winds through Harvey, goes as far south as Chatham, and then returns to Marquette.

In 2001 the race had a record entry of 36, 12-dog teams. A $30,000 purse provides an incentive for mushers to do well. First place in the 244-mile, 12-team race is $6,000 (not a lot of money when considering the expense involved in mushing). Factoring in the cost of caring for and transporting 12 Alaskan

Huskies, costing as much as $3,000 a dog, it doesn't take long to have a big investment in competitive dog racing.

The travel expense alone can be astronomical. Teams from as far away as Alaska and Poland rarely ever recoup their expenses, no matter how much prize money they win. The dedicated mushers who make the sled dog circuit do it for the challenge and excitement. To the musher, there is no greater joy than being on the trail with your companion dogs towing you through some of Michigan's Upper Peninsula spectacular scenery. These are the driving forces that propel mushers to stay the course.

The International Federation of Sled Dog Sports sanctioned the shorter of the two races, the Midnight Run, in 2001 for the first time. This recognition allows mushers to compete for points that accrue for the world championship. With this new status, the mid-length Midnight Run has drawn competitors from Norway, Finland, Poland, Russia, New Zealand, Quebec, Australia, and Belgium. The race was capped at 50 competitors. It is the first championship race held in the continental United States.

> Dog owners are meticulous in the care they lavish on their sled dogs. A properly cared for dog is not only a companion, but an expensive investment that provides up to ten years of service as a sled dog.

Lyle Ross crossing the finish line in 8th place at Mattson Park in the U.P. 200. Pleased with his finish, Ross said, "These are the best dogs I ever had."

With dogs as the primary athletes in the U.P. 200, veterinarians provide an essential service in maintaining the health of more than 500 dogs. Eight to ten veterinarians provide medical assistance to the canine athletes before, during and after the race.

Veterinarians are stationed at check points to examine the dogs for any signs of illness, lameness, or other conditions that may be exacerbated by the animal continuing to race. Most veterinarians feel that mushers take excellent care of their dogs and would do nothing to jeopardize the health of their animals.

In the U.P. 200, dogs are examined at the beginning of the race in Marquette, then again at the Rapid River, Escanaba and Gwinn checkpoints. Making sure the huskies have sufficiently recovered to progress to the next stage is one of the major roles of the veterinarian. Most Upper Peninsula veterinarians disagree that sled dog racing is inhumane, as suggested by some animal rights activists. Tom Gustafson, lead veterinarian in the 2001 race, said, "The dogs thrive on the competition – they are enthused about it; they wouldn't do it if they didn't enjoy it."

All services provided by the veterinarians are volunteered (they are part of 500 total volunteers); they do it just because they like to work with canine athletes.

THE UPPER PENINSULA'S

"NATIONAL" SPORT

Deer outnumber the population 2 to 1: 300,000 residents and 600,000 deer inhabit the Upper Peninsula.

The stealthy hunter, dressed in a soft blaze-orange, two-tone Armani jacket with a rain repellent Gortex exterior, slides quietly into his $300 portable, camouflage-colored, propane-heated deer blind. To avoid wrinkling his Thinsulate insulated Tommy Hilfiger taupe pants, the nimrod cautiously picks up a high-energy compound bow and confidently places a graphite arrow into position. Polypropylene undergarments yield an agreeable fragrance of fresh lilac. Meticulously, he uncaps a steel-shelled Stanley thermos and pours a piping-hot hazelnut cappuccino into a handmade Aztec ceramic coffee cup.

In final preparation for the morning hunt, the well-appointed hunter places a DVD headset into position and tunes in Charlotte Church singing "Pie Jusu." Finally set, he leans back in a comfortable canvas-backed steel-framed chair and casually observes the smoke drifting lazily in the air from a Cuban cigar he just lit with a personalized inscribed Ronson titanium lighter.

This is deer hunting in Michigan's Upper Peninsula in the year 2001? Well – perhaps. It may be, at least for some of the more affluent hunters. But, it's certainly a far cry from the Upper Peninsula a century ago when hunting was not a ritualistic fall-rite, but a daily chore carried out because of economic necessity. A hundred years ago, hunting was not a recreational excursion for Dad; it was a mission to supply the family with meat for the coming winter.

Two occurrences made the Upper Peninsula a desirable place to deer hunt: logging and a transportation system. Extensive logging in the 1880s made deer browse more available;

and the opening of the Detroit, Mackinac and Marquette Railroad from Marquette to St. Ignace made the Upper Peninsula more accessible.

With these changes, professional hunters from Lower Michigan were now lured to the Upper Peninsula deeryards; and the railroad connection facilitated shipping the game out of the Upper Peninsula. Commercial deer hunting in the 1880s and 1890s in the Upper Peninsula was devastating to the deer population. Professional hunters bagged U.P deer by the thousands, stacked them up like cordwood and shipped them off to downstate markets. The Upper Peninsula became a "killing field." Prior to any regulations, the commercial deer hunting in the Upper Peninsula was catastrophic. Of the seventy-thousand deer taken in 1880, professionals who hunted for profit took sixty-thousand.

The State of Michigan first responded to this deer decimation with the establishment of the Office of State Game and Fish Warden. Some early regulations were passed that restricted hunting with dogs, shining and snaring deer. In 1895, the first deer quota bill was passed, which allowed only five deer per year to be taken by each hunter. This number restriction would be reduced to two deer per hunter in the early 1900s. Other practices outlawed in the 1880s were: digging pits along deer trails, driving deer into the water and cornering deer in a fenced-in area.

With new deer regulations in place and the creation of the Department of Natural Resources (DNR), the wholesale slaughter of deer ceased. The DNR then embarked on a mission to have a healthy, sustainable deer population in the State of Michigan. The success of their efforts is evident today with a statewide population of 1.7 million deer and an Upper Peninsula deer population of 600,000.

The middle of November is the time when most Upper Peninsula hunters pack up their hunting gear and head to camp for two weeks of serious deer hunting. However, for many nimrods, this is more than a hunting excursion; it is hiatus to paradise, a visit to nirvana and a respite from earthly shackles.

This is a place where there is no responsibility for two weeks. This is where cholesterol is consumed by the gallons at nightly wild game feeds and the camp chef is the high priest of camp cuisine. This is where the devil's libations are the only available consumable liquids. Poker is considered a high art form and using profanity is the only acceptable form of communication. Pictures of lightly clad women adorn the walls of many of these old cabins, and the visual pleasure they provide for the young neophyte hunters are a source of amusement to the seasoned veterans.

But, men, be ready! There is a specter lurking on the horizon. Women of the Upper Peninsula have united. There are now all-female hunting camps spreading across the Upper Peninsula forests.

One of the longest tenured and most successful all-female hunting camps is the Lindquist Camp on the Kingston Plains in Alger County. (Under the threat of death, the author was required to take a secret oath never to divulge the precise location.)

Brenda Lindquist and her seventy-nine year old mother, Doris, along with her sisters Jean, and Sandy, and friend Kathy Witcher form the nucleus of the famed "Lost 20 Girls" camp. These women are serious hunters. The clan matriarch, Doris, has bagged 15 bucks over the past 25 years, while Brenda has tagged 6 bucks in her deer outings, including a four-pointer she easily dispatched on the opening day of 2001. The ladies are always looking for trophy-sized bucks; does are not part of the equation. Other females join the Lindquist's clan at their woods retreat; the number of hunters at the camp varies from year to year. Who gets invited to this select hunting camp? Serious hunters who love the outdoors, know how to have a good time, and above all, aren't wimps.

The gals' November 15th residence is a hunter's camp paradise. Entry to the hunting camp is achieved only by a four-wheel-drive vehicle traversing a water-logged two-rut road. The tar-paper camp is located on a 20-acre site in the middle of nowhere; it is difficult to find and that's just the way the girls like it. The old camp is in the best tradition, a "hunting camp" with few amenities, but lots of rustic charm. It's old, but sturdily built. The small two-room cabin houses an old pot-belly stove that generates more than enough heat, capable of quickly getting the camp up to 90 degrees on the coldest winter day. Two large bunk beds occupy half of one room where 10 women can comfortably bunk down for the evening; sleeping quarters where visions of prize bucks dance in their heads. The other room is a small kitchen with a stove and the necessary liquor cabinet.

Located right next to the camp is the all-important camp privy; the outhouse is tastefully decorated (according to the camp residents) with colored glossies of nude males; some of the pictorials are more suggestive than others. The prints provide visual amusement to the ladies while sitting on the all styrofoam toilet seat. Brenda Lindquist swears by this toilet seat adaptation saying, "The Styrofoam keeps your bottom warm no matter how cold it gets outside." These ladies are rugged and take on any task necessary to have a successful hunt. On one occasion, Doris shot a large trophy-size buck that was too heavy for her to get out of the woods. To solve the problem, Doris and Brenda Lindquist harnessed themselves with rope and secured the other end of the rope to the deer carcasses. The prize deer was now

The early years of deer hunting in the Upper Peninsula were much different than today. Up to the Civil War, few hunting regulations were in place, and those that were did not apply to the Upper Peninsula. (Apparently the Lower Peninsula was still reluctant to recognize the Upper Peninsula as a part of the state.)

ready for his unsolicited journey back to the camp. The Lindquist duo heaved and tugged their heavy load over hill and dale until the exhausted couple finally got their captive stag to his final resting place — the cook stove at camp. You could have asked no more from stalwart Clydesdales. No four-wheeled RV was needed to haul a deer for these take-charge ladies.

Pre-hunting season planning that includes dance rituals is part of the Lindquist preparation. Several weeks before the start of the season, the lasses go to their blinds, located near the camp, and prepare the bait pile. Later they check on its condition to see if any deer have been dining at their prepared feast. If the bait pile has been consumed, the ladies perform a "deer-bait ritual dance" around the empty food site. No one but the camp members have seen this dance, so its movements are unknown to the outside world. And, there is no hard evidence whether this ritual dance guarantees a successful hunt for the year; despite this the lasses continue with the ceremony — science be damned.

Brenda's love for the woods and hunting is contagious and filters easily to those around her. With enthusiasm, she talks of a recent tree rub or disturbed ground where rutting had just taken place near her blind. Brenda said, "I love the smell of the woods; there's nothing like a crisp, clear sky on a chilly November evening. This is the most peaceful place I can be."

The Lindquist camp hunters after a successful day in the woods. Left to right: Jeanie Gramm, Sandy Keeler, Kathy Witcher, Brenda Lindquist.

The "Lost 20 Camp" represents what hunting is all about in the Upper Peninsula. The women of Alger County exemplify the spirit and skill that is characteristic of an Upper Peninsula deer hunter, whether male or female.

Hunting is big business for the Upper Peninsula; it is estimated that hunters in the year 2001 spent between $170 and $250 million dollars in the U.P. buying gas, food, lodging, and of course, tavern refreshments.

Between 250,000 and 370,000 hunters pursue deer in the Upper Peninsula forests the last two weeks of November. Overall, the Upper Peninsula deer count is within sustainable limits. The geographical distribution, however, is skewed with a surplus population in the lower Upper Peninsula counties (Menominee has the highest count), while the northern half of the Upper Peninsula has a slightly lower count than what the DNR would like. The larger, trophy size bucks are more numerous in the northern U.P. counties.

In the world of athletics, geographical areas are identified with a particular sport: Wisconsin has the Packers, New York has the Yankees, and Indiana has Notre Dame, but the Upper Peninsula has deer hunting. It may not be the glamour sport, or the greatest in revenue producing, but it is loved and revered by the natives who cannot wait for the opening day when the crisp smell of the forest reminds them that once again they are in "God's Country."

The Lindquist female hunters were not the first to hunt. These ladies from the eastern Upper Peninsula proudly bear their hunting weapons. (circa 1900)

THE BENNETT
HERMITAGE

*The cozy cabin
built with boulders.*

Duane and Joan Bennett longed to be away from the clamor and bustle of semi-urban life and were looking forward to the day when they could resettle in more peaceful surroundings. In 1999, when Joan retired from the Harbor Springs Schools and Duane retired from investigating airplane crashes, this became an opportune time to make a much anticipated life change. They searched for a remote but charming place to live. After considerable exploration, they found just the spot – a rustic, run-down cabin(s) (two attached units) located on an overgrown road nestled on the shores of the Michigamme River, just south of Republic. Their first visit to the cabin quickly alerted them to the awesome task awaiting them; repairing the old, sadly neglected homestead was going to be a big job. In the older cabin, the roof and floors were caving in, and the neighboring forest creatures had established residency. It would be work to get it livable, but the Bennetts were ready for the challenge. Republic would be their new home.

The cabin sits on two acres with 400 feet of frontage on the river. It is a choice location; the river widens out in the front of their cottage, giving the cabin frontage a "lake-like look." The vista from the log home, situated on a gentle rise just off the river, provides an unparalleled view of the wooded landscape leading down to the water. The attached units make one cabin: a one-story spruce log structure built in 1935 and a three-story addition built in 1973. Although the '73 addition is new construction, most of the materials used in its fabrication are over a hundred years old and give the appearance of being built a century earlier. All the log material used in this construction was obtained from old neighboring barns and houses that were no longer in use. Etched in the wall logs are names and dates of previous owners of the house and barns that years earlier, had served as sanctuaries for early settlers to the Republic area.

The expression, "a solid foundation," is used loosely to describe any variety of situations, but deemed most appropriate when describing the footings for the three-story section. This sector rests, unbelievably, on a 12-foot concrete bed. This is not a case of over-construction, as these twelve foot deep footings are needed to support walls made entirely of huge boulders! Each weighs anywhere between 2,000 and 4,000 pounds and are large enough to be used by the U.S. Corps of Engineers for a break-water. The supportive footings meet the load requirements to support the Washington Monument and the John Hancock Skyscraper together.

The living room of the Bennett Cabin. The boulders, weighing between 2,000 & 4,000 pounds, rest on 12-foot-thick footings.

Placed immediately in front of the boulder wall is a wood stove used for heating. Duane Bennett said, "The boulders are great for reflecting heat from the wood stove in the cold winter months... it keeps the place cozy." The boulders are the most unique feature of the house – making it one-of-a-kind.

Dick Lawrence, the previous owner and builder of the log and boulder addition, had the immense boulders hauled to the cabin site by Republic residents Edwin and Charles Neimi.

One at a time, the immense boulders were brought to the

The Bennetts in front of their unique cabin. Built in 1935, the structure has dovetail and overlap joints with a knurled lilac door handle.

cabin in a front end loader. Lawrence and his son meticulously mortared each boulder into place. The boulders are now the walls in the first floor living area. Unbelievably, Lawrence and his son did this Herculean task with no other assistance. To the casual observer, the building of the Egyptian pyramids would have been easier. Apparently, Lawrence did the boulder wall for aesthetic purposes, knowing there would be none other quite like it. He was right.

The ceiling and floor joists in the three-story section are 12x12 timbers that could support the weight of the Superior Dome. The walls are 8x8 square logs with dovetail and overlap corner joints. The flooring is two inch pine with wooden dowels. Lawrence noticed on a highway, near the cabin, a semi-truck had overturned with its cargo of tongue and groove flooring. The lumber company found it more economical to sell the lumber to Lawrence at a nominal price rather than to reclaim it. Being an effective and tasteful scavenger, he bought the lumber and hauled it back to the cabin and made an impressive doweled wood floor on the second floor of the addition. The Bennetts sanded off the old finishes and restored it to its original appearance.

The first and second-floor living areas are furnished eclectically and comfortably, while the third floor, with a small vaulted ceiling, serves as the master bedroom. The spacious second-floor living area, with a brick fireplace and open kitchen area, is where the Bennetts spend most of their time

The older '35 section was built by Carl Johnson and was in need of immediate repair. In reclaiming this one-story section, the first order of business was to replace the sagging, leaky roof and the rotting floor. Prior to the floor repair, one could have easily disappeared into some unknown cavern if one chose to tread on its deteriorated surface. The Bennetts repaired the floor and roof in the fall of 1999, barely out-racing the early November snowstorms.

The cottage has many unique features. The entry doors have been well-worn, but have functional, knurled lilac wood handles. Sitting benches line the breadth of the windows in both the living areas of the first and second floors. Three-inch-thick, triple layered, solid wood doors could double as bank security doors.

Housed on the two-acre lot are 15 kenneled Siberian and Alaskan huskies that the Bennetts harness up in the winter to enter in dog races. They race in the U.P. 200, the premier dog race, hosted by Marquette mushers.

"Stridor" was once the lead dog, but now he enjoys the amenities of being the house pet. On his own accord, Stridor decided that racing was a bit much and opted to retire to a more leisurely lifestyle which included moving his sleeping accommodations from the cold kennel he shared with his furry colleagues to the Bennetts' warm king-sized bed. During heavy, thunderous rainstorms, he burrows himself in the covers and waits for the comforting sounds of his master or mistress to assure him that all is well.

This house is not for everyone. But if you are inclined toward charming, rustic quarters on a remote but beautiful river bend and know that your home will be a work in progress for some time, then this house is for you – something the Bennetts knew from the start.

One room in the old structure, the summer kitchen, was re-chinked, and the pine floor rustically restored; a nook bench and a table are tucked in one corner of the windowed, well-lighted room. This is a perfectly delightful place to greet the morning while enjoying a sunrise breakfast.

THE SAWMILL
SANCTUARY

THE FLEURY SAWMILL HOME

Henry Ford never envisioned his sawmill becoming a fashionable home.

Urban dwellers look pridefully at their new downtown loft – a converted factory done over in a rakish art deco motif and possessing all the accoutrements of any civilized yuppie apartment. The cost can be astronomical for a well-appointed loft complex in an urban setting. A pre-ordained accompaniment to living in a converted factory in a city area is the clatter and clamor generated by your asphalt surroundings.

Emerson and Linda Fleury also have a factory home – a sawmill factory home to be exact – with 4,800 feet of living space located in Big Bay on the periphery of the remote Huron Mountains. The Fleurys ingeniously transformed part of an old, unused Henry Ford lumber mill on the shores of Lake Independence into a cozy, eclectic, comfortable home. It has all the amenities of any urban factory loft/apartment, but without all the traffic, pollution, congestion and price tag that most urbanites experience in owning a similar home.

The dwelling sits on 45 acres with over 1,000 feet of choice lake frontage. The Fleurys occupy only a small part of the old mill; the remaining building is empty or serves as a storage facility. The massive brick structure, perched on Lake Independence's shore, imposingly welcomes early morning sunrises that streak across the lake and bathe the old mill with fresh morning warmth.

From 1912 to 1926 the Lake Independence Lumber Company operated on the Fleury site. The corporation was a subsidiary of the Brunswick Company, the largest producer of bowling pins in the United States.

The aged mill has a rich history. White pine from the adjacent forest was milled and shipped out to the east coast where it was used for the construction of ships in the 1880s and 1890s; by the turn of the century it was a large-scale operation.

From the early 1930s to 1943, The Kerry and Hansen Flooring Company rebuilt and operated the mill with some success, but were forced to close their doors when they could not meet the wage directives ordered by the War Labor Board.

The great financier and automobile tycoon, Henry Ford, bought the lumber mill in 1943. The town was jubilant. Great things were expected from the huge Ford Corporation; this was to be the village's renaissance. Ford modernized the mill with a towering landmark feature: a 190-foot smokestack that is still visible from almost any point in Big Bay.

The old Ford sawmill on Lake Independence in Big Bay with its skyline-dominating, 190-foot smokestack. The Fluery's home is built inside of the sawmill on the opposing side of this picture.

Under Ford, the plant hummed with activity, manufacturing wood side-paneling for the popular Ford station wagons. However, this prosperity was short lived. Wood paneling on the station wagons fell out of favor as a car treatment, and Henry Ford – the driving force behind the lumber mill – died in 1947. With Ford gone and a decreased demand for the wood, the inevitable happened: the plant closed in 1949.

The mill, unused and deteriorating, was pillaged by scavengers for the next 25 years. Emerson and Linda Fleury looked at the site (in spite of being told they were crazy by their friends), and thought of the possibilities it had. They proceeded to purchase the mill and 46 acres in 1975. The Fleurys rescued the old mill from further plundering. They took it off the junk pile, tucked its brick, repaired its sagging roof, and made a unique and comfortable home out of the old mill.

Converting an old sawmill into a living space is not an easy task. There were gaping holes, cement outcroppings, and immovable walls that made the transformation challenging.

The kitchen is dominated by an impressive and exceptionally large walnut and maple island that seats 19 people comfortably. The island sits on a large cement slab that once was the resting place of sawmill machinery. Making an "eating island" out of the cement slab was just one of the Fleury's many creative innovations in converting the barren factory into a showcase home.

The kitchen's south wall has a large expanse of windows that provide a view of a spacious lakeside front yard. A green carpet of grass creeps to the water's edge where a dock and pontoon boat are ready and waiting to convey guests about the sizable lake.

The wing of the sawmill the Fleurys converted was a

16-foot one-story structure. In order to accommodate two levels, the second floor had to be limited to a 6' 2" ceiling. This was fine for Linda and Emerson who are both under 5'8," however, their taller offspring wished at times that mom and dad had been of more towering proportions. The limited height in the bedrooms, however, does not detract from the warmth and snugness you feel when entering the tastefully appointed quarters.

The section of the old sawmill that the Fleurys converted into a comfortable 4,800-square-foot home.

The exterior shake siding and brick blend well with the old mill; a wraparound porch with east and south exposures maximizes the use of available light and presents one with a grand vista of the expansive, meticulously manicured lawn.

This vast green space imaginatively plays with one's sense of time. At any moment, the mistress of the manor, wearing a colorful wraparound shawl and sporting an umbrella that delicately shadows her face, could stroll casually across the expanse, giving those on the deck charming coquettish glances.

Although the Fleurys have been in the house 25 years, they still consider it a work in progress. Converting a small, unused storeroom, just off the kitchen, into a bathroom, is the latest project in this continuous renovation.

Emerson and Linda are both photographers and market their wildlife notecards and postcards throughout the county. They are renowned for capturing photographs of native moose in the wild – unique in outdoor photography. The affinity they have for moose is evident in their home decorating. In the living area, a set of palm moose antlers, resting on a table, are used as a receptacle for knickknacks. A creative way to functionally use what nature has provided.

Converting an old sawmill into a showcase home is time-consuming and demanding; not everyone can do it. The Fleurys have done it – and they did it with style.

Emerson and Linda Fleury in their kitchen, with an island that comfortably seats up to 19 people.

DRUMS ALONG THE KEWEENAW

*Native Americans and the
Baraga Pow-Wow.*

The largest social
and spiritual Indian
gathering occurs
yearly at the Baraga
tribal grounds.

The deep rhythmical beat of the large ceremonial drum pulses steadily as the high-pitched, chanting voices of the drummers blend eerily with the strong percussion. The melodic resonance glides ethereally into the imposing white pines where the diminished tones trail off to a whisper in the sky.

This is the setting for the 24th annual Baraga Native American Pow Wow, a spiritual and social gathering of over 1,500 Chippewa, Lakota, and Oneida Native Americans. The Pow Wow site is a thickly-forested spot one mile north of Baraga on Highway U.S. 41, a short distance from Keweenaw Bay. Several thousand Native Americans and non-Natives take part in the activities over the weekend. This gathering of Native Americans is one of the largest in the Upper Peninsula.

Native Americans being called "Indians" is a misnomer. Christopher Columbus mistakenly called the Native Americans "Indians" or "Los Indios" believing that he had landed in India and not the Caribbean Islands. The term Native American applies to all groups that originally occupied both North and South American continents.

The Native American migration to the Upper Peninsula occurred 10,000 years ago when their Anishnabe forefathers moved westward from the east coast and reached the Straits of Michilimackinac where the tribe split up into three groups: the Ottawa remained near the Straits of Michilimackinac; the Ojibwa moved north and west; while the Potawatomi moved south along Lake Michigan. A small band of Potawatomi settled near the Cedar River in what is now called Hannahville.

The tribe numbers about 600.

Today, there are five reservations located near the following Upper Peninsula towns: Baraga, Sault Ste. Marie, Bay Mills, Hannahville, and Watersmeet. All the reservation tribes are Ojibwa (Chippewa and Ojibwa are used interchangeably), except for the Potawatomi of Hannnahville.

Nationally, the Ojibawa Tribe is an Indian community of 29,000. The Sault Tribe of Upper Michigan has 15 non-gaming businesses and five casinos that employee 2,500: it is the Upper Peninsula's largest employer. The Sault Ste. Marie Tribe Casinos are located in the Sault, St. Ignace, Manistique, Munising and Hessel. Native unemployment was as high as 70% in pre-casino days; it is now near the national average of four percent.

The Baraga Pow Wow is a gathering place for Native Americans from the Upper Peninsula and Wisconsin, who come together every summer for a spiritual and social celebration. The dance area is the physical and spiritual focal point for the Pow Wow. It is a large circular space with a cedar covered canopy shelter in the center. The first order of business is to bless the dance area with sage and prayer. With the blessing completed, the area is now clean and becomes a spiritual ground that serves as a resting place for the elders and a congregational place for the dancers and singers. It is not an area for non-Native Americans to transgress; this would be considered rude behavior.

One of the many food vendors at the Baraga Pow Wow. It is the largest of the Upper Peninsula Pow Wows.

Dancers, dressed in opulent Native American regalia, parade and dance in their own unique style to the pounding rhythm of the community drum. The drum provides a background beat for the dancers. To the Native Americans, each chant, each beat of the drum, and each dance step have significance; to those unfamiliar with the sounds and sights of the music and dance, the celebrations, while interesting to watch, have little meaning.

The dancer's regalia is nothing short of splendid. Much of the elaborate clothing is hand made and has been handed down for generations. They are priceless. Many have eagle feathers in their bonnets; the feathers are illegal for non-Natives to own. Often, it takes years to collect the items for a regalia; each article of clothing has a special meaning. The regalia is an expression of spirit and has been prayed over and blessed. To the Native American it represents living history.

A colorful opening ceremony is replete with rich native regalia and a tally of bright-hued flags.

Prior to 1978, many of the dignified spiritual ritual dances were banned. The Federal Religious Freedom Act of 1978 permitted Native Americans to practice and pass on these rites without fear of reprisal from any malcontent, ill-advised social activist, or government agency.

Physically stereotyping a Native American is a mistake. They come in a variety of skin pigmentations that range from milky skinned and blue eyed, all the way to dark brown skin and black hair. They are not any different than other races, possessing a wide variety of physical characteristics, all related to the lineage of their heritage.

The Native Americans are proud warriors and honor that tradition in the entry ceremonies. They pay tribute to all those who have served in battle: veterans from World War II, the Korean War, the Vietnam War and the Persian Gulf War. Each solemnly placing a flag from that conflict in a prominent place in front of the shelter in the arena's center.

Trading is a significant part of Native life. For centuries Native Americans traded with each other. Bartering goods with other tribes was a way of life, and this tradition is alive and well today. The Baraga Pow Wow had over 40 vendors selling jewelry, rugs, hats, beads, leather goods and a host of other craft items. Natives have long honored the talents and crafts from other tribes and the prized possessions they obtained from a neighboring tribe. It is important for the Native vendors to sell their creations, as many depend on the revenue received as a primary source of income. As a result, the craft items are competitively priced and a shopper at the Baraga Pow Wow will do no better price wise. The quality and authenticity of the vendor's goods are reputable.

Native Fry Bread is the most popular and sought after food at the Pow Wow. Over 13 vendors sold Fry Bread and competed for the honor of having the best fry bread at the Baraga Pow Wow. Native Fry Bread is deep fried dough; the results are a flaky, brown-coated staple that delights your pallet and expands your waistline. (It's worth it.) On the final day of the Pow Wow, 4,500 pieces of Fry Bread were sold. For a real delight, try a Fry Bread Burger smothered in cooked onions; it is a moment your taste buds will cherish forever.

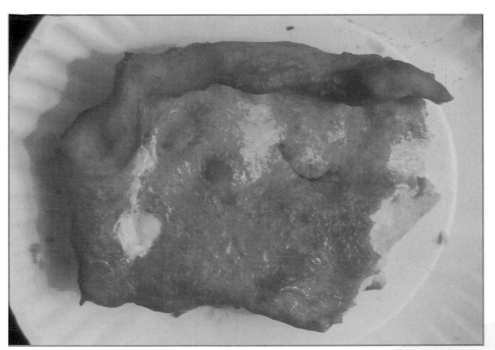

The Baraga Pow Wow and other Upper Peninsula Pow Wows provide the Native Americans with a spiritual and friendship renewal – a gathering that celebrates their uniqueness in the rich tapestry of Upper Michigan's people.

Native Fry Bread, a tasty morsel of deep fried dough, is the most popular food at the Pow Wow.

DAILY PRESS

EXTRA! EXTRA!

Gun Battle Rages In Ludington Park – Armed Conflict Leaves Dozens Killed Or Wounded

Escanaba – Two armed groups, each with as many as 40 men, engaged in bloody battle in Ludington Park's east end early Sunday afternoon. The fortified groups, one dressed in navy blue, the other in gray, were locked in a struggle to the death that left causalities on both sides strewn in a field of blood – exact number of dead and wounded is not known.

Apparently, the conflict erupted over secessionist statements that the "grays," or South, made to the "Yankee," or North group. It appears the Yankee group took exception to the South's secessionist rhetoric and demanded they retract the seditious statements or suffer the consequences. The South, in defiance, held steadfast and refused to withdraw the comments. A captain for the South group stated, "We have a moral obligation to determine our own destiny." All attempts to reconcile the grievances failed. With no agreement in place, the two sides clashed in the park shortly after 1 p.m.

Both sides brought in heavy artillery; eight-pound cannon balls pierced the air with a deafening roar, leaving billowing white clouds of smoke and death in their wake. In addition to the large cannon weaponry, each man was armed with a musket that had the capability of shooting accurately at 300 yards. The exactness of the weapon was evidenced by the carnage that lies on the field – bloated bodies baking in the hot summer sun.

During the battle, the Yankee physician, nearing complete exhaustion from treating the wounded in the nearby municipal dockside park, toiled on despite an endless line of battered bodies. After several hours of battle, with casualties mounting on both sides, and no apparent winner, the grays and the blues retreated to campsites located a short distance from the battleground. The ferocity of the engagement bears testimony to the commitment by both sides; judging by this action, it appears likely that even greater and more brutal conflicts are likely to occur.

(Longtine news release)

For the past four summers, this Civil War re-enactment has taken place in Escanaba's Ludington and Dockside parks. This Civil War re-enactment is a "living history" – a recreation of life during the war years (1861-1865) that seeks to preserve the memory and the ideals of the war era. Organizers Tom and Maureen Gardner of Escanaba are instrumental in bringing this event to the city; it is one of two civil war re-enactments in the Upper Peninsula. The other being at Fort Wilkins, in Copper Harbor. Tom Gardner said, "We have about 140 participants with about 40 being from Escanaba, a very good turnout for our 4th annual re-enactment."

The campsite was located at the Municipal Dock, while the battle site was a cordoned off area at the east end of Ludington Park. The campsite had the look and the feel of the 1860s, with over 50 white pup tents dotting a field of green, each tent with a fire pit in front. Rifles nearby are neatly stacked in upright groups and ready for action in a moment's notice. A stroll through the campsite is an emotional filtration with the past.

The area near the Municipal dock in Escanaba provides the ideal location for the weekend warriors to set up their campsite.

The encampment is divided into three areas: a civilian section where the women, children, and other non-combatants stay; a North military campsite; and a South military campsite. (In actuality, civilian camps were not mixed in with military camps, but in the re-enactment mode it makes it possible for the entire family to participate in the event.)

Early morning hours on the re-enactment weekend find the campsites bustling with activity as the women prepare the morning breakfast (often hardtack and salt pork), and the soldier husbands clean their rifles and ready their uniforms for the day's battle. The small tents and meager sleeping bags that keep the partakers sheltered and warm are minimalist in comfort. No Sheraton-Hilton accommodations here.

The male participants dress in typical Civil War uniforms; the North clad in navy blue while the South is in their traditional pewter gray. The women and children also dress in authentic period clothing. The full-length cotton dresses worn by the women are often self-made and extend four inches above the ground; generally the dresses are crowned with a vintage bonnet or hat. Maureen Gardner, smiling coyly, said, "The younger women wore hats while the older women wore bonnets – as you can see I'm wearing a stylish 1860s hat." These heavy garments can be stifling on a warm summer's day. Mrs. Gardner also noted that she honored the tradition that women did not enter the men's camp area unless escorted by their husbands. She hesitantly approved of this – for the re-enactment weekend only. As was the custom of the Civil War time, Maureen wore a broach with a picture of her husband in it, and had a pocket watch gracefully draped from a fob at waist height; women wearing pocket watches was accepted fashion during the Civil War.

Plumes of smoke in the air from a Union-fired cannon in Ludington Park.

After a generous breakfast, several soldiers in the South military camp completed clean up and then gathered under a towering oak to sing Civil War ditties. The blended voices emanating from the South's camp hung sweetly in the morning air as the prophetic words of "Somebody's Darling" glided harmoniously through the camp recess.

"Where the dead slept
and the dying lay;
Wounded by bayonets,
sabers and balls,
Somebody's darling
was borne one day."

Robert E. Lee said, "Without music there would be no army." The Southern soldiers, on this day, proved no exception.

After the last song drifted into the wind, the soldiers fell into formation to receive last minute directions from their commander about the ensuing battle.

Previously, the leaders of both contingents met to decide who would be the winner for this day. It is the only time in history when both sides jointly determine the outcome prior to the battle taking place. On this particular morning the North troops were addressed by a likeness of Abraham Lincoln. The actor, dressed in solemn black, with Lincoln's trademark stovepipe hat, gave the troops a departing statement: "You must do your best, for the fate of the nation rests on your courage." After this brief address, the Northern troops marched out of the campsite to the eerie beat of a lone drum; the Southern soldiers, in a march cadence, followed the North troops to the battle site.

The muskets used by the actors are Civil War reproductions capable of firing live ammunition; but for the re-enactment they will only belch ignited powder. Today, the enactment has three smooth-bored cannons used in the battle; they are original Civil War heavy artillery. (One of the gleaming bronze-barrel cannons can sell for as much as $50,000.) Likewise, a soldier's garments are fairly expensive, upward of $1200 or more with all the paraphernalia (saber, medals, etc.).

In a brief respite from the mock battle, Tom Gardner enjoys a meal prepared by his wife, Maureen.

After the battle on Sunday afternoon, the participants go back to their campsites; pack their equipment and bid their weekend friends adieu. Many of the Escanaba participants were from Wisconsin and Lower Michigan.

The Gardners participate in 4-5 re-enactments a year. You sense the enjoyment the participants had in putting on period clothing and living in a tent for a weekend; then stepping back in time by recreating a historical happening. The soldier/civilians return to their home communities, only to be resurrected and die again the following weekend. But, on that warm Sunday afternoon in Escanaba, they briefly lived in a time long ago and brought history closer to the residents of the Upper Peninsula.

THE FROZEN Fairyland

MICHIGAN TECHNOLOGICAL UNIVERSITY'S WINTER CARNIVAL

Tech engineers build the world's most elaborate snow statues – some as high as a four-story building, others a city-block long.

It's Michigan Tech's largest event of the year – the annual Winter Carnival. What could be more appropriate than for a city (Houghton) that has twice the annual snowfall of Juneau, Alaska, to sponsor a winter carnival with a host of winter games that include: hockey, snowshoe races, skits, ski meets, and of course the signature event – the unbelievable, carefully crafted snow sculptures.

Female students battle it out in an ice broom-ball event at the Winter Carnival. It is one of the many activities that is scheduled on the busy Winter-fest weekend.

The Winter Carnival has a long and colorful history going back to the first carnival in 1922, which can best be described as an ice circus held in the Amphidrome. By 1924, the winter circus became an established event and played to over 1,000 attentive spectators in the local ice arena. The day prior to the big performance in '24, the "circus band" paraded down Shelden Avenue and caused a near riot as eager spectators crowded from the buildings to see the winter parade spectacle.

After the Amphidrome appearance in 1924, the sponsoring Blue Key National Honor Fraternity, attempting to build on the carnival's local success and raise money for student activities, sent the ice carnival troop on the road. One of the stops on their entertainment pilgrimage was Marquette, where they performed at the Palestra Ice Arena. The traveling troop was not successful raising money, but served the college well in public relations.

The 1927 carnival saw the addition of one of the more curious winter circus activities. Ski riding was the feature of the '27 carnival, a dangerous event that called for a brave (or foolish) skier to be towed by a low flying aircraft. No statistics are available at the Houghton County Hospital as to the number of dismemberments that occurred as a result of this activity.

Nineteen twenty-eight inaugurated a carnival queen at the gala winter event. For many years the queen was selected from the local population because Tech was an engineering school and attracted few women. Recently, with more women entering the engineering field at MTU, the queen candidates are now students at the university. In 1955, the queen candidates were judged in skiing and skating competition. Apparently this limited the number of queen applicants and so the sporting qualifications were dropped.

The 1930s saw the first snow statues, and by 1935 the snow sculptures had become part of the carnival tradition. Local school children helped the college students build the ice marvels in the early years. Today, the snow statues are the premier attraction, drawing national attention in major newspapers across the country.

On two occasions, the Winter Carnival was suspended: from 1930-1934, the early years of the great depression, and during the war years from 1943-1946.

Celebrities who have performed at the Winter Carnival include the Chad Mitchell Trio, the Four Preps, the Highwaymen and Julie London.

This snow sculpture illustrates the incredible detail that goes into these ice masterpieces. The students spend hundreds of hours sculpting the snow monoliths.

Tech's Carnival is a grand celebration that infuses life into the community during the long, dark winter months. The snow sculptures (calling them statues does not do them justice) magically turn Shelden Ave. from just another main street into a road of captivating monuments. For one week the primary city corridor becomes a magical frozen fairyland.

HENRY FORD
Meets
John Tobin

Marquette resident John Tobin frequently repaired Ford's cars when he stopped in Marquette on his way to the Huron Mountain Club.

Henry Ford made frequent trips to Marquette; usually he was en route to the exclusive Huron Mountain Club at Big Bay. He often stopped at the Ford dealership in Marquette, located on the south side of Washington Street between Fourth and Fifth Streets. The building has a brick facade and the company name, *Upper Michigan Motors Corporation*, etched in the front and center of the structure. Presently, Fagan Antiques and Love Notes are the businesses that occupy the site.

Lifelong Marquette resident John Tobin (now 96 years old), was a mechanic at the Ford garage (1934-1936) where Henry Ford had his car repaired. Tobin met Ford on several occasions at the garage. Tobin said of Ford, "The chats were brief – he was kind of cranky – didn't say much." On one occasion Tobin told Ford of a repair problem; the leaf springs on the rear of the Ford cars were extremely difficult to lubricate. Ford immediately went to examine the car, and after an inspection, declared that the car's leaf springs needed a hollow center bolt that would distribute the oil evenly without having to do extensive leaf removal. He devised a new bolt, and the following year all Ford's new cars came out of the factory with the adaptive bolt. Tobin respected the mechanical genius of Ford, but said, "You wouldn't like him. He was a slight man, hard-headed and didn't have any sense of humor."

Tobin amusingly stated, "When Ford came to the garage, he had with him several hard-boiled characters with fur collars." They apparently were Ford's burly bodyguards. He never did explain to Tobin the need for this kind of protection in the remote Upper Peninsula.

Marquette resident John Tobin (96 years old) repaired Henry Ford's car at the Ford garage on West Washington Street in Marquette. Love Notes is now in the old garage building.

WITNESS TO A MURDER

On July 30th, 1952, Marquette residents Ken Goldsworthy and his wife Grace were sitting with Mike Chenoweth at the Lumberjack Tavern in Big Bay on a warm summer evening, unaware they were about to witness the most celebrated murder in Upper Peninsula history. Tavern owner Mike Chenoweth would be killed shortly after the Goldsworthys' arrival. With uncanny recall, 49 years later, Ken relates what happened that fateful night.

KEN GOLDSWORTHY
(in his words)

I "I picked up Grace at the Fleury Grocery Store in Big Bay at 8:30 on the evening of the 30th. It was a normal day, nothing unusual happening in town. I suggested to Grace that we go to the Lumberjack Tavern, as we occasionally did when she got done with work. We were going to have one beer and then head out to our cottage on Lake Independence, where our children were staying. We arrived at the tavern shortly, about 8:40 or so, and went to a booth in the bar. We weren't there more than ten minutes when Mike Chenoweth, the bar owner, joined us at our table. Mike was in good spirits that evening. Nothing out of the ordinary about him or in the tavern that nightfall. After a short period of time, Mike asked a friend to get an old scrapbook he had in an upstairs apartment that he thought might interest us. He said there was a picture of a Goldsworthy in the scrapbook that he had from when he was in the State Police and was curious to know if I knew him, or was related to him. We found the picture he thought might be my relative, but as it turned out, the guy wasn't any long-lost relative. However, what really struck me – and this didn't happen until much later – was the picture in the scrapbook that showed a murder scene that Chenoweth investigated as a state police trooper. Later on it struck me how close to home that picture was.

We continued the small talk for five minutes or so, when Mike was called to assist bartender Bud Wentzel with customer Orville Alexander. Wentzel was busy, so Mike came to his assistance. Chenoweth went behind the bar to get the six-pack for Alexander who was standing just on the other side of the bar.

Chenoweth got the beer from the cooler, turned around to give it to Alexander, who, moments earlier, was directly across the bar. Instead, there stood Lieutenant Coleman Peterson, just three feet away, with a revolver aimed right at Chenoweth. Grace and I were about ten feet away at the time. We didn't see Peterson come in the bar; he entered unnoticed by us, and went straight to where Chenoweth was located. At point blank range, Peterson unloaded his pistol into Chenoweth. Within seconds, Chenoweth was lying dead in a pool of blood behind the bar. It all happened so fast – it was hard to believe what we were seeing.

Marquette resident Ken Goldsworthy revisits the Lumberjack Tavern where he witnessed a murder over 50 years ago.

The place went crazy – customers ran in all directions, women were screaming and crying; Alexander ran into the women's bathroom. Grace and I were stunned and we just stayed in our booth. Bud Wentzel, the bartender and an ex-police officer, immediately approached Peterson after the fracas and attempted to stop him. Peterson then pointed the gun at Wentzel and said, "Do you want it, too?" Wentzel wisely backed down. Peterson then left the bar. Still dazed, but realizing something had to be done, I went up to the Thunder Bay Inn, a block away, and found the commander of the Big Bay military post, who was Peterson's superior, and brought him back to the Lumberjack Tavern. The commander, after briefly looking over the bloody mess, called in the State Police, who arrived at the scene within the hour.

Grace and I were eager to leave the Lumberjack and return to the cottage where our children were waiting for us. I told the police I had to leave because my daughters were back at the

Mike Chenoweth, the ex-police officer, was sitting with Ken Goldsworthy just prior to being murdered in the Lumberjack Tavern.

camp alone. The police complied and took our statements and we then left the bar. Sometime later, Grace and I were called to testify at the trial.

The day after the murder I was driving from Big Bay to Getz's Department store where I worked, when the impact of what happened the previous day hit me. All of a sudden, I started to shake; this went on for several minutes while I was driving. I thought, what if Peterson had turned his gun and Grace and I were killed? What would have happened to our daughters? [Ken and Grace had 5 daughters at the time ranging in age from 4 to 12.] It's something I'll never forget."

The killing would be immortalized in the John Voelker book, *Anatomy of a Murder,* and would eventually be made into a movie classic with Jimmy Stewart and Lee Remick. Ken is 85 years of age and resides in Marquette. His wife, Grace, died in 2000.

LEGENDS

ANATOMY
OF AN ICON

JOHN VOELKER

Few people become an icon during their lifetime.
John Voelker did.

"Trout fishing is a lot like chasing women, there s not much chance catching them when they re not in the mood."

John Voelker, 1989

The famed jurist, novelist and Ishpeming native, catapulted into national prominence in 1957 with his thinly veiled fiction book, *Anatomy of a Murder*. Voelker wrote three novels prior to *Anatomy*, all with moderate success, but *Anatomy* put him over the top and into the national spotlight.

Anatomy of a Murder was not only a best selling novel, but it also captured the attention of Hollywood moguls who turned it into a smash movie hit in 1958. Voelker changed overnight from a being a semi-obscure jurist and writer to a glitzy celebrity with a homespun demeanor.

Clarence Randell, a Sunday school teacher and lawyer, became John's mentor during his teenage years. Randell recognized John's potential and told him he would co-sign his loans, thus enabling him to attend college.

For the first two years of his academic life, John attended Northern Michigan University (1924-26), but then decided the law was his true calling. He enrolled at the University of Michigan law school where he graduated with a law degree in 1928. Of greater importance, however, John met Grace Taylor while at the U of M; he fell in love and then pursued her doggedly until she finally married him in 1930. John said, "I knew the jig was up for me when I saw this dark, lovely lady in her swishing black dress."

After graduating from law school, Voelker returned to the Upper Peninsula where he took a job with a Marquette law firm. After a short period of time in Marquette, he moved to Chicago to practice law. Before he left for Chicago, Judge Frank Bell told

Voelker, "You'll be back. In the meantime, good luck." Bell was right. John lasted three long years in the Windy City before he fled back to his beloved Upper Peninsula. He told his wife Grace, "It's better to starve in Ishpeming than wear emeralds in Chicago."

John Voelker's boyhood home near downtown Ishpeming, and not far from the Carnegie Library, where John spent much of his youth.

Back in Marquette County, Voelker ran for and was elected prosecuting attorney in 1934. He was the first elected Democrat to the county prosecutor position in many years. Of this miraculous break in the Republican hold on the office, Voelker called it, "The first one since Noah's Ark or the Flood." Later, he would recall with amusement the cases on his docket the first year. "There were three grand larcenies, two auto thefts, three burglaries, a brace of bastard cases, one indecent exposure, one assault with intent to murder, two wife desertions and one dog-tired prosecutor."

Voelker would hold the prosecutor's office for the next 14 years. In spite of having a good judicial record that reflected both common sense and legal expertise, he was defeated in 1950 by a slim margin of 39 votes by Edmund J. Thomas. Ironically, Thomas, within two years of his victory, would be locked in a deadly court duel with Voelker in a sensational murder trial in Marquette County. Voelker would represent the defendant, while Thomas would be the prosecutor in the famed 1952 Chenoweth murder case. The barrister combatants shared the public stage where Thomas was the reluctant recipient of Voelker's charm, wit, guile – and legal expertise. Thomas never had a chance. John Voelker would win the celebrated murder case, and though he never acknowledged it, I'm sure delighted in defeating – in court – the man who cost him the prosecutor's job.

Voelker quickly discovered that losing the 1952 election was a blessing in disguise: he now had more time to write. Earlier in life, he had written *Troubleshooter* and *Danny and the Boys* under the pen name of Robert Traver. John said this was necessitated by his being the country prosecutor at the time. He didn't want the public to think he was writing a novel on their time.

He continued to use the Traver pen name for all of his books.

John went into private law practice with moderate success. He still had time to cast a fly at his favorite fishing hole, but mostly it gave him time to write. And write he did. Fermenting in his facile brain during the early 1950s was what every author dreams of – The Great American Novel. He was always tinkering and tweaking a manuscript, but this was to be the blockbuster – the one that would vault him into literary history. It was, of course, *Anatomy of a Murder*.

Anatomy, published in 1953, quickly became the Book-of-the-Month selection and national sales sky-rocketed. Voelker will wryly say of his new found fame, "At 52, I'm a promising young author."

The novel was followed in 1957 by the blockbuster movie *Anatomy of a Murder*. Filmed entirely in Marquette County, the movie featured the silver screen legends of Jimmy Stewart, Lee Remick, and Duke Ellington as well as other Hollywood notables. The county buzzed with the excitement of Tinsel Town coming to Marquette. The movie would be as successful as the book, capturing six Academy Award Nominations.

John Voelker relaxes with Jimmy Stewart during the filming of "Anatomy of a Murder."

In addition to the book and movie accomplishments, Voelker, in 1957, would be appointed to the State Supreme Court by Governor Williams. The once reclusive fly fisherman, who enjoyed being in the woods, fishing, or culling morel mushrooms from the forest floor, could no longer hide from the luminosity of his national stature.

He served on the Supreme Court from 1957 to 1960, running for court office only once during this time. Being an elected official, John now had to campaign: he hated it. Voelker's Jeffersonian mistrust of urban areas made him a reluctant campaigner in Detroit's factories. He said of his factory campaigning, "This is a cynical invasion of privacy, the final denigration of democracy." He quit factory campaigning, but won the election anyway. He resigned shortly after his election win.

Voelker wrote 99 opinions in his brief stay on the Supreme Court; his decisions were frequently embellished with his wit, but all were imbedded with his northwoods common sense. Voelker's most

John Voelker was born in 1903 to George and Ann Voelker in the mining town of Ishpeming, Michigan. He lived within a stone s throw of the Ishpeming Carnegie Library, a place where he spent a considerable amount of time. Later in life, he would describe himself as "moderate literate."

noted case on the State Supreme Court involved a ruling on Battle Creek nudists that were convicted in a lower court of indecent exposure. Voelker, while not a champion of nudity, convinced the other justices of the naked clan's right to associate unclothed, as long as they weren't bothering anyone. To Voelker, this was just common sense. As a result, the Supreme Court set aside the lower court decision and let the bare-skinned bevy off the hook.

When asked about his judicial responsibility, Voelker said: "I believe in the responsibility and dignity of the court. On the other hand, I have no notion that judges are made in Heaven or decisions are ordained by the stars. We may err just as other men do. Our special responsibility is to see we don't err too often."

John resigned from the court in 1960 saying, "While other lawyers may write my opinions, they can scarcely write my books." If he could not be a writer and a State Supreme Court Justice at the same time, then writing it would be.

John would spend the next 30 years penning four more novels and doing what he loved most: stopping for an early morning cribbage game with his cronies and then fishing for the elusive trout at Frenchmen's camp. None of his later novels would ever capture the magic and notoriety of *Anatomy of a Murder*, but as a writer he was always pregnant with a new book.

John Voelker would die of a heart attack in March of 1990 while driving his car on Deer Lake Road, near his home. The titan of trout slipped quietly that day into another world. No longer would his tin cup brim with bourbon, or his mouth cradle a crooked cigar. The common sense jurist, the brilliant writer, and the trout impresario is gone, but he left a legacy that captured the hearts of his fellow Upper Peninsulans.

As a child, his mother frequently read stories to him, many times the same ones, over and over. As a youth, John penned his first story: Lost All Night in the Swamp. Voelker, always the master of understatement, said, "With a title like that there was not much story left to tell."

JOHN VOELKER PUBLISHED BOOKS

TROUBLESHOOTER (1943)

DANNY AND THE BOYS (1951)

SMALLTOWN D.A. (1954)

ANATOMY OF A MURDER (1957)

TROUT MADNESS (1960)

HORNSTEIN'S BOY (1962)

ANATOMY OF A FISHERMAN (1965)

LAUGHING WHITEFISH (1965)

JEALOUS MISTRESS (1967)

TROUT MAGIC (1974)

PEOPLE VS. KIRK (1981)

CALUMET'S
JOAN OF ARC

BIG ANNIE CLEMENC

She spat in the face of "scabs" and dared them to cross her union line.

She was outspoken and tough, and would verbally challenge anyone who attempted to obstruct her union marches. Annie Clemenc was not a wallflower.

Annie (Anna) Clemenc (pronounced "Clements") made a life-changing decision in the summer of 1913: she resolved to march in the famous copper strike in Calumet. The decision transformed her life forever. She was only twenty-five when she made this momentous decision. Few at the time knew who Annie was, but shortly, her name became a household word. She – almost single-handedly – galvanized the beleaguered miners into a cohesive force.

Annie was born in 1888 to George and Mary Klobuchar, Calumet residents who had migrated to the Copper County from Croatia. Annie's father worked for Calumet and Hecla Copper Mining Company for thirty years, while her mother worked as a cook and maid for the more affluent in the community.

Annie married Joseph Clemenc when she was eighteen years old. Joseph, a Croatian miner, never achieved the notoriety that eventually came to his wife. He was a big man at six-feet four-inches tall, but his size did not reflect his quiet and mild-mannered nature. Annie was a towering woman; standing six-feet two-inches tall, with a dominant personality that matched her physical size. As one reporter described Annie, "She was not unattractive, though dressed in the manner of the working class." Annie and her husband were very different in their views of life, and what they could do to improve their lot. She was an activist; he was not.

Annie witnessed her father and mother scrimping for the basic necessities of food and clothing. Her younger sisters wore Annie's old, worn-out hand-me-downs. The brothers followed their dad into the mine, destined for a life of pauperism. At the time, Annie's husband was making $2.50 a day at the Calumet and Hecla Mine; and she – if she were lucky – could earn fifty cents a day scrubbing the floors of the wealthy.

This pleasant-appearing portrait does not reflect the toughness the six-feet, two-inch "Big Annie" Clemenc demonstrated in the union marches.

In 1913, there was labor unrest in the copper mines in the Keweenaw Peninsula. The miners were concerned about their low wages and the long, 11-hour working day. They were most troubled, however, about the C&H policy of making a two-man drill a one-man drill. For thirty years the drill was a two-man operation, but in a belt-tightening move, the Calumet and Hecla Company insisted that only one man operate the drill. The miners felt it was extremely unsafe. The second man on the drill watched out for his partner in case of an accident – or even worse – a cave-in. The infamous drill wore the dreaded moniker, "the widow maker." These unresolved grievances led to the strike in 1913.

The miners wanted a better life than what they could afford as copper miners in 1913. A pay raise was necessary to be able to properly feed and clothe their families. An 8-hour workday would allow them to spend more time with their wives and children. But all-important was the two-man operation on the frightful drill.

Annie was aware of the poverty wages, the long workday, and the infamous widow maker. She knew the mines were atrociously unsafe, and on the average, claimed one life every week. Annie would now dedicate herself to improving the miners' working conditions.

Once the strike began, Annie, the housewife, responded and came to the support of the miners. On the third day of the strike, she led 400 miners, four abreast, down Calumet Avenue. Annie, wearing a gingham housedress – defiant – led the parade bearing a huge American flag on a 10-foot pole. Along with Annie and the miners were the children and the miners' wives who bravely marched through the streets of Red Jacket (Calumet). Annie knew that being prim and proper would not do it – womanish behavior would not commandeer respect from her adversaries.

The strike that Annie led did not have large worker support when it first began. Most of the workers in the largest mine in Calumet were opposed to the strike. However, once the strike began, many reluctant workers got on board with the union.

The Western Federation of Miners (WFM) organized the copper miners. Annie Clemenc spearheaded the Calumet auxiliary of WFM. Calumet and Hecla refused to recognize the miner's union. To do so would have given the strike credibility, something the mining company would never do.

She continued her marches seven days a week and became a serious irritant to McNaughton, the C&H President, and other mine officials. Annie became the symbol of defiance as thousands of miners daily marched behind her on the five-mile trip to the mines. Her imposing figure towered over the miners as she marched down Calumet Avenue, toting an oversized American flag with a confident gait.

Anti-Socialists in 1913 making a statement about the left-wing influences on the copper mine strike in Calumet.

Annie and the strike gained national prominence when famed attorney Clarence Darrow and Mother Jones marched with Annie through Red Jacket. Big Annie and the striking miners became the darlings of the media; much to the chagrin of the Calumet and Hecla mine owners.

Annie was arrested in September of 1913, along with five other women, when they tried to stop a scab (non-union worker) from going to work. Annie's loyal followers cheered wildly when she was released after spending several hours in jail.

On one occasion, Annie was knocked to the ground during a march; lying in the mud, she hugged the flag to her chest and shouted, "Kill me, run your bayonets and sabers through this flag and kill me, but I won't move. If this flag won't protect me, then I will die with it." Fellow marchers rescued her from this confrontation, but she was to have more encounters with the Waddies (strike-breakers hired by C&H). Big Annie was physically defiant; she spit on and kicked her adversaries. On some occasions, she doused a broom in a pail of human excrement and brandished those who attempted to thwart her march.

Her activism resulted in her being arrested three times, and spending 10 days in jail. This, however, did not deter the feisty union agitator. In one instance, she had to ride to jail in a car. Annie reportedly said, "It was her first ride in an automobile and she was proud of the occasion."

The union movement suffered a severe setback with the occurrence of the Italian Hall (see "Seventy-Three Die In False Alarm Fire") disaster on December 24th, 1913. The tragedy that ended in the death of 73 miners and their children, for the most part, took the energy out of the strike. Many of the miners now believed to return to the mines under any conditions would be an act of heresy. They left the Copper Country by the thousands after the Italian Hall tragedy; eight hundred and fifty left every week for Detroit, where Henry Ford promised them five-dollar-a-day employment.
Annie and 4,000 miners stayed in the Keweenaw Peninsula and saw the strike to its final conclusion in April of 1914. Annie vowed she'd stay to the end – and she did.

The union had a partial victory in the final settlement. They didn't get their union (WFM) recognized, and they lost the bid to have two men returned to the operation of the widow maker. They did, however, get an eight-hour day and a wage increase to three dollars an hour.

Annie's husband left her during the 9-month-long strike. With the strike over, Annie went on a Midwest lecture tour. When the tour was completed, Annie headed to Chicago with Frank Shavs, a Chicago reporter who covered the strike. She married Shavs in 1914 and they had a child the following year. Their child, Darwina, matured into an attractive woman, who bore a striking likeness of her mother. Annie, no longer a union activist, ended up working sixteen hours a day at two different millinery companies. Her husband Frank turned into a wife-beater and a drunk. Annie died from cancer in 1956. She was 68. Annie's legacy was not forgotten. In 1980, the U.S. Congress passed a resolution recognizing her (and others') remarkable contributions. She was the first woman to be nominated into the Michigan Women's Hall of Fame. In a lasting tribute, her portrait was hung in the state capitol in Lansing, Michigan.

Big Annie was not a suffragette, nor did she march for the equality of women. She marched because of her deep concern about working men making an adequate wage so they could provide a decent living for their families. To accomplish this, Annie grabbed her flag and marched for justice; she achieved equality the old-fashioned way – she earned it.

Annie soon became known as the American Joan of Arc. A Detroit newspaper said that Annie and the women were the heart and soul of the strike.

A militia officer once said of Annie, If McNaughton (president of C&H) could buy Big Annie, he could break the strike.

90

THE FLYING
Bietilas

THE BIETILA BROTHERS

"When it got dark we skied with lanterns placed on the end of the ski jump."

RALPH BIETILA

Seventy-seven-year-old Ralph Bietila is the last survivor of the famed Flying Bietilas. Ralph, along with his brothers, is enshrined in the National Ski Hall of Fame.

A Legend: "a notable person whose deed or exploits are much talked about in his own time." How about six legends in one family? The Flying Bietila Brothers of Ishpeming are a family of legends; their accomplishments on treacherous ski slides propelled them from being local icons into national celebrities. For nearly three decades, the Bietilas launched off ski jumps at 65 miles per hour, soared above the trees for hundreds of feet, and landed on precipitously steep slopes: all with the grace of a Baryshnikov pirouette. Unlike the fabled Icarus, they succeeded in flight; when others talked of soaring with the eagles, the Bietilas did it with Suicide Hill as their launch pad.

Jacob, the Bietila family patriarch, and a local iron miner, was born in Finland where skiing was not only a way of life, but was your transportation in the rugged Finnish winters. When Jacob emigrated from Finland to Ishpeming, little did he know that the six sons he would sire would become a skiing dynasty.

The Bietilas learned their craft on homemade jumps in the backyard. By the age of four they had strapped on their first set of crude hickory skis with only toe straps to hold them in place. They skied every day after school until the sun went down, and often into the dusk, when the only source of light were kerosene lanterns placed precariously at the end of the ski jump. After years of patiently honing their skills on their primitive backyard hill, they eventually migrated to Suicide Hill, where their earlier training resulted in record-setting performances.

Today's Olympic athletes have an elaborate support system. When the Bietilas skied, there was little financial aid – or any other support for the aspiring Olympic athletes. Olympic training sites, corporate sponsors, and fiberglass skis were unheard of in the 1930-1950 era.

The Bietila brothers dynasty. From left to right, Paul, Walter, Roy and Leonard Bietila. Notice the natty ties that were part of ski-jumpers' apparel. (circa 1940s)

Ralph (77), the youngest and only surviving brother, said, "We skied all the time, we didn't have television to watch or cars to drive like the kids do today." He lamented that not many kids were taking up ski jumping today because of so many other things for them to do. However, he did note that there appears to be a recent resurgence of interest in ski jumping by Ishpeming's youth.

Paul, the fourth son, had the most promise as a ski jumper; but never had the chance to achieve his potential. His life was tragically cut short; he died as a result of a ski accident in St. Paul, Minnesota, in February of 1939. He crashed into steel rope supports on the hill landing, breaking two ribs and suffering multiple fractures of his jaw. He died three days later of pneumonia – a direct result of the ski accident.

Paul's skills with the hickory boards were recognized early in his life. At age seven, Paul made a jump of 77 feet on the ski hill in his backyard. At age 11, he won the Class C title with a jump of 160 feet. He set a world record for his age (12) at Suicide Hill with a leap of 185 feet, breaking the old record by an unbelievable 19 feet. As a Class B rider in 1936, he won eight tournaments and set eight hill records.

By the time he was a teenager, Paul was the toast of the town; he was the guy that other youths his age wanted to be. You bragged about just knowing him. With his youthful good looks and athletic skill, he became a local "phenom." He had all the right stuff.

In 1939, he was 20 years old, and had just been named to his first Olympic team. He never made it; death beckoned first. He would soar into the sky – not with fellow skiers – but on the wings of angels.

Ralph Bietila in classic 1940s form at a ski jumping tournament in Iron Mountain.

The Bietila accomplishments were many: the brothers were on Olympic teams from 1936 to 1950. A trophy room in the National Ski Hall of Fame has a special showcase that houses just the Bieitila trophies. Another showcase, illustrated with family pictures, traces the history and contributions the Bietilas made to ski jumping. In locations through the Hall of Fame Building are pictures or artifacts from the Bietilas' memorabilia collection. Their presence blankets the Hall of Fame.

When Ralph was asked, "Were there any regrets in your skiing career?" He responded with a mild incredulity, "Regrets, no – I just met a lot of nice people – and I still get Christmas cards from fellow skiers in Europe."

Many of today's athletes, when asked the same question, would bemoan the fact that they never were appreciated, didn't make enough money, or failed to win a gold medal because of bad judging. This was not Ralph Bietila.

Ralph Bietila skied because the hill was there, and he loved to ski. The medals and trophies were nice, but a good jump on a hill lined with appreciative spectators was all he really needed. Those were the days when athletics were played for the love of the sport. Ralph Bietila knew that – he had it right – decades ago.

THE COPPER COUNTRY'S
GENTLE GIANT

BIG LOUIE MOILANEN

The world's tallest man.

Let's Get Acquainted	I Am Worth $1,000,000
Introduce Me To Yourself	In My Dreams

Let Me See Your Smile
Do Not Spurn Me
LOUIS MOILANEN

A Ragtime Millionaire
Am Not Married
Willing To Be

Never Flirt	Regards To Friends
Looking For Someone To Love	And Knockers

A life-size mural of "Big Louie" proudly hangs in the lobby of Republic Bank on Main Street in Hancock. It is only fitting that Louie's portrait be displayed in the tallest building in the Copper Country.

This was Louie Moilanen's calling card. At eight-feet one-inch, he was the Copper Country's most famous resident at the turn of the century. The phrases are telling; silent statements about what he feels, but cannot say. In spite of his enormous size, Louie was a reticent man; the card was his voice, his communication with a world that often viewed him as a life oddity. He never did flirt, he never did find love, and he never did marry. His card served as a lifelong reminder of what he wanted, but could not have.

Louie Moilanen was born in Finland in 1885 to Louis and Annie Moilanen. Ironically, his parents were extremely short; his dad was barely five feet tall, while his mother was well under five feet. The family immigrated to the United States when Louis was just four years old; they settled on a farm just north of Houghton.

It was apparent early on that Louie would be no ordinary child, by the age of nine he was the height of the average man, and by sixteen he was eight-feet one-inch and weighed over 400 pounds.

Louie liked to dress sharp; he decked out his tailor-made wearing apparel with a broad-rimmed Stetson hat, making his immense stature even more imposing.

Louie's legs, just over three feet in length, were more suited to a man of average height; this irregular body proportion made him awkward, resulting in frequent falls.

His first job was at the local copper mine where he labored as a timberman. Although he was a hard worker and had the respect of his fellow miners, the restrictive conditions of a mine-shaft made it difficult for him to work. The low heights and cramped quarters in the drifts were a constant difficulty for Louie; these troublesome conditions eventually made Louie leave the mine and seek other employment.

With little opportunity for other employment, Louie capitalized on his towering height and became a circus sideshow "freak." He toured the country with several circuses, including the world famous Ringling Brothers and the Barnum and Bailey circus. In spite of his soaring height, Louie did not garner much attention as a circus "oddity." This, in large, was attributed to his shyness and reluctance to be a side-show entertainer. Promoters were disheartened about Louie's low attendance numbers and encouraged him to seek other employment. This was just as well for Louie, who was not enamored with circus life and lonesome for his home in Houghton.

Big Louie Moilanen, standing eight-feet one-inch, was an oddity in the Keweenaw Peninsula. He died at the age of 28.

Louie had several other jobs in Hancock during his short life, but he always returned to the family farm. For a while he bartended and operated a tavern in the center of Hancock's business district. On another occasion, he entered the political arena and served as a Justice of the Peace for the township. He didn't stay long with either job and always migrated back to the family farm, where, in later years, he cared for his widowed mother and where he was most happy.

Louie was not destined to live a long life. Physicians said that his heart was undersized for an eight-foot, 400-pound frame. Louie became ill in December of 1913 and was rushed to the hospital where he laid for three days, finally succumbing to tubercular meningitis of the brain. On his final day, Louie was found peacefully slumped in a chair in his hospital room with a bible in his hand. He was 28.

After the funeral service at the Lutheran Church, eight men transported his nine-foot casket to the nearby Lakeside Cemetery. The oversized coffin had to be strapped to the horse-drawn wagon in order to navigate the steep inclines in the cemetery. It was feared the ponderous casket would slide off the wagon if it were not adequately secured. No accident occurred and "Big Louie" was finally laid to rest.

Local gossip declared Louie died a millionaire. He was not; he died destitute.

THE GODFATHER

DOMINIC JACOBETTI

"Some of the people call me 'The Godfather' and I don't mind it. I am The Godfather for the U.P. and I'm proud of it."

July 1990

Dominic, "Jake," Jacobetti delighted in his moniker, "The Godfather." To him, it meant power and respect. Like the Mafia boss in the movie *The Godfather*, Jake was as tough as nails and used his toughness to fight fiercely for his Upper Peninsula constituents. Political opponents aware of Jacobetti's tenacity were frequently out-muscled by his aggressiveness and relentlessness. Jake was aware of his clout and reveled in his strength, but said there was more to him than just the tough guy image. He thought his tough persona was often exaggerated and that his soft side was often overlooked. "I like to help people," he said. "I have a soft spot for poor people. That's where I come from."

Known as "The King of Pork" in the legislative body, Jake wielded his power for the Upper Peninsula. He brought home the bacon with no apologies.

While political purists were repelled by the notion of pork barrel legislation, Jake was proud that he was delivering the goods to Upper Peninsula residents, an area he felt was just a poor stepchild to the wealthier downstate districts. Anything he brought to the U.P. he felt was deserved.

Jake was born in 1920 to Nicholas and Josephine Jacobetti, poor Italian (Sicilian) immigrants who lived in the Patch Location in Negaunee. Laboring in the mines, Jake's father barely earned enough to feed the family. There were hard times and the family teetered on the edge of poverty. During the Depression Jake cut wood and stole coal (in the middle of the night) just to keep the family warm during the bitter cold winter months. He had no qualms about stealing the coal. "My mother told me,

Adversaries, aware of his intense Upper Peninsula allegiance, were quick to comment that Jacobetti brought so much money over the Mackinac Bridge they feared it would collapse from the weight.

"it's no sin to steal to keep yourself warm."

The Patch Location was a tough neighborhood; fighting was a necessary survival tool. Jake learned it well. "There was always somebody there to challenge you, to hit you in the nose, just to show they were tough." Later in life, Jacobetti found his toughness served him well when he was locked in political struggles in Lansing. He never backed down from a good fight. The Southern Michigan lawmakers quickly learned that the man from the remote Patch Location in Michigan's Upper Peninsula wasn't a lightweight and was tenacious as hell.

A distinguished Dominic Jacobetti received an honorary Doctorate from Northern Michigan University. Jacobetti worked tirelessly in the State Legislature on behalf of Northern.

It was in the Patch Location that Jake got another of his nicknames – "Puga." His childhood friend Jimmy Maino dubbed him Puga. Maino gratuitously nicknamed others in the neighborhood as well, but felt Puga was most fitting for Jacobetti. Jake said that Maino told him that he was the guy that was going someplace and that's why he named him "Puga."

Jake grew up during the Depression; those poverty years were a great lesson in life, which he never forgot. He knew that if he ever got into a position to make decisions that affected other people he would do things on behalf of the poor. He said, "I lived with that in mind and I think I'll die with that in mind."

Dominic Jacobetti was a star athlete in Negaunee's St. Paul's High School where he captained both the basketball and football teams. He graduated from St. Paul's in 1938. His son "Duke" would follow his athletic leadership at St. Paul's – becoming one of the most prolific scorers in the history of Upper Peninsula basketball.

After high school, Jake went to work in the iron ore mines like many other young men his age. He followed in the footsteps of his father and plunged into the deep abyss of the dank and sunless Athens shaft mine, where he and other miners toiled from dawn to dusk.

Early on, his mother encouraged him to join the union. Jake followed her advice and joined the union, soon becoming one of the more active members and an eventual steward. He then became the grievance chairman and within a short period of time was President of the United Steel Workers Local.

By 1954, Jacobetti was a union staff representative and had worked in the mines for 16 years. It was at this time that he was encouraged by John McNamara, the local Democratic Chairman, to run for a State House seat. McNamara told Jake he probably wouldn't win, but it would make it more difficult for the Republican. Typical Jacobetti, he said, "If I'm going to run, I'm gonna win." He did – by 162 votes. Jake would never have another close election.

By the time the dust settled on Jacobetti's illustrious career in 1994, he had been elected 21 times, becoming the longest serving politician in the State of Michigan. During his 40-year tenure in the House, he rose to power, eventually becoming chairman of the powerful Appropriations Committee, a post he would hold for 18 years. As Appropriations chairman, Jake controlled the purse strings for the State of Michigan. Even governors had to pay homage (reluctantly at times) to Jake. His iron-fisted, no-nonsense leadership style earned praise from his friends and enmity from his foes.

The Jacobetti Home for Veterans, located in Marquette, is one of several facilities named after the legendary lawmaker.

During his record-breaking tenure in the House he drew his share of controversy. In 1991, Jake refused to support a resolution honoring Erwin "Magic" Johnson for his community service. Johnson was a Michigan State and National Basketball Association icon and prominent in speaking out on behalf of those with AIDS. The media exploited the fact that Johnson had AIDS and that was the reason why Jacobetti denied support to the resolution. Jake disputed all accusations that he was prejudiced.

The House Fiscal Agency scandal in 1993 was the most serious attack on Jake's lengthy legislative career. John Moberg, the agency's director, bilked $300,000 in state agency funds for his own personal use. Jacobetti was Moberg's superior and was the one ultimately responsible for the agency's expenditures. Although Jake was cleared of any wrong doing, he was dumped from his powerful Appropriations chairmanship. Moberg did prison time for pilfering the taxpayers' money.

The removal of Jake from the Appropriations Committee diminished his power in Lansing, but not with his Upper Peninsula constituency. They loved Jake back in the Upper Peninsula regardless of what accusations swirled about him. After his ouster, Jake vowed to regain his chairmanship of the House

Appropriations Committee. But, at age 73, time was running out for the veteran lawmaker. Multiple illnesses were now ravishing his once sturdy body. Jake was battling a rare skin disease, walking pneumonia, a bleeding ulcer, and leg, heart and lung problems. His spirit was willing, but his body was failing. In spite of these medical difficulties, Jake ran again for his house seat. For the 21st time the old warrior strapped on his campaign clothes. He was re-elected by a 4-1 margin. Jake was untouchable when it came to elections.

Time, however, was not his ally. On November 20, 1994, he died in his home from a massive heart attack. Marie, his wife of 52 years, was at his side. Jacobetti made a telling comment in 1990 when he said, "...So I guess maybe I'll retire when the good Lord says 'I'm going to take you.' That's the way I feel about life."

Ironically, Republican politicians criticized Jacobetti, just a year before his death, when they learned that Jake had the largest state legislative pension in the nation at $45,967 a year. Bryan Flood, a Republican spokesman said, "Here's a legislator who has 'Been There Too Long' written all over his shirt." The Republican tirade was premature; Jake never collected a cent of the pension money. He died while in office at the age of 74.

Perhaps his wife Marie made the most fitting tribute – and the one that meant the most to Jake – in 1990 when she said, "Sometimes I look at him and think, what a delightful man you are." Jake enjoyed the accolades he received from the public, but basked in the support of his life-long friends and family.

He was, "Mr. Upper Peninsula."

Most U.P. residents felt that Lower Michigan politicians purposely engineered scandals about Jake; they believed that Lower Michigan politicians had a vendetta against the beloved Upper Peninsula lawmaker.

THE LAURIUM LEGEND

GEORGE GIPP

Laurium's legend gave movie star Ronald Reagan his most famous quote –
"Win one for the Gipper."

It looked bad.

The score: Notre Dame 0, Army 6. Notre Dame was on their heels and facing yet another loss to a powerful Army team.

It was 1928, and Coach Rockne, with a 2 – 4, record was desperate. The season was slipping away. For the first time, sport critics were harsh on him, asserting that his golden touch was gone. Now was the time to pull out all the stops and use his one last ace in the hole. Rockne had saved this one motivational tool for eight years. If ever there was a time to use it – this was it. At half-time he would drop his usual fiery rhetoric, and with solemnity, deliver a heart-rending oration that would inspire his team to decimate a superior Army team. This had to be his best half-time discourse – maybe his best ever.

With that in mind, he faced his beleaguered team at the half and told a story – a story with a wish – a wish by the Notre Dame legend George Gipp. Rockne related to his players what Gipp had said while clutched in the throes of death, "I've got to go Rock, it's all right. I'm not afraid. Sometime when the team is up against it, when things are wrong and the breaks are beating the boys, tell them to go in there with all they've got and win one for the Gipper. I don't know where I'll be then Rock, but I'll know about it, and I'll be happy."

When Rockne finished telling of the Gipper's last wish, there was not a dry eye in the locker room. After a moment of silence, the psyched-up players burst out of the dressing room, nearly tearing the hinges off the door, and went on to thrash the Army team in the second half. The final score: 12 – 6. The

The Gipper incident was immortalized by Ronald Reagan playing Gipp in the 1940 movie, Knute Rockne — All American. This was not lost sight of by politicians who supported Reagan in his drive to the White House in 1980.

winning touchdown was scored by seldom-used reserve, Johnny O'Brien. O'Brien never played another down of football after this historic touchdown, but along with Gipp, he became a Notre Dame legend known as "One Play O'Brien."

George Gipp's legendary coach, Knute Rockne, described Gipp as Notre Dame's greatest back.

George Gipp was born in Laurium in 1895. Records are scant about his early years, but in high school his feats in track and baseball were well known in the community. Observers noted that Gipp could traverse 100 yards on a football field in 10.2 seconds, and tear the cover off a baseball he just launched on a 400-foot journey.

Although Gipp was a Methodist, he and a friend opted to attend Notre Dame, a Catholic university. While at Notre Dame, Gipp was a force to be reckoned with, both on and off the field. In his last 20 games, the football team had 19 wins, no losses and one tie. Gipp crushed opponents with lightning speed and brute strength by scoring 83 touchdowns in 32 games.

Off the field, Gipp was just as active. Academia was not his long suit; socializing in dance halls was more to Gipp's liking. On one occasion, Gipp was expelled from the exalted university for cutting classes; reports, however, surfaced that he was dismissed because of his attendance at a disreputable dance hall that was strictly off limits to the student body.

This expulsion led to thunderous protest from the alumni and other Nortre Dame fans. Eventually, the administration caved in under the relentless pressure and shortly Gipp was back on the field terrorizing the defense of some hapless opponent.

Gipp was a confident man. In a game against Northwestern, Nortre Dame was down 17 – 14 at the half. Coach Rockne was livid. He was delivering one of his fiery half-time recitations when he noticed Gipp gazing about indifferently during his serious tirade. Rockne glared at Gipp with a contempt reserved only for those you wish an early departure from life – then snapped at Gipp, "I don't suppose you have any interest in this game?"

Confidently, and unemotionally, Gipp responded, "I have $400 bet on this game and I don't intend to lose it." This was quintessential George Gipp.

In 1920, Rockne held Gipp out of a game against Northwestern; Gipp was ailing with a sore throat and injured shoulder. Notre Dame was losing, and with Gipp not playing, the highly partisan crowd was irate; they wanted Gipp on the field. After several minutes of repetitively chanting his name, "Gipp, Gipp," Rockne relented and sent his star player into the game. As usual, Gipp responded with a winning touchdown. But the price was high.

The Lake Superior stone monument honoring Laurium's hometown legend, George Gipp. He was only 25 at the time of his death.

Two weeks later, Gipp entered the hospital; he was deteriorating quickly and immediately diagnosed with pneumonia and strep infection. Teammates rushed to his side and donated blood in an effort to save his life. The blood donations from his teammates and the medical intervention were to no avail. It was at this time that Gipp made his deathbed wish to Rockne with the immortal phrase, "Win one for the Gipper." Shortly after the Rockne visit, Gipp slid quietly to his death. He was 25.

George Gipp, Notre Dame's first All-American, is honored with a pocket park in his hometown of Laurium. A Lake Superior stone memorial with a stone fountain dominate the small pocket park. A plaque with an inscription adjacent to the stone memorial is the center-piece of the park. Providing park definition, a backdrop of cedar trees wreathes the back perimeter of the quaint setting. George Gipp, Laurium's favorite son, was not forgotten.

THE SAGACIOUS SCIENTIST

GLEN SEABORG

Ishpeming resident and famed world-class scientist discovered plutonium at the age of 28.

Glen Seaborg, born in Ishpeming in 1912, was raised in a modest home on New York Street at the east end of town. His father, a machinist for the iron mines, provided a livable but marginal income for the family. This limited economic backdrop was hardly predictive of the fame that Glen would gain in later life. From these humble beginnings, Glen would become a world-class scientist.

Glen Seaborg never forgot his Ishpeming roots and always considered himself a "Yooper." In later years, when he achieved global status and was a speaker at prestigious conferences, when he took the podium he would ask those in attendance if they knew where Ishpeming was. To a gathering of world-class scientists, this rhetorical inquiry always went unanswered. Seaborg would then wryly state, "...Well, it's right next to Negaunee."

Glen Seaborg's modest childhood home on New York Street in Ishpeming. Glen spent ten years of his life living in this now dilapidated dwelling.

Glen spent the first ten years of his life in this quiet, remote mining community. His upbringing was typical of the time and gave no indication of the greatness that was to come. In grade school, Glen was big for his age; this served him well as he was in demand as a caddie at the local golf course: few other boys his age could tote the heavy golf bags. In re-telling others about his time in Ishpeming, Glen was fond of describing the heavy winter snows and how he could ski out of his bedroom window after a snowfall. He had a life-long love affair with his native Upper Peninsula.

Glen T. Seaborg, holder of 43 patents and winner of the Nobel Prize in 1951.

When he was ten, the family moved to California, where struggling to survive was a daily concern. The family weathered the depression, at times with little to eat. Glen's family indigence made the thought of a college education something he could only dream about. Glen knew the only way he could go to college was with financial help. To do this, he was advised to take chemistry. In his junior year of high school, he enrolled in chemistry; this was a turning point for Glen – he loved it. Physics was taken the next year and Glen now knew that scientific exploration was to be his life's work.

He enrolled at UCLA where he worked as a stevedore (one who loads and unloads ships), and a linotype assistant. Packing fruit and distributing handbills were other small jobs that Glen did to make money while working on a college degree. Glen was ambitious; this would be a lifelong trait.

Seaborg earned a Bachelor's degree from UCLA in 1934 and a doctorate from Berkley in 1937.

Success came early to the youthful Seaborg. At the age of 28, Glen, along with other colleagues, discovered plutonium, a fissionable element that would forever change the world and usher in the era of atomic weapons. By the age of 30, Seaborg was in Chicago working on the Manhattan Project (building the atomic bomb) with famed and brilliant scientist Enrico Fermi.

Glen met fellow scientist, Ernest Lawrence's, secretary Helen Grigg in 1941 and was smitten by her. Like many successful relationships, Glen needed a friend to assist him with getting the courtship underway. Eventually he won Grigg's heart and they eloped in 1942. The marriage produced three children and lasted 56 years, until Glen's death in 1997.

Glen's importance to the scientific community was well recognized by the presidents of the United States. He was an advisor to all the presidents from Harry Truman to George H. W. Bush. First Ladies, from Eleanor Roosevelt to Hillary Clinton, met and admired Glen Seaborg. Few attain the lofty stature and high regard that was his.

Seaborg loved sports. He had an affinity for football and loved hiking. Northern California was Glen's and Helen's hiking domain where they spent countless days traipsing the forest all the way to the Nevada border.

His lifetime accomplishments in science are hard to imagine: The discovery of 10 atomic elements, discoverer or co-discoverer of more than 100 isotopes, and a reorganizing of the periodic table (much to the chagrin of many of his colleagues). His many contributions made Glen a giant in the scientific world.

Although his research was instrumental in developing atomic weapons, Glen was a strong advocate of the peaceful use of atomic power. Throughout his illustrious career, Glen pushed for uses of atomic power that would profit mankind. While chairman of the Atomic Energy Commission, he was instrumental in negotiating The Limited Nuclear Test Ban Treaty of 1963. Sixty nations witnessed Glen touring their countries promoting the peaceful use of atomic energy. Northern Michigan University in Marquette, only 12 miles from Seaborg's birthplace, honored him by naming their new science building the Glen T. Seaborg Center for Teaching and Learning Science – a fitting honor for one of the great men of science in the 20th century.

The Glen T. Seaborg Center for Teaching and Learning Science on Northern Michigan University's campus was named in honor of the Ishpeming native.

Author of more than 25 books, holder of 43 patents and winner of the Nobel prize in 1951 are but a few of the many achievements of Glen Seaborg's long career. He was a man for all seasons, brilliant, accomplished and above all, a caring human being. An unassuming, gentle, likable man, with an extraordinary gift – this was Glen T. Seaborg.

THE SKUNK WORKS

WONDER

CLARENCE "KELLY" JOHNSON

The Ishpeming native designed the world famous U–2 spy plane that was piloted by Francis Gary Powers and shot down over Russia in 1960.

There was none better – Clarence "Kelly" Johnson – an Ishpeming native, jet-age pioneer, and a brilliant engineer who was on the cutting edge of airplane design from the mid 1930s to the mid 1970s. He was an unequaled world-class plane designer for over 40 years.

Johnson spent the first 13 years of his life growing up on Summit Street in Ishpeming. Rambling about Ishpeming in sartorial splendor while sporting his trademark bright green ties, he appropriately acquired the nickname "Kelly."

Johnson had an early interest in planes, his neighbors recalled; he was continually working on models. On one occasion, he ingeniously built a submarine that could go around in circles and then dive and surface. Johnson could be found demonstrating the submarine's capability in a large water holding tank near his house on Summit Street.

He named one of his model planes "Merlin," after the legendary famed magician. He deemed the name appropriate, as the model could do unrealizable things. Kelly Johnson's real-life pursuit would parallel this childhood fantasy; he would create planes that designers thought impossible.

Kelly Johnson was the son of Peter Johnson of Ishpeming, one of the finest stone masons in the area. Many of the grand buildings in Ishpeming are the result of Peter Johnson's skilled labor.

Kelly attended the Ishpeming schools until the 7th grade. In 1923, at age 13, Kelly, along with his family, moved to Flint. Johnson graduated from Flint Junior College and went on to receive a degree from the University of Michigan. His first job

Celebrated woman aviator Amelia Earhart used a Model 10 Electra, designed by Johnson. She attempted an around-the-world trip in a Johnson-designed plane.

was working for General Motors as a consultant on the aerodynamics of cars running in the Indianapolis 500.

From General Motors, Kelly went to Lockheed Corporation where he spent the next 30 years designing more jet aircraft than any other person in history. From the beginning in 1933, Lockheed recognized Johnson's genius. He assisted in designing the Orion, an aircraft piloted by the famous Jimmy Doolittle.

This Kelly Johnson photograph was signed to Miss L. Tucker, an Ishpeming librarian.

During World War ll, Johnson designed aircraft for both the United States and Great Britain. The most famous of his WWII planes was the P-38 Lightning, a planc that served in every theater of the war. In 1943, Johnson was given one of his most ambitious assignments – design a plane in 180 days. To complete this task he was housed in a temporary facility that became known as the Skunk Works. The Skunk Works was Lockheed's secretive operation where the best brains in aeronautics labored to build the next generation of military aircraft.

Johnson did not disappoint Lockheed officials; out of the Skunk Works came the embryonic P-80 Shooting Star, the U.S.'s first jet fighter. The P-80, traveling in excess of 550 miles per hour, was described as the most exciting aircraft since Kitty Hawk. The plane was developed too late to see World War II combat, but the Shooting Star was the forerunner to the jet fighter used in the Korean War.

In the 1950s, Kelly Johnson developed the famous F-104 Starfighter, described as "the missile with a man on it." This streamlined fighter set a world speed record of 1, 400 miles per hour.

The limelight came to Kelly Johnson in 1960 when his famous U-2 spy plane, piloted by Francis Gary Powers, was shot down over Russia on a high altitude reconnaissance mission. The incident caused an international stir. The Russian premier, Nikita Khrushchev, paraded plane remnants before a worldwide television audience. In the aftermath, Powers was sentenced to ten years in a Russian prison, but served only two years when he was exchanged for a Russian spy.

The 1960s witnessed Johnson's continued progress in plane development with the creation the SR-71 Blackbird. His aeronautical eminence was evidenced again as Johnson used titanium rather than standard aluminum in the construction of the Blackbird. Titanium's advantage over aluminum was its ability to withstand 800-degree temperatures at supersonic speed. The Blackbird flew from New York to London in an unbelievable one hour and 55 minutes.

Clarence "Kelly" Johnson spent his early childhood in this home on Summit Street in Ishpeming.

Johnson was brilliant and immensely competent, and he expected those selected to work with him to be equally competent. If you screwed up, you were subject to Kelly's wrath. Staff members who attempted to finesse a mistake around Kelly would quickly wish they were never born. Nothing got by him.

In 1964, President Lyndon Johnson awarded Kelly Johnson the prestigious Collier Trophy for aeronautical accomplishments.

Kelly Johnson's personal life was marred with tragedy. His wife died in 1970 after a long struggle with cancer. Before she died she told him to remarry – recognizing that Kelly had a difficult time living alone. She was concerned about his eating and drinking habits when left by himself.

Kelly heeded his wife's advice and within a year married MaryEllen Mead, a spirited redhead, twenty-five years younger. She admired Kelly and was very attentive to him. MaryEllen got Kelly to give up drinking scotch; she hated the smell on his breath. Not to be denied his spirits, Kelly switched to Vodka, which he assumed did not leave an odor.

MaryEllen was diabetic and didn't take care of herself. As a result she became quite ill, and by 1980, she was in a serious condition. By the end of 1980 her weight had dropped to 80 pounds and she died shortly thereafter. She was only 38.

Before MaryEllen died, she suggested to Kelly that he marry her best friend, Nancy Horrigan. Wasting no time, Kelly married Nancy a few weeks after MaryEllen's death. He was always worried about what others thought of him marrying so quickly after the death of a wife – however, not enough to deter him from a quick trip to the altar.

In 1998, the Marquette County Board of Commissioners considered naming the new county airport after Kelly Johnson. The board eventually rejected naming the new facility after Johnson and decided to have a walk of fame honoring other local air pioneers, as well as Johnson. Kelly Johnson, a national aeronautical icon, deserved the honor of having the new county airport named after him.

In 2001, the County Commission decided to name the new access road to the K. I. Sawyer International Airport, "Kelly Avenue." This was only fitting for the genius of airplane design whose roots are firmly secured in the craggy rock outcropping on Summit Street in Ishpeming, Michigan.

After a long career, Kelly Johnson retired as a senior vice-president of Lockheed in 1975. He lived to age 80 and died in Burbank, California in 1990.

THE SNOWSHOE PRIEST

FREDERIC BARAGA

This church, built with logs and bark, near Manistique, is a replica of Bishop Baraga's first one on this site in 1832. Frederic Baraga was Upper Michigan's first Roman Catholic Bishop.

Frederic Baraga was born in 1797 into a well-to-do Slovenian family. Orphaned when he was only eight, his inheritance provided for an excellent education by private tutors. A diligent scholar, he earned a law degree from the University of Vienna. Upon graduation, however, he renounced his inheritance, put aside his legal training, and entered the seminary.

After his ordination he found himself in conflict with church authorities. Jansenism, a creed that mandated God's predestined salvation for only the select, ran contrary to Baraga's view that God's love was universally bestowed. This dispute led to his emigration to the United States in 1830 to serve as a missionary.

He began his ministry in Harbor Springs, Michigan, but his missionary work soon spread to the Upper Peninsula where he established churches at Sault Ste. Marie and L'Anse.

Baraga labored tirelessly, spreading the Catholic gospel to the Ojibwa Indians. Fluent in six languages, including Indian dialects, he baptized, held marriage ceremonies, heard confessions, said Masses, gave communion, comforted the sick and buried the

Bishop Frederic Baraga (1797 – 1868) renounced his inheritance to enter the seminary. For 35 years he traversed 80,000 square miles as a Catholic missionary.

dead. In 1853 he published *A Grammar and a Dictionary of the Otchipwe Language.* That same year, Frederic Baraga became the first bishop of what would become the Marquette Diocese.

For 35 years, the Snowshoe Priest traversed an 80,000-square-mile area including present-day Michigan, Wisconsin and Minnesota. Traveling from outpost to outpost on snowshoes during the winter and on foot during the summer, he was glad to catch a ride horseback or on a wagon if he could. Whenever possible he traveled over water, by canoe, sailboat and an occasional ride on a lake steamer.

After a severe stroke in 1866, he lost the ability to speak and lingered on for another year and a half until January 1868. He was buried in a crypt at St. Peter Cathedral, only two blocks away from the home where he spent the last years of his life.

The Bishop Baraga Association is attempting to have him canonized. His positio (declaration for sainthood) is being edited and prepared. Intercessions, or miracles performed after his death, are a necessary proof; church authorities attribute over 100 such intercessions to Baraga. If the positio is approved, his case then proceeds to the next level, consideration for beatification. Canonization supporters have been working for over 70 years to have him declared a saint.

His square brick house on the end of Fourth Street stands empty, but the name of Frederic Baraga is still remembered in the village and county that bear his name, and in the old Baraga School and Baraga Avenue in Marquette.

This modest dwelling in Sault St. Marie was Bishop Baraga's first home. Built in 1864, this unpretentious house was Baraga's residence for only two years. Missionary travel prevented him from establishing any long-term residency.

THE TWO HEARTED
TALE

ERNEST HEMINGWAY

In 1919, the famed author spent a week in the Upper Peninsula.

As many Upper Peninsulans know, world famous wordsmith Ernest Hemingway wrote about fishing the Two-Hearted River near Newberry in Michigan's Upper Peninsula. But, few know that Hemingway, the master of crisp prose, was never near the Two-Hearted River. In the short span of time that Hemingway was in the Upper Peninsula (one week), it would have been impossible to get from Seney (his arrival point) to the Two-Hearted River. Closer to the truth is that he fished the Fox River near Seney, but chose to use a more "romantic" title for his piece, "Big Two-Hearted River." The Fox River just didn't cut it for a story title – obviously much too prosaic for a writer with an intimate connection to the English language. Hemingway knew what he was doing.

In 1919 Hemingway made his one and only visit to the Upper Peninsula. He was twenty years old and embarked on what he thought would be an adventure to a wild and untamed Upper Peninsula frontier. He and his two friends, Jack Pentecost and Al Walker, arrived at the Seney Railroad Depot ready for a challenging escapade. Hemingway envisioned Seney as a wide-open logging town with its tawdry 1880 reputation intact. He was, however, 30 years too late; when he got to Seney all he found was a desolate community rife with empty, deteriorating buildings. The wild era of Seney as a tavern and brothel-haven for lumberjacks on weekend missions was long past.

Rumor has it that after their arrival, Hemingway and his friends walked a short distance east of the depot to the Fox River. From there, it is theorized, they followed the river north for two miles and then camped out near blueberry pickers in the area. They remained in the area hunting and fishing for a week before returning to the Lower Peninsula. (The Hemingway family had a camp on Walloon Lake near Petoskey, Michigan.)

Hemingway wrote the "Big Two-Hearted River" in 1924. A noted collection of stories titled *In Our Time* featured the now famous short story. In his story Hemingway says that Seney was burnt to the ground. This was not true – areas around Seney had burned down over the years (a frequent happening in logging communities). Hemingway, however, did view the charred remains of the Grodin Hotel that burned down a year earlier. Hemingway, taking literary license, called the hotel the "Mansion House Hotel" in the Big Two-Hearted River. He could never be accused of not dressing up a piece

The old train station, and now the Seney Historical Museum, where Ernest Hemingway arrived in 1919. The museum houses a Hemingway pictorial.

After leaving Seney in 1919, Hemingway would move to several cities before becoming an expatriate on Paris' avant-garde West Bank. Who would have thought the great American writer, and winner of the Nobel Prize for literature, would choose Paris as a place to live rather than Seney. Nonetheless, Upper Peninsulans have "big hearts" and forgave him for that one transgression.

When Hemingway made his visit to the Upper Peninsula, he was in the last stages of recuperation from a severe leg Injury he received while driving an ambulance in Italy during World War I. He was only 18 at the time of his war injury.

THE UNREWARDED INVENTOR

JOHN BURT

John Burt sued the federal government for his Sault Ste. Marie lock invention that the government used and then refused him compensation.

In June of 1891, the Justice Department of the United States Government issued an order to close the Soo Locks for three days. General Poe, a federal administrator in Detroit, issued the closing order. He had no idea why the Justice Department issued the closure, but, being a faithful government employee, he didn't question the directive and was prepared to execute the decree.

The shipping magnates and owners of the boats (the word "boat" is preferred to "ship" on the Great Lakes) that used the locks were outraged at a possible temporary lock closing. This would not only cost them time and money, but it would create an unmanageable flotilla of boats bottled up at both the east and west ends of the St. Mary's River. The shipping companies were steaming mad over the projected closing, and the government was not forthcoming in telling them why they were proceeding with a closure recommendation.

The reason the Justice Department was ordering the closure was a source of intrigue. It seems the Department was in a protracted and unresolved lawsuit with John Burt's son, Hiram, over an invention John had patented years earlier (1867). The invention was incorporated into the construction of the Weitzel Lock in 1881. The government never acknowledged the use of the Burt invention in the building of the lock.

John Burt, the first Locks superintendent (1855-59), patented a way for water to enter and exit the locks more efficiently and with greater safety. His system of water exchange reduced the lock time by half and made the loading and unloading of ships in and out of a lock much safer. His invention was simple, but

John Burt never received one cent for his inventive system that was used in all the locks that were built in the 20th century at the Sault, saving the government countless millions of dollars in the process.

ingenious. Under the old system the locks were using, water entered and exited the locks through ducts (sluices) in the entry and exit gates. The water had to be let in and out slowly or the turbulence could seriously damage the boats by bouncing them around in the lock.

Burt drew up a plan where the water would enter and exit the lock from ducts in the floor of the lock. This enabled the lock to be filled and emptied more quick and safely. When the new Weitzel lock was completed in 1881, the Burt system was used, but the government failed to give him credit for his invention; they built the lock without providing him with any recognition or remuneration. The use of the Burt system saved the government two million dollars alone in construction costs.

Shortly after the completion of the Weitzel Lock, John Burt became aware of the government's use of his patent lock. Perturbed at the government for usurping his invention, John sued the federal government in 1882 for $500,000. Burt died four years later (1886) and never saw the completion of his lawsuit.

His son, Hiram, continued his father's legal action, hoping for some compensation by the government for violating his father's patent rights. The bureaucratic, lethargic, government failed to take action on the Burt lawsuit in a timely fashion and seven years later found themselves unprepared and facing a court deadline on the suit in 1891. The government failed to inspect the lock to see if Burt's invention was used as specified in the patent. The government needed to close the lock down in order to have a visual inspection. The Justice Department proposed closing the locks for three days to do so.

Hiram Burt got wind of the projected closing and realized it would paralyze shipping for three days. He suggested to the government that the lawsuit be postponed until the locks were closed for the winter season and thus enable an easy inspection. The government readily agreed to Burt's magnanimous offer – Burt saved the day. This charitable offer, however, did not soften the government's position or the Burt compensation claim – they still denied culpability. The trial was post-postponed until a later date and the locks remained open. Had the conditions been reversed, one wonders if the government would have been as understanding as Burt in resolving the matter.

Hiram Burt doggedly pursued the infringement suit. A bill was introduced in congress in 1900 to rectify the injustice to John Burt that was committed by the U.S. government. The bill was never acted upon and died when the 56th Congress adjourned.

Sometimes it pays to fight city hall. For John Burt and his descendants, it was an exercise in futility.

THE WRIGHT Stuff

FRANK LLOYD WRIGHT

At age 70, world-renowned architect Frank Lloyd Wright visited Marquette.

Frank Lloyd Wright, the genius of American architecture, paid a visit to Marquette in 1936 to oversee the construction of one of his home designs. Abby Beecher Roberts, the surviving daughter of pioneer developer John Longyear, had commissioned Wright to design a house for a wooded 240-acre site just west of the city.

Nestled into a hillside, the house blends naturally into the environment. Sweeping glass panels and beige-colored bricks, framed by an impressive roof overhang, dominate the lower level. All the windows look out on a thickly wooded forest.

A Frank Lloyd Wright designed house built in 1936 in Marquette. The residence has the classic "Prairie" look with the low profile and extended eves.

The living room, with a unique corner fireplace, is 25 feet by 40 feet, "Big enough," owner Abby Roberts said in a contemporary news story, "to swing a tiger!" Stained cypress trim complement the beige brick walls which are continued in the interior.

Described variously as "elusive, impish, arrogant," Wright was 70 years old when he visited Marquette. According to a newspaper account, he was still a human dynamo: "If someone doesn't tether his feet, he will start soaring like Peter Pan." His vibrant personality and enormous talent made him a dominant force in American architecture during the first half of the century.

ASSASSIN
In Our Midst

LEON CZOLGOSZ

The presidential assassin spent time in the Upper Peninsula.

Old logging hands from the area demeaningly described Czolgosz as being ill suited to the work of being a lumberjack. "Not a rough-neck," was how one old timer described him.

On September 6, 1901, Leon Czolgosz, without attracting any notice to himself, worked his way through a crowd of admirers to where President McKinley was greeting throngs of well-wishers at the Pan-American exhibition in Buffalo, New York. When he was close enough to McKinley, Czolgosz extended his hand that concealed an automatic revolver. After firing two shots into the president, the handkerchief that neatly hid the weapon burst into flames and dropped to the ground.

The gun wounds proved fatal, but not immediately. McKinley hung on to life for seven more days before succumbing to an infection caused by a bullet that was still lodged in his back.

The now infamous Czolgosz drew national attention and every detail of his life was fodder for the press. Records indicate Leon Czolgosz spent a summer at a lumber camp in Seney, Michigan. He was known as an agitator while at Seney. Supervisors were disgruntled at Czolgosz's pontificating about workers' rights to his fellow lumbermen. He promoted anarchism (violent overthrow of the government) to solve the inequities in society.

Within two months of the assassination, Czolgosz would be electrocuted and buried in the Auburn Prison Cemetery. Prison authorities disintegrated the body with sulfuric acid. Just before he was electrocuted, Czolgosz said, "I killed the President because he was the enemy of the good people – the good working people. I am not sorry for my crime ."

DEATH
At Lake Gogebic

REIMUND HOLZHEY

WANTED

FOR:
ROBBERY
&
MURDER

REIMUND (REINHARDT)
HOLZHEY

REWARD $2,800

CONTACT:
SHERIFF DAVID FOLEY,
BESSEMER

AUGUST 27, 1889

"You'll get nothing out of me," a defiant Arnold Macarcher said to Reimund Holzhey who had a .44 caliber side arm jammed into his abdomen. With that, the angry Macarcher pulled out the revolver he had hidden inside of his coat and fired at Holzhey who was attempting to rob him.

Macarcher's errant shot went wide and missed his attacker. Twenty-two year old Holzhey responded with a volley from his handgun. One of his shots hit Macarcher in the mouth, seriously wounding him. Macarcher was one of four passengers on a stagecoach in the Western Upper Peninsula.

In the ensuing confusion, the frightened stagecoach horses bolted and careened wildly down the road. Reimund Holzhey blazed away with his six guns at the departing stage. Two accurate shots hit passenger Adolph Fleischbein in the abdomen, sending him toppling off the stage and crashing to the earth. Two frightened female passengers inside

118

the stage screamed in horror as they watched the bloody melee. Fleischbein was dead. Macarcher was seriously wounded.

A youthful and unconcerned Reimund Holzhey (center) is hand-cuffed and guarded by a well-armed sheriff. Holzhey would serve time in the Marquette Branch Prison.

This was the last stagecoach robbery in Michigan. The year: 1889; the place: the quiet hamlet of Bessemer, Michigan. The robbery took place on a lonely and primitive stretch of road that ran from the Gogebic Station to the plush Lake Gogebic Resorts, close to the town of Bessemer. It was an isolated area – ideal for a robbery. Highwayman Holzhey knew what he was doing. Both Macarcher and Fleischbein were bankers and probably were carrying a good deal of cash. He thought it would be easy pickins; after all, he just finished several successful heists in Northern Wisconsin and Upper Michigan. Holzhey didn't think the robbery would end up with him committing murder and having the law hot on his trail.

Reimund Holzhey was a transient German immigrant who just migrated to the Bessemer area from Milwaukee, believing there were riches to be found in the Gogebic Range. He was bright but uneducated, didn't have any job skills and didn't get along with people.

Rumors of gold, silver and diamond mines in the Gogebic area lured Holzhey into a belief that quick riches were soon to be his. He just needed a stake.

After the robbery debacle, Holzhey scampered off into the woods with his ill-gotten booty. He lived in the woods for the next several days, eating berries and begging meals from unsuspecting fishermen and campers whom he encountered along the way. After several days of this nomadic existence, he hopped a train to Republic, some 100 miles from the scene of his holdup.

In Republic, Holzhey's crime spree was about to come to an end. The desperado, with a price on his head, was unceremoniously captured by vigilant law officials from the small mining community. Historical records vary as to how the actual apprehension took place – some descriptions more colorful, but perhaps less accurate, than others.

One newspaper account of the nabbing of Holzhey comes close to describing the "Gunfight at OK Corral." The article states that Holzhey stepped out of his hotel in Republic on a bright sunny morning, only to be quickly surrounded by an angry mob. The law officers subdued him just before he could reach for his gun and then he was kicked unconscious by a self-righteous rabble that demanded his immediate lynching. He survived the capture, was incarcerated briefly in Republic and then sent to Bessemer for trial.

His trial garnered the most attention in the community, even though it was competing with the town s most colorful prostitute on trial for selling whiskey, and a local judge being litigated for embezzlement.

The 21-year-old Holzhey was tried in Bessemer Circuit Court in October of 1889. The Holzhey incarceration was drawing so much attention that the local sheriff decided to capitalize on the "media frenzy" by agreeing to have Holzhey photographed in a local studio, wearing a "macho" ammunition vest and touting a long rifle. The sheriff, with entrepreneurial adroitness, sold the pictures to the curious as well as to souvenir seekers. Young children were shown the photograph of the ominous looking Holzhey and told in stern terms that bad things happen to children who don't obey their parents.

The 12-man jury convicted Holzhey in 45 minutes, in spite of his defensive plea that he had unnatural feelings and spells of amnesia after a horse had kicked him in the head. Playing the "victim" card in 1889 did little good, and he was sentenced to a life term at the Marquette Branch Prison.

Holzhey began serving what would be a 24-year incarceration. Prison records report that Holzhey had "recovered from his criminal tendencies following a surgery to remove a bone splinter lodged in his brain." He was a model prisoner, eventually becoming the head prison librarian and editor of the penitentiary paper.

Upon his release in 1913, he took a job as a guide for the exclusive Huron Mountain Club (a posh retreat for the wealthy), just north of Marquette. He worked there for the next 20 years, and then at the age of 63 he moved to Florida and began a new career as a freelance writer. (Beware of men who become freelance writers late in life.)

Throughout most of his adult life, Holzhey complained of severe headaches and nightmares. Whether these reoccurring terrible dreams had anything to do with a conscience, weary of 63 years of guilt over the murder he committed, is unclear; but one thing is certain: at the age of 86 he took his own life by putting a bullet through his brain while sitting quietly on a rocking chair on his back porch.

MURDER
IN MENOMINEE

THE McDONALD BOYS

*Frontier justice in the Upper Peninsula
in the 1880s resulted in
vigalante hangings.*

In 1880, Menominee was the lumber port capital of the world and home to a rugged lot: lumberjacks – tough, crude men – who worked hard during the week and raised hell on the weekends.

Two of the lumberjacks were Frank and John McDonald. The McDonald cousins (not brothers) were from Nova Scotia, Canada, and had a reputation as bad men, particularly when they were drunk – which was all too frequent.

The McDonalds repeatedly caused disturbances at the lumber camp. On one occasion, Sheriff Julius Reprecht was sent up to the lumber camp where the McDonalds were in the midst of a camp commotion. When Reprecht arrived at the camp and attempted to quash the disturbance, Frank McDonald, the younger of the two, took offense to the Sheriff's interference and pulverized the hapless sheriff until he was unconscious.

Shortly after the beating of Reprecht, Deputy Sheriff George Kittson, a burly 200-pounder, pursued and arrested the McDonald boys and brought them to the Menominee jail for trial. The McDonalds were tried, convicted, and sentenced to one-and-a-half years at the Jackson State Prison. They served their time uneventfully, and were released early for good behavior. They returned to Menominee where they resumed their old ways – working during the day and drinking and raising cain at night.

The McDonalds began drinking one night at the Montreal House, a bar in Frenchtown. Bartending at the Montreal House was Norman Kittson, brother of the deputy sheriff who was responsible for the McDonalds' Jackson Prison incarceration. The McDonalds let Kittson know they were out to even the score with his brother.

The McDonalds
are buried in an
unmarked grave
in the potter's
field section of the
Riverside Cemetery.

In the 1930s a federal employment project renovated the old jail that housed the McDonalds. Bloodstains left from the infamous day over 50 years earlier were clearly visible in the McDonald cell — a reminder of a past when justice in a frontier Upper Peninsula town retreated into the murky depths of mob vigilanteism.

After a short stay at the Montreal House, the McDonalds paid a visit to the Three Chimney House, a nearby well-known house of prostitution. Fortuitously, the brothers ran across their old nemesis, Billy Kittson, brother of George Kittson, the man responsible for their jail time. The "ladies" immediately began to shower attention on the McDonald Boys. This angered Kittson and a melee ensued with Kittson hitting Frank McDonald over the head with a bottle and then leaving the Chimney House. The McDonald boys, true to their vow of vengeance, followed Billy Kittson to the street where John McDonald clubbed Kittson with a heavy metal pipe called a Peavy; not satisfied with dropping him to his knees, John McDonald then plunged a six-inch dagger into his back. Billy's brother Norman, witnessing the brawl, sped to his brother's rescue when a McDonald stabbed him. Billy, wounded and bleeding profusely, got back into the fray to help his now beleaguered brother. In desperation, Norman Kittson, lying on the ground, pulled out a gun and shot Frank McDonald in the leg. Billy Kittson, the life blood draining out of him, feebly staggered to the Montreal House where he gasped his last breath and fell over dead in the street.

With the blood bath now concluded, the McDonalds seized a nearby horse and buggy and went directly to Dr. P. T. Phillips, where the physician attended to their wounds. After getting medical treatment they quickly departed north to Cedar River. On the way to Cedar River they were arrested and jailed by David Barclay, the new Menominee sheriff.

Somewhere in Potter's Field in Menominee's Riverside Cemetery are the unmarked graves of the notorious McDonald cousins.

When Judge Henry Nason attempted to have an inquest the next day over the Kittson murder, he decided to forgo the proceeding when he learned the citizens of the community were in a rage over the murder the McDonalds had committed. Judge Nason felt that by delaying the inquest he would defuse a potentially explosive situation, a decision he would come to regret.

On Monday, the local paper, *The Marinette Eagle*, speculated on the "...serious threats of lynching the McDonalds," but the night passed without any further violence.

But, Tuesday, it began to turn ugly. Local men gathered at the Forvilly House, a large hotel and saloon, and proceeded to ply themselves with liquor. By evening the drunken rabble decided that lynching the McDonald boys was the surest and quickest way to have justice. Armed with liquor and self-righteousness, the angry vigilante band marched down the street to the jail and demanded the McDonalds.

When the rabid, liquor-laced mob was denied the McDonalds, they grabbed a telegraph pole, and cursing wildly,

122

smashed open the entry door. After a brief scuffle, the deputies were subdued and the McDonalds forced out of their jail cell, clubbed with an ax and taken from the jail.

The McDonald cousins were lynched by drunken villagers in Menomincc in 1881. No one ever served time for the vigilante executions.

A local priest, Father Heliard, unsuccessfully attempted to stop the uncontrollable mob; they cursed and spat on the priest and pushed him into the gutter. The lynch party tied one end of the rope around the McDonalds' necks and the other end to a horse and buggy and then proceeded to drag them down the street, jumping up and down on the defenseless bodies – savagely ripping off flesh with their lumberjack boots as they traveled down Ogden Avenue.

Pandemonium spread down the street; the gathering crowd along the route hurled rocks and garbage and cursed the McDonalds. When the lynch party approached an intersection with a railroad crossing, they apparently had temporarily spent their energy and decided this was as good a place as any to hang the McDonalds. They hoisted the two men onto the crossing sign with a rope around their necks and left the carnage of their handiwork for eager spectators to view. The McDonalds were dead long before they were hung from the sign.

The mob, still in a drunken rage, took the bodies down from the sign and hauled them to the brothel on Belview Avenue. In a further act of debauchery, the necktie party forced a prostitute to lie with the dead McDonalds. Then they burned down the brothel and hung the cousins from a nearby jackpine.

The next day, the McDonalds were still hanging from the tree next to the smoldering rubble of the house of prostitution. The drunken frenzy was over.

A jury indicted several leaders of the mob for murder, but nothing ever came of it. Charges were dismissed for various reasons. One man did eventually go to trial, but was found not guilty. No one was ever convicted of the crime.

When justice is denied does it seek other avenues to express itself? Perhaps it did in the McDonald case; several of the men suspected of being involved in the McDonald lynching also met with a violent death:

Albert Beach, a log driver, fell out of his boat and drowned.
Louis Porter died after apparently being bitten by a rattlesnake.
A mill owner was fatally injured in a lumberyard fire.
A witness named Dunn was later cut in two by a sawmill.

NAZIS ROAM
The Upper Peninsula Forests

GERMAN PRISONER OF WAR CAMPS

In a small but comfortable room, several men casually lounged after a hard day's work. Small talk and light laughter emanated throughout the cozy quarters. At a table in the center of the room, two men were intently playing a chess game, while another was curled up reading comfortably in a corner. At the far end of the room, a would-be artist sketched on paper, while the other occupants leisurely engaged in idle chit-chat.

This was not a relaxing evening in an officers' club on a military base somewhere in the United States. It was (hard to believe) a typical Sunday in German Prisoner of War (POW) camps in the Upper Peninsula during World War II.

Nationwide, the United States was the home of 400,000 German POWs; of that number, 1,200 were in the Upper Peninsula. The five POW camps in the Upper Peninsula were located in AuTrain, Wetmore, Mass, Sidnaw and Raco. Most of the camps housed between 200-300 prisoners of war. There was usually one guard for every ten POWs.

With a shortage of man-power to harvest pulp for the war effort, the German prisoners became a vital part of the work force in logging Upper Peninsula forests. The logged timber was used to make crates for transporting military supplies.

Most of the U.P. prisoners of war were enlisted men. Wetmore, however, had some of the feared SS infantrymen who were members of Erwin Rommel's famed Afrika Corps. These soldiers acknowledged each other in camp with the traditional raised arm and a "Heil Hitler" salute.

Scurrying for freedom was probably on the minds of many

Nearly 1,200 German soldiers were housed in civilian conservation camps throughout the Upper Peninsula from 1944-46

German POWs, but few attempted it. On one occasion, a number did escape from the Wetmore POW camp, only to be caught in Skandia the next day. Undoubtedly, most realized that attempting to escape from the remote Upper Peninsula was difficult at best, and with no friendly boarders nearby, it made an escape near impossible. Most prisoners upon first arriving in the U.P. thought they were at the end of the world. (In light of the geography they had quickly made that astute judgment.) This was unlike American POWs in European camps where the possibility of escape to a friendly territory was more likely.

A German African Corp soldier in the Raco POW camp looks admiringly at a photograph of Adolph Hitler on the camp wall.

In AuTrain, guards made an attempt to safeguard the German POWs during hunting season by placing red arm bands on the sleeves of their captives. This identification, hopefully, would protect the POWs from an errant (or not so errant) shot by a U.P. deer hunter. The prisoners were amused at this and probably did not understand the possibility of them becoming a menu item for black bear after they were inadvertently shot by a much too eager hunter.

Most of the POWs were industrious; the Prussian work ethic and self-discipline were characteristically German. One exception, however, occurred at Camp Sidnaw when the POWs refused to work. In defiance, they broke saw blades and punctured truck tires. Retribution by the camp authorities was swift. After the day of sabotage, the prisoners were forced to walk 12 miles back to camp in a snowstorm; they went to work the following day – eagerly! Apparently, the harsh Upper Peninsula winters had a purpose.

Ironically, it wasn't the German POW camps that gave the Upper Peninsulans grief, it was the American camp of

Conscientious Objectors (CO) at Germfask (Seney) that proved to be the most difficult. In the United States, close to 12,000 COs were interred; eighty were in the Germfask camp. The Conscientious Objectors were unmanageable prisoners who continually created camp disruptions. The mostly college-educated group included teachers, lawyers and college professors. They engaged in acts of property destruction and sabotage, frequently employing "slow downs" while working.

The Conscientious Objector principle belief was that the only way to stop war was simply not to join in the fighting. Many were COs based on religious principles; Jehovah's Witness followers were a large contingent of the COs.

The local population detested the conscientious objectors. The Upper Peninsula natives had more respect for the German POWs than the Conscientious Objectors. They felt the German POWs were fighting for their country – be it not well intended – but COs were just aristocratic, obnoxious traitors. Some of the 80 COs proved to be so difficult that 22 were sent to federal prisons on other charges.

The logging was monotonous for the interred visitors, but many of them knew it was far better than being on the front line facing the Allied armies marching east to Germany, or worse yet, being on the Eastern Front retreating from the Red Army.

Life in a POW camp did have some amenities. They had libraries, put on theatrical productions, played chess, held track events, and at Sidnaw there was even a 12-piece orchestra. To augment their spiritual life, the local clergies offered religious services to the camp prisoners.

The camps were closed after the German prisoners departed, and today there is little evidence that the camps ever existed. Although it has been reported from time to time by hunters in the Sidnaw area, that if they are quiet – and listen carefully, they can faintly hear the sweet refrain of a German ballad whispering in an autumn wind.

When the war ended, some of the POWs wished to remain in the United States. However, allowing them to stay in the United States would have violated the Geneva Convention. In honoring the Geneva provisions, the prisoners of war were returned to Germany.

POVERTY ISLAND Gold?

Is there gold from the Civil War at the bottom of the Poverty Passageway in Bay De Noc?

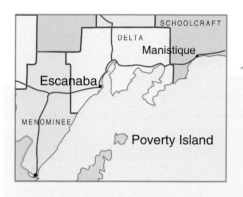

Sunken treasure located just off Big Bay de Noc in the Poverty Island Passageway — just waiting for some lucky maritime scavenger to scoop it up? Could be.

Purportedly, there is a treasure, long dormant, and waiting for some enterprising treasure hunter to rescue it from its murky depths. This is the seafaring rumor that circulated among Lake Michigan treasure hunting buffs for decades. Several attempts to retrieve the obscured bullion have been unsuccessful.

During the final days of the Civil War, a cargo-carrying barge made its way from the east end of Lake Erie to Chicago, carrying a chest of ingots (gold bars) that were to be converted into coins for the Union war effort. It was speculated that the ingots were booty from Confederate banks.

During its long and harrowing journey, the barge, being towed by a tug, ran into a violent storm near Poverty Island just off the coast of Big Bay de Noc. The lighthouse keeper on Poverty Island witnessed the tug and barge battling heavy winds in Poverty Passage, about a half-mile north of the island. With conditions worsening, the crew from the tugboat boarded the barge, transported the beleaguered sailors off the barge to the tug and then cut the lashings of a large chest on the barge and sent it overboard. Within moments the barge sank in the heavy seas; the tugboat then disappeared into the storm.

In 1936, Escanaba deep-sea diver Dale Vinette was approached by Sol Meyer of Milwaukee to search for the presumed sunken treasure chest off Poverty Island. Meyer assured Vinette he had researched archival records and indeed the story of gold bars lying at the bottom of Poverty Island Passage was true. Meyer was confident the treasure was there, just waiting for some enterprising salvagers to retrieve it.

The lighthouse keeper with a telescope was a witness to this near catastrophic occurrence. The chest, according to some maritime records, contained valuable ingots.

Dale Vinette, underwater explorer from Escanaba, dove for gold in Big Bay de Noc in 1936.

After some hard bargaining, Meyer and Vinette finally agreed on a contract for Vinette's services. At first, Meyer wanted Vinette to dive for the treasure on a contingency basis, paying Vinette only if they were successful in finding the cache of gold. Vinette knew the chances of finding the gold were slim and told Meyer that he would work for $60 a day when diving, $10 a day for standbys, and 5 percent of all the gold recovered. The men agreed on this arrangement and the search for the missing gold began.

Vinette contacted friends in Escanaba, attempting to ascertain the reliability of the stories of underwater gold in the Poverty Passageway. Reports he obtained in the Escanaba area gave credibility to Meyer's belief that there was gold in the bottom of the Passageway. With this additional information, Vinette concluded that his time spent diving for the elusive gold bars may be well worth the while.

Vinette secured a large enough fish tug for scavenging, the *F.S. Howard*, from the Geirke family in Fairport, a small fishing community at the southern point of the Big Bay de Noc peninsula.

Meyer and two friends, one a diver, came up from Milwaukee and joined Vinette at Fairport where the foursome embarked on the *Howard* to the suspected site of treasure, five miles from the diminutive coastal village. For two days, the crew scurried about the passageway, repeatedly diving into the cold, 45-foot water depth, all to no avail. On one occasion, their dragline hooked on something suspicious. Vinette dove to the bottom in his diving gear only to find that the wire was hooked on several rolls of barbed wire. Meyer, however, took this as an encouraging sign, believing that it may be wire from the deck of the old gold-carrying barge. Further dives in the area, however, proved fruitless and the scavenger crew returned empty-handed to Fairport.

The crew relentlessly continued their search; on one occasion they turned up wood pieces that belonged to an unidentified barge. Another time they found an old anchor and chain, but again the evasive barge, laden with treasure, was not found.

At times, Dale Vinette was limited to the number of dives he could take in a given day. Any dive 65 feet or more could only be done once a day. The danger of the "bends" (bubbles in the blood that cut off oxygen to the nerve endings, causing excruciating pain and possible death) is a risk with deep dives. A sudden change in atmospheric pressure causes the bends or "diver's sickness." To avoid this, deep-sea divers must ascend slowly from significant depth, allowing the body to adjust to the changes in atmospheric pressure.

For nine days, Vinette, Meyer and his crew searched for the riches that were alleged to be in the depths of the channel;

Dale Vinette as he appeared in his Moris canvas and rubber one-piece diving outfit. The metal helmet was used primarily for shallow water diving. Vinette made his own cast-iron sandals.

each day the crew returned to Fairport empty-handed, always hoping the next day would be the lucky one.

It was not to be.

After a week and a half of unproductive searches, Meyer returned to Milwaukee, his dream of instant riches faded into the murky depths of the Poverty Island Passageway. He took with him only a pine decking plank and a few decking nails from a sunken barge that at one time he thought might be the elusive mystery barge.

Vinette was not so disappointed. He knew the chance of finding buried gold bars was remote – and he was well paid. Dale, ever an optimist, said, "The diving assignment was a good one: no water over 70 feet deep, fairly good visibility under water, and water temperatures no colder than 50 degrees." Others have searched for the gold before and after Vinette, but no one has yet claimed to unearth the precious yellow metal from its watery grave. Whether there are gold ingots at the bottom of Lake Michigan in Poverty Passageway is uncertain. What is certain is that as long as treasure hunters believe there is a chance that gold bars exist somewhere in the depths of the Island Passageway, they will continue to slide into its watery depths in hopes of finding what others could not.

Was the gold found by one of the many scavenger groups that searched for it?

Perhaps. Any successful treasure hunter might disappear into the night with the plunder without reporting their lucrative find to anyone. (Fearing repercussion, IRS comes to mind.) No one knows for sure. If, however, the gold is in the frigid abyss off Big Bay de Noc, the waters have jealously harbored its whereabouts for 135 years, and chances are that it will continue to conceal the gold's whereabouts well into the next millennium.

THE SINKING
Of The "Fitz"

EDMUND FITZGERALD

When launched in 1958, the Edmund Fitzgerald was the largest carrier on the Great Lakes. Then in November of 1975, disaster struck the 'Fitz.'

(November 10th, 1975, 7:10 p.m.) In a vicious November storm on Lake Superior, gale force winds of 80 to 90 miles per hour pierce the *Edmund Fitzgerald's* bow as she rides the crests and valleys of 16-20 foot waves just off Whitefish Point. Monstrous breakers, smashing over defective hatch covers, allowed water to seep into the taconite-laden hold, lowering the boat even further below the critical load line. Titanic whitecap action hurtled the iron ore pellets in the hold to the bow of the ship, creating a dangerously heavy front end. Crashing headlong into a wall of water, with an overweight bow, the *Edmund Fitzgerald* was unable to recover from the impact of the massive wave, pulling the front end of the boat, submarine-like, into the icy depths of Lake Superior. It crashed hard on the bottom some 600 feet below the surface, breaking in two on impact, with the bow remaining upright and the stern, 70 feet away, resting upside down on the disintegrated middle section of the boat. Experts say the ship could have gone down in as little as 10 seconds.

Although there is some controversy as to what actually did happen on that fateful night, most authorities agree the preceding description is most likely what occurred on that stormy evening on Lake Superior.

The *Edmund Fitzgerald* was named after the president of the Northwestern Mutual Life Insurance Company, a prominent Milwaukee executive and the fourth family member to have a ship named after him. Edmund's grandfather and five grandfather's brothers were all captains of Great Lakes sailing vessels. The "Fitz" was named after a family with a proud nautical heritage.

The Edmund sailed the Great Lakes with smugness; she was the largest ore carrier navigating the Great Lakes from 1958 to 1971, and a record setter, becoming the first vessel on the Great Lakes to carry more than a million tons of ore through the Soo Locks.

The Northwestern Mutual Life Insurance Company built the boat (Great Lakes seamen prefer the name "boat" rather than "ship") in River Rouge, just south of Detroit. She was imposing and touted as the "American Flagship" of the Great Lakes.

The *Edmund Fitzgerald* as she appeared in the early 1970s. The great iron ore carrier sank off Whitefish Point in a severe 1975 storm.

An "old salt," sixty-two-year-old Ernest McSorley was the Captain of the *Edmund* and a seasoned sailor, having his first job on an ocean-going freighter when he was only 18 years of age. He was the youngest to make captain on a freshwater freighter.

For her time, the *Fitzgerald* was immense; at 729 feet long (over two football fields) and weighing over 13,000 tons, her size was tailor-made to just squeeze through the Poe Lock, the largest of the Soo Locks at Sault Ste. Marie, Michigan.

The *Fitzgerald* began the doomed voyage in Superior, Wisconsin on November 9th, 1975. Laden with 26,000 tons of taconite iron pellets, the 'Fitz' was on her last run for the year; it was routine, something the venerable boat did 40-50 times a year for the past 17 years. This trip would be no different, a comfortable last run to Detroit where she would hold up for the winter. In early spring, with the ice beginning to melt on the Great Lakes, the *Fitz* would again ply the icy waters of the lakes, delivering the ore pellets to the steel mills in America's heartland.

The trip from Superior began uneventfully, but near the end of her first day on November 9th, she received weather reports of a nasty storm coming in from the northeast, but later the storm would shift to the northwest. At 7 p.m. on November 9th, The National Weather Service predicted the brewing storm to have gale force winds (39-46 miles per hour). Seven hours later, at 2 p.m. on November 10th, Captain McSorley of the Fitzgerald became concerned with the deteriorating conditions and headed north to the protective Canadian shore in an attempt to reduce the impact of the storm.

The *Arthur Anderson*, a nearby ship, accompanied the *Edmund* to the shelter of the Canadian side. At 7 a.m. the savage storm started across Lake Superior, turning to the northwest, just as the Weather Bureau predicted. The relentless winds reached hurricane level, twice the velocity the Weather Bureau anticipated. With the wind shift, the shielding Canadian coast no longer was effective. The two ships, recognizing the seriousness of the situation, decided to make course across Superior to Whitefish Bay in Michigan.

At 2:45 p.m., the *Fitzgerald* reported minor rail damage and that water was entering her hull. In the midst of one of the worst storms on Lake Superior, and some four hours later, at 7:10 p.m., Captain McSorley reported to the nearby *Anderson* (10 miles away) that "We are holding our own." That was the last word from the *Fitzgerald*. Within minutes, the '*Fitz*' disappeared from the *Anderson's* radar. The *Edmund Fitzgerald* sank. She was only 13 miles from Whitefish Point.

At the time of the sinking, the air temperature was 49 degrees and the water temperature 40 degrees. Under these conditions, if you did not quickly drown by being entombed in the ship's hull, shock and death would be inevitable within 30 minutes in the open sea.

The next morning, the only evidence that the *Edmund* ever existed was a black oil slick 1,000 yards long, floating lazily on Superior's surface. Days later, lifeboats, bottles, splintered wood and a crumpled raft with the *Edmund's* name on it washed up on the Canadian shore.

The bodies were never recovered. An old mariner adage says, "Lake Superior never gives up her dead." This is not because of some eerie mysticism about Lake Superior; the dead do not surface because the depth and cold temperatures of the Lake prevent body decomposition. Oxygen needed to produce organisms that decay matter is non-existent at 600 feet. When the *Fitzgerald* was located and photographed on a dive in 1991, the decision was made that if any corpses were found they were to remain with the ship. The boat bell was removed from the *Edmund* (one of the few objects permitted to be removed) and

In the history of Great Lakes disasters, the Edmund Fitzgerald is only one of 6,000 commercial shipwrecks, less than half of those were ever found. The Fitzgerald, however, was the biggest ship to go down and the one that took the most lives in a single vessel sinking on Lake Superior.

is now housed in the Great Lakes Shipwreck Museum at Whitefish Point.

Gordon Lightfoot popularized the disaster in 1976 with his song, "The Wreck of The Edmund Fitzgerald." A memorial service was held in a Detroit maritime cathedral to honor those that met their untimely death in a watery grave in the depths of Lake Superior. Lightfoot, in what has become his signature song, captured this solemn ceremony in his mournful elegy:

> *"In a musty old hall in Detroit they prayed*
> *in the maritime sailor's cathedral.*
> *The church bell chimed 29 times*
> *For each man on the Edmund Fitzgerald."*

The *Edmund Fitzgerald* nearing completion in dry dock in 1958. The "*Fitz*" was named after Edmund Fitzgerald, the president of The Northwestern Mutual Life Insurance Company and a man with a nautical heritage.

Landmarks

A BRIDGE
Of Beauty

RAMSEY KEYSTONE BRIDGE

There may not be a more picturesque bridge in the Upper Peninsula than the charming Keystone Bridge located near Bessemer. The stone bridge is unique. It's constructed in a series of arches, each with a center keystone at the top; the design locks the structure and gives it strength and beauty.

Also known as the Black River Bridge, the Chicago and Northwestern Railway Company built the stone overpass in 1891 for $48,322. This durable and distinctive bridge is constructed of limestone quarried from Kaukauna, Wisconsin.

The charming Keystone Bridge, built in 1891, is located two miles south of Bessemer.

The Black River, a popular trout stream, flows under its graceful arch. Hugging the perimeter of the Bessemer Township Memorial Park, the bridge is in an idyllic setting with its sweeping green lawn and spacious picnic area.

Located two miles south of U.S. 41 (from Bessemer), it is one of the few arch bridges of its kind in existence and well worth a side journey on a Sunday afternoon drive.

THE BRIDGE
That Binds

MACKINAC BRIDGE

*Before the bridge was built, a 19-hour wait
to cross the straits was not uncommon.*

"And what man has joined together – let no man put
asunder." A phrase most often heard in the exchange of vows at
a wedding ceremony. The State of Michigan would like to believe
this aphorism is applicable when speaking of the two separate
Michigan Peninsulas that were wedded in 1957. The completion
of the Mackinac Bridge finalized that geographical bond. With
the long awaited marriage, the bridge would do more than attach
two land masses; it would facilitate the linking of its people.

FERRY TOLL RATES

1. Passenger	**5. Truck, Tractor and Combination**
Adults.....................$0.25	Not wider than 8'—0"
Children over 12.................. 0.25	Length under 20 feet over-all........$2.75
Children under 12....—NO CHARGE	Length 20 to 30 feet over-all........ 4.50
(When accompanied by an adult)	Length 31 to 40 feet over-all........ 6.00
	Length over 40 feet over-all......... 8.00
2. Passenger Car...................... 2.50	Additional for Width More than 8'—0" 5.00
(Includes Driver)	Additional for carrying Livestock....... 5.00
3. Trailer Drawn by Passenger Car	
Other than coach................. 1.75	**6. Motorcycle**.......................... 1.25
Coach 3.25	
4. Passenger Bus	**7. Horse-Drawn Vehicle**................. 5.00
Passenger seating capacity under 32.. 4.00	(Drivers of all vehicles are included in above rates)
Passenger seating capacity 32 and over. 5.00	(ABOVE RATES EFFECTIVE MAY 1, 1955)

ALL SCHEDULES ON EASTERN STANDARD TIME

Ferry toll rates in 1955.

The state was hopeful that connecting the two
land masses would discourage the periodic dialogue
by the Upper Peninsulans, (Yoopers) of creating a
51st state. The State achieved partial success;
most northern Michigan residents knew realistically
there was little chance of Upper Michigan becoming a separate state, and the new bridge would only
serve to further integrate the populations of the
two peninsulas. But U.P. residents still cling to
the belief that they are unique; and though a part
of a larger political/geographical unit, still think of
themselves first as Upper Peninsulans and secondly
as members of the State of Michigan.

Although the bridge was completed in 1957, discussion on
a need for a bridge began back in 1884 when a Lansing newspaper
stated: "If a great east-west route were ever to be established
through Michigan, a bridge or tunnel would be needed."

In 1888, the great financial tycoon, Cornelius Vanderbilt,

said, "We now have the largest well-equipped hotel of its kind in the world for a short season business (the Grand Hotel on Mackinac Island). Now, what we need is a bridge across the Straits."

During the 1920s, the state highway commissioner suggested a floating tunnel to join the two peninsulas. Even in the "Roaring '20's" age of optimism, the tunnel suggestion was viewed as improbable and nothing ever came of it.

Progress was made in the early 1920s with plans for a ferry service. In 1923 the first car ferry service began with one ferry boat – this expanded to five boats by 1956 with the ability to transport 462 cars per hour. Today, the bridge can accommodate 6,000 vehicles per hour.

The ferry, *Chief Wawatam*, was used to transport railroad cars across the Straits of Mackinac from 1911 to 1986. The rail link to St. Ignace was discontinued in 1986, negating any need for the old ferry.

Although the ferries finally linked the peninsulas, travel between the two could be lengthy and exasperating. It was not uncommon to sit in a 17-mile line of cars on U.S. 27 and wait 19 hours for a ferry to transport you across the five-mile Straits of Mackinaw. Motorists frequently felt they could have circumnavigated the globe – at the equator – in a shorter period of time.

After years of planning and replanning, the bridge became a reality; in 1954 work began on the three-and-a-half-year, $100 million project. It was an amazing building feat – many thought it could never be done. But in November of 1957 the five-mile-long suspension bridge (longest in the Western Hemisphere) opened for traffic. Supporting the huge structure is 42,000 miles of wound cable attached to twin towers that soar 552 feet above the Straits of Mackinac (The Washington monument is 555 feet). Some of the statistics of the bridge construction boggle the mind: 85,000 blueprints, a labor force of 3,500 men on the site, with another 7,500 off-site. Five workers died in the process of building the bridge. A positive spin-off of the bridge's erection was the economic boom for the Straits communities of St. Ignace and Mackinaw City.

Built to last a millennium, the bridge has withstood gale force winds of 96 mph (engineers say it can withstand winds up to 632 mph); and will move as much as 35 feet side-to-side during a windstorm – built to bend but not break.

When the bridge opened in 1957 the toll was $3.25; this

was increased to $3.75 in 1961. The rise in the fare resulted in a howl of protest by the frequent bridge users who then boycotted the bridge; the consequence was a decrease in bridge traffic. The Bridge Authority, responding to the rate criticism, reduced the fare to $1.50 in 1968. Even with the reduced rate, the Authority managed to retire the last bond on the bridge in 1986. Revenues now go into maintenance and updating.

The Mackinac Bridge, built to withstand winds up to 632 miles per hour. The "Mighty Mac" will move as much as 35 feet from side-to-side during severe windstorms.

The Bridge is in a constant state of repair. Major repairs scheduled are: a new paint job at $75 million; an updated brighter lighting system to be completed in 2001; and in 2016-2017 a new bridge deck at a cost of $180 million.

Yoopers have somewhat gotten used to the fact that they will forever be linked to the Lower Peninsula and reluctantly admit to some benefits that derive from the span. The bridge facilitates tourism to the Upper Peninsula. Although some residents consider this a mixed blessing, most view the economic benefits as desirable. Many Upper Peninsulans enjoy sharing with visitors, be they friends or acquaintances, the beauty of "God's Country."

But not to be denied is the overwhelming fact that many Upper Peninsulans see the bridge as a speedy way for Upper Peninsula high school athletic teams to get downstate to collect yet another state high school athletic trophy. Big Mac – "Mistress of the Mackinac" – mighty, magnificent, miraculous.

THE HIDDEN Bridge

The "fortress-like" stone supports at the bridge ends provide a passageway for visitors.

CUT RIVER BRIDGE

Unless you're a keen observer, you can drive over the Cut Ridge Bridge unaware you are traveling over one of the highest steel cantilevered bridges in the Upper Peninsula. Signs delineating the bridge's impressive statistics, located at each end of the bridge, are one of the few indicators that alert motorists to the bridge's existence. A further investigation of this seemingly inauspicious bridge reveals it to be anything but inauspicious.

Because it doesn't have a ponderous above-ground superstructure, as suspension or covered bridges do, travelers may be unaware they are traversing a massive girded steel structure. The road spans a deep gorge (147 feet above the river) that was created by the Cut River. The tourist who takes the time to park at either end of the bridge, and is then willing to walk a short distance to a staircase that descends to the underside of the bridge, will be pleasantly surprised. Only from this vantage point can the massive steel erection that supports the roadway be observed. The monolithic bridge, built in 1946, is a pleasant stop for the vacationer who enjoys taking in sights that are lesser known, and is willing to take the time.

The incredible steel structure of the Cut River Bridge weighs 888 tons.

THE KEWEENAW CONNECTION

THE PORTAGE LAKE LIFT BRIDGE

The world's heaviest lift bridge.

This bridge spanned the Portage Canal until 1905 when it was rammed by a steamship and made unstable.

When we think of a great Upper Peninsula bridge, most residents and non-residents believe the Mackinac Bridge (Mighty Mac), is the greatest. This may be true, but the bridge connecting Houghton and Hancock deserves recognition for its uniqueness.

A little known fact: the Portage Lake Lift Bridge cost more per foot to build than the Mackinac Bridge. While the Mackinac cost $100 million, and the Portage Lake Lift bridge cost only $11 million, it was the cost of the huge double deck lift-span on the Portage Canal bridge that propelled the per-foot expenditure. Another obscure fact: the Portage Lake Lift Bridge is the heaviest lift bridge in the world.

Uniquely, the bridge center span can easily be moved vertically into three positions. The lowest position allows trains to move on the bottom level and vehicle traffic on the upper level (no boats can go under the bridge in this position.) The intermediate position allows vehicles to cross the span and permits

Weighing in easily at 4.5 million pounds, the bridge's caloric intake of nuts, bolts, and steel during its construction easily outdistanced any of its pantywaist competitors in material consumed during its erection.

boats needing a clearance of 35-feet or less to pass underneath. The top position prevents any rail or car traffic from crossing the bridge, but allows for large vessel passage (ore carriers) that need a clearance up to 100 feet.

The Portage Lake Lift Bridge was erected in 1959. Two other bridges existed on the site prior to the Lift Bridge: The first was a drawbridge constructed in the 1890s; it lasted until 1905 when a steamship careened into the structure and made it unusable. A second drawbridge replaced the first one and provided the link to the northern Keweenaw Peninsula for the next 54 years. Children loved the old drawbridge with its wooden walkways. Riding the swing span as it opened its portal for a freighter to pass was the highlight of the day for many children from Houghton and Hancock.

The portage Lake Lift Bridge connects the Keweenaw Peninsula to the Upper Michigan Mainland.

Driving on the narrow, old, wooden structure was not without its scary moments. A semi-truck coming from the opposite direction on the bridge struck terror into the heart of more than one motorist.

The current bridge has remained relatively unchanged for decades. To keep her from getting tarnished with age, she periodically is spruced up. The most recent being a $3.2 million dollar expenditure that upgraded the approach and sidewalk surfaces as well as providing a new coat of paint. The upgrade was completed in the fall of 2000.

With its massive, oversized, steel frame, the bridge is a solid and unyielding link between the Upper Peninsula mainland and the Keweenaw Peninsula. Securely anchored on each end by two multi-ethnic villages tucked into the neighboring hillsides, it is the gateway to the Keweenaw Peninsula. It doesn't have the graceful sweeping lines of a suspension bridge, or the quaintness of an old covered bridge, but it doesn't need it. It makes its own bold statement.

THE CASE OF
The Courthouse Caper

IRON COUNTY COURTHOUSE

In the 1880s, Crystal Falls and Iron River feuded over the location of the new courthouse.

In the dead of winter, two men dressed quietly in the dark and lowered themselves out of a back window into waist-deep snow. The below-zero outside temperature was biting cold. They quickly made their way down a dark alley to a shack that housed important records. The documents they sought were quickly moved out of the shack and onto a sled and then to a waiting train. The two men then disappeared back into the black cold night.

This was the beginning of a famed rivalry – not the Hatfields vs. the McCoys, the North vs. the South, or the Montagues vs. the Capulets, not even the Packers vs. the Bears, all great rivalries – but none matching the intensity of the famed Crystal Falls vs. Iron River rivalry.

It's been going on for over a century and the animosity they have toward each other may well continue into the next millennium. Usually town vs. town rivalry is limited to the high school basketball or football programs, mostly harmless, but nonetheless a rivalry. However, this is a political rivalry and the antagonism goes much deeper than traditional town competition.

Conflict between the two began back in the 1880s when Iron County, with its two equal-size cities of Crystal Falls and Iron River, was a part of Marquette County. The distance of these cities from the county seat at Marquette made it difficult for their residents to participate in county affairs. During the hard, cold winters, it was a seven day journey on old logging trails from the west end cities to Marquette. This hardship on the county representatives from Crystal Fall and Iron River led them to

Over a hundred years later, the restored and dignified building still casts its stately shadow from its lofty perch over the proud city of Crystal Falls.

pursue the creation of their own county seat in the west end of Marquette County. To their delight, the State Legislature granted their request, and in September of 1885 granted the petition. Iron County was formed.

But all was not well. The newly formed county needed to decide which city would be the county seat. It was resolved that in the next general election in November 1886, the voters of the newly-formed county would decide if Crystal Falls or Iron River would become the legal seat for the county government.

Meanwhile, the county records were housed in Iron River.

The grand Crystal Falls County Courthouse, built in 1890, was a cause of considerable rivalry with Iron River in the 1880s.

Crystal Falls put all their efforts into getting out the vote for their representatives. Residents of the local cemetery were suddenly, Christ-like, resurrected to cast ballots in favor of their beloved city. Crystal Falls won the majority of seats on the county government, but haggling at the next council meeting prevented the vote for the new Crystal Falls Courthouse from becoming known. Frustrated, Crystal Falls representatives then petitioned the state for a writ of mandamus; this would compel the board to canvas the council vote and legally declare Crystal Falls the county seat.

Crystal Falls residents were aware of how slow and cumbersome the state judicial bureaucratic process could be and were quite concerned that the Iron River politicians would deny moving the records that were stored in their city – writ or no writ.

The Iron River residents were just as adamant in keeping the county records in their town; after all, the last election was illegal and Crystal Falls was merely trying to hijack what was rightfully theirs.

Suspecting this would never get resolved, Crystal Falls residents decided to take matters into their own hands. Dr. A.L.

Frederickson, Frank Scadden, C.T. Roberts, and other conspirators, hatched a "James Bond" plot to steal the county records from Iron River in the dead of a cold, winter night. After their removal, the bandits (they would disagree with the name) would take them back to Crystal Falls, bury them in a secretive place and wait for the slow wheels of justice to finally declare Crystal Falls the new county seat.

The plan was simple but effective. Frank Scadden and Bert Hughitt were to engage the Iron River county representatives in a poker game in Iron River after the county meeting was adjourned. During the poker game, Roberts and Scadden would feign tiredness, go off to bed, and later in the evening while the poker game was in full swing, sneak out of their room, go to where the records were stored, load them on a sleigh and take them to a waiting train. The train would swiftly depart with the stolen booty and head back to Crystal Falls where they would secretly hide the records in the Mastodon Mine.

The sweeping oak balustrade staircase with pointed newel posts leads to the second-floor courtroom.

The plan was executed with "Mission Impossible" precision. However, it was not without its scary moments. The Iron River hosts were suspicious of their fellow Crystal Falls county commissioners. With that in mind, they had guards protecting the records. But the Crystal Falls commissioners, knowing the proclivities of the guards, plied them with free drinks and a chance to watch the hottest poker game in the county. With the derelict guards now joining the festivities, the theft became easier.

After the records were loaded safely on the train, Scadden and Hughitt stealthily went back to their hotel room. When they heard the train whistle blow they knew the records were now on the way to secretive hiding in Crystal Falls. The thieving twosome were jubilant as they drifted off to sleep while visions of sugar plums danced in their heads.

The next day when the great caper came to light, there was celebration in Crystal Falls, while Iron River residents were seething with rage. The angry Iron River residents made retaliatory threats, but nothing ever came of it.

The case of the stolen courthouse was finally laid to rest in

February of 1889 when a second vote was put to the constituents of the communities and Crystal Falls won a narrow victory. With the legal questions now settled, and the state's five-year moratorium on building a courthouse expired, Crystal Falls began the construction of their grand, new building. In 1890 the majestic structure rose in all its elegance on a grassy hill at the highest point in the city.

A memorial to Finnish pioneers rests on the front lawn of the Iron County Courthouse.

THE HILLSIDE
COURT

HOUGHTON COUNTY COURTHOUSE

An architectural gem built in 1887 for $75,000.

The front of the courthouse has an impressive porch supported with Gothic arch brackets embroidered with quarterfoils that enhance the porch's character.

Perched halfway up a ridge on Houghton's south side, just off downtown Main Street, is Houghton's imposing county courthouse. The stately, polychromatic (multi-colored) four-story structure looks down on the village. The building's occupants have administered justice (presumed) to the town's inhabitants for over 100 years.

The first courthouse was built on this site in 1862. With copper mining rapidly expanding, the old courthouse quickly became inadequate, and a new and larger facility was needed. Fifteen years later, in 1877, the old courthouse was torn down, and an elegant new courthouse was completed at a construction cost of slightly over $75,000. By 1913, the burgeoning copper mining industry was flourishing and the county population swelled to over 80,000. Eventually, in 1987 the courthouse underwent a major expansion and is now amply large to service the still growing population comfortably.

The asymmetric, high Victorian design of the building incorporates several architectural styles. The solid massiveness of the building is characteristic of Romanesque architecture, while the parapet (low railing) dormers are classic Gothic architecture. The courthouse is a rectangular block with attached north and west wings, clustered around an impressive four-story tower.

The exterior is cream-colored brick from Lake Linden, while red sandstone lintels (the horizontal piece over a door or window) from Upper Peninsula quarries blend harmoniously with the oxidized green mansard roof made from native copper.

Two bands of red sandstone encircle the structure, fusing the

146

irregularly-shaped building into powerful, yet elegant proportion of line and mass. An ornately carved wooden cornice (decorative trim just below the roof line) adds a detailed beauty while uniting the wings of the building into a singular presentation.

The front of the courthouse has an impressive Victorian porch supported with posts and Gothic arch brackets embroidered with quarterfoils (a circular design consisting of four converging arches) that enhance the porch's character.

A grand hand-carved oak bannister staircase greets visitors entering the main entrance.

The interior of the courthouse is as imposing as the exterior. A grand, hand-carved oak banister staircase greets visitors entering the main entrance. The floors are covered with a warm, rich, yellowish-brown tile. Yellow pine wainscoting on the walls adds a decorative touch.

Energy-saving acoustical tiles cover much of the ceiling that encircles the plaster walls. A decorative frieze (an ornamental band around a room) dominates many of the rooms in the venerable old courthouse. John Procissi, a local craftsman who trimmed and garnished two other Copper Country landmarks – the Calumet Theater and Shute's, did much of the interior work in the courthouse.

Fireplaces were at one time the central attraction in many courthouse rooms. Today, however, only one remains. Nancy Fenilli, the county clerk, restored the fireplace in her office. When she first occupied the room, the fireplace was shielded with plywood. Removing the wood covering and cleaning the old fireplace was the first order of business. She then inserted an electric firebox in the cavity. The result: a step back in time, and a warming touch that recaptures the ambiance of an earlier century.

The Probate Court now occupies what was once the jail. In the original jail, the sheriff's wife cooked the meals for the inmates and served them by passing the morsels though a small window slot. No such luxury as home cooking exists in today's county jail.

By the 1960s, the old courthouse was showing its years of wear and tear. Having served the community well for over 70 years, it was in desperate need of both repair and space for the court's expanding services.

A jail condemnation in 1961 declared the facility to be hazardous, and prompted officials to seriously consider expansion. As a result, a $200,000 jail, adjacent to the courthouse, was completed in 1963. This freed up interior space in the courthouse for other functions. The Friend of the Court, Juvenile and Probation Offices and Probate Court were added with the increased space.

In 1987, after a hundred years of service to the people of the county, the courthouse underwent a major renovation. A service core was added to the southwest corner of the building. The location, shielded from a frontal view, preserved the integrity of the building. The new addition also removed a cluttered area that made the courthouse less attractive. Making the service core user friendly, an elevator was added, as well as more parking.

Interior renovations at the courthouse included expanded office space, an employee lounge, and a new waiting area. Space was made available for a drain commissioner, a civil defense director, a controller office, the equalization department and the department of public works.

Exterior improvements included roof repair, tuckpointing the brick, caulking and insulating the windows and painting the wooden areas.

This asymmetrical, high Victorian county courthouse is nestled in a Houghton hillside. Built in 1877, the structure has peninsula-quarried red sandstone and a native copper mansard roof.

The Houghton County Courthouse is a magnificent building, rivaling any of the great courthouses that were built just prior to the turn of the century. From its lofty position on the hillside, the Houghton County Courthouse presents a picture postcard elegance. This unique and breathtaking courthouse is the pride of the Copper Country and its restoration says much about the respect the Keweenaw people have for their cherished landmarks.

ONE HUNDRED
AND TWENTY-FOUR
YEARS OF JUSTICE

CHIPPEWA COUNTY COURTHOUSE

The Chippewa County Courthouse is the only courthouse in the state of Michigan that has been in continuous operation since its construction in 1877.

If ever a courthouse were built on hallowed ground, the Chippewa County Courthouse, on Portage Avenue in Sault Ste. Marie, would be a good example. Prior to its construction in 1877, the site was the location of the American Baptist Missionary Society, the driving force behind the Temperance Society in the Sault in the 1840s. Somehow, justice and sobriety seem to be desirable handmaidens.

The elegant courthouse was built for $18,153, when the population of Sault Ste. Marie was only 1,500. For its time, it was an opulent and over-stated structure, considering the remoteness of the location and the scant population, but the residents wanted a grand courthouse – and they got it. It was one of many imposing courthouses built in the Upper Peninsula during the latter half of the 19th century.

The courthouse is classic Second Empire architecture; a style that predominated the American landscape in the late 1800s and is characterized by high mansard roofs, pavilions (ornamental extensions jutting out from the main building, e.g., a widow's walk tower), and opulent decorations of fifteenth century origin. Another Second Empire architectural feature of the building is "constructional polychromy." Simply stated, it means incorporating different colors and textures into a building's exterior. The polychromy theme is evident in the facade of the Chippewa courthouse; composed of light-colored limestone brick from a Drummond Island quarry and rich-colored brownstone from a Marquette quarry, it personifies the Second Empire look. The light-colored limestone handsomely embroiders the brown sandstone

The front presentation of the building is impressive. A tower harbors a statue of mother justice; the wooden sculpture, holding the scales of justice, was completely restored in a 1986 restoration project by skilled woodcarver, Leno Pianost.

on the three-story structure. This new combination of varying colors and textures was a spirited Second Empire architectural change from the more monochromatic look of earlier periods.

The solid, fortress-like courthouse has stone walls two-feet thick and gives the erection a ponderous, but classy look. The use of indigenous stone gives the courthouse an Upper Peninsula feel, and created regional pride in the legal edifice, one of the earliest stone structures in Sault Ste. Marie.

The elegant Chippewa County Courthouse, built in 1877, is architectural "Second Empire," with a high mansard roof and opulent ornamentation.

A convincing clock and bell tower dominate the skyline of the front facade giving the building a historic regality. When the courthouse was built, a wrought-iron railing, complete with a widow's walk, graced the tower, but was eventually removed.

In 1904, the first addition to the courthouse was added. This renovation, and one again in the 1930s, added more office space. The result was an interesting Pavlovian maze of offices connected by private staircases. This labyrinth of small offices and connecting staircases was tangled and confusing, but seemed to work.

In the 1904 renovation, a time capsule was unearthed with some interesting items. Newspapers housed in the time capsule were extremely partisan for either the Democrats or the Republicans. The bias was not limited to an editorial page but was also reflected in the general news articles. Fortunately for the residents, the Sault had two papers, one for each political party. The partisan papers made no attempt to conceal their bias; they were proud of it and made no bones about it.

In 1904, betting on election outcomes was not only accepted, it was encouraged. The Empire, a local bar and hotel, was the scene for much of the election betting that took place in Sault Ste. Marie. The popular bar set up a betting booth to accommodate those who wished to wager money on the success (or lack of) of their candidate. (It would have been interesting to see how the election contest in Florida between Al Gore and George Bush would have been played out on the betting scene.)

In the center of the clock and bell tower, new scales of justice were carved and put in place in 1987.

In 1988, a $1.7 million renovation upgraded the courthouse to meet safety standards and provide barrier-free access. Other changes in the '86 renovation were installation of an elevator, new interior oak doors, and the removal of the ceiling in the courtroom to expose the original skylight. This restoration was not easily achieved; renovation opponents wanted to demolish the historic building and replace it with a contemporary structure. The preservationists won the decade-long battle, much to the delight of most of the citizens of Chippewa County.

The front grounds of the courthouse are graciously intertwined with well-appointed flowerbeds. At the front of the building, and near the sidewalk, are two lawn sculptures: one shows a wolf nursing two children and represents the myth of Romulus and Remus, the founders of Rome. The other sculpture, the "Crane of Sault," shows two Indian children who, according to local folklore, were transported across the St. Mary's River on the bird's back.

The 124-year-old courthouse is modernized, but has retained its strong architectural link to the past; it continues to faithfully serve the residents of Chippewa County, and will likely do so for generations to come.

T.R.'S COURT
OF VINDICATION

MARQUETTE COUNTY COURTHOUSE

*A trial at the stately courthouse in 1913 witnessed
Teddy Roosevelt defending himself
against a charge of being a drunk.*

The frontier village of 1855 Marquette, recognizing the need for law and order, authorized the building of a town jail. Charles Johnson agreed to put up a wooden building for $1,187. Accordingly, a two-acre parcel of land was purchased from the Cleveland Iron Mining Company for $600. Shortly thereafter, the site was enlarged by the purchase of two adjoining properties for a grand total of $3,050. The final site was an entire block that gently sloped toward the lake.

The refurbished interior of the courthouse is resplendent with wainscoted Italian marble and inlaid ceramic tile. The upper walls were painted in rich, dark hues highlighted with friezes of gold stenciling.

Two years later, a two-story wooden courthouse costing $4,300 was constructed. With shuttered windows and a portico supported by four substantial pillars, it was probably the first Greek Revival building to be built in the Upper Peninsula. Twenty-four years later, in 1881, a sizable addition was affixed to the original building. The wooden jail had been replaced with a more substantial stone building, later doubled in size.

In 1902, bonds in the amount of $120,000 were issued for the construction of a new courthouse. The local architectural firm of Charlton, Golbert, and Demar drew up plans for a Beaux Arts building composed of a three-story central section flanked by two-story wings. The final cost came to $240,000.

The old, wooden courthouse was moved to a corner of the lot to make way for construction until it was sold to the Catholic Church, which dismantled it and used the timbers in the construction of the Baraga School.

Marquette's grand County Courthouse was built with Portage Entry redstone and Marquette quarried brownstone. The edifice was completed in 1904 at a cost of $240,000.

The courthouse was opened to the public with great fanfare on September 17, 1904. This must have been a day of great civic pride, since Peter White Public Library, another grand public edifice, was opened on the same day.

The lower portion of the exterior was constructed of rain drip sandstone from local quarries; the upper portion was of Portage Entry redstone and sandstone from the Keweenaw Peninsula. The four imposing twenty-three-foot columns that support the portico were each carved out of a single block of granite, transported by ship and rail from Maine. The roof was crowned by a gracious dome clad in copper. The grounds were extensively planted by the Manning Brothers, landscape architects.

Walls were wainscoted in Italian marble, the steps leading

up the grand stairwell were also of marble, and the floors were inlaid ceramic tiles. The interior revealed ornate Victorian decoration that was the height of style. The upper walls were painted in rich, dark hues highlighted with friezes of gold stenciling. Elaborate stained glass designs highlighted windows and the ceiling of the dome.

While in Marquette, Teddy Roosevelt took time to pose with Spanish-American War Veterans.

A $2.25 million addition was constructed to the rear of the building in 1977. In contrast to the palatial turn-of-the-century elegance of the old courthouse, the newer annex is sleek and modern.

As the years passed, the courthouse became shabby, a bit down-at-the-heels. In 1984, under the supervision of Lincoln Poley, the whole building was lovingly and gloriously restored.

A gala event on September 24, 1998 celebrated 150 years of local democratic government. Tours of the courthouse, musical events, and an enactment of the historic Roosevelt-Newett trial were staged. The Marquette County Board of Commissioners announced plans to erect a $5,000 outdoor sculpture on the grounds.

BUILD IT
And They
Shall Come

SAULT HYDROELECTRIC PLANT

*At one time the only larger electric
plant was at Niagara Falls.*

In the 1890s, the community leaders of Sault Ste. Marie envisioned their town on the St. Mary's River as a city destined for greatness. They saw it becoming a flourishing metropolis to rival Detroit, Chicago and Minneapolis as one of the nation's most important cities in the northern United States. Wealthy travelers and industrial moguls would seek out the Sault as a destination place to build their future. The beautiful city on the St. Mary's River would become the heartbeat of the Midwest.

It never happened. The dream died when the thoughtful plan to bring the Sault into economic prosperity failed.

This ambitious plan to make the city the Mecca of the north hinged on one gigantic project – the creation of a behemoth hydroelectric plant to provide cheap energy for industries located in the Sault. This cheap power would stimulate economic growth and turn the Sault into an industrial giant in the Northern Hemisphere.

With these grand goals in mind, the Sault hydroelectric plant construction began in 1898 and was completed in 1902. The huge structure was built on the St. Mary's River in the south end of the city. After four years of difficult construction, the finally completed power plant drew "ahs" from spectators passing the impressive quarter-mile-long superstructure.

The new electric producing plant harnessed the power from the St. Mary's River and illuminated the city. The lower part of the St. Mary's rapids was a natural place for a hydroelectric plant. The plant was located at the terminal point of the rapids where it benefited from the Lake Superior water descending 28 feet to Lake Huron. This 28-foot drop was channeled through a newly created power canal that wound its way through the city, terminating at the power plant. The force of the canal water descending for several miles reached the power plant at a tremendous velocity, easily turning the turbines that generated electricity. Uniquely, the power plant had many functions; in addition to generating electricity, it served as a dam and a factory. The second-floor factory was over a quarter-mile long. Above that, an additional third floor was one-eighth-mile long.

This was not just another power plant – it was *the* power plant. The size of this project drew national attention. The most prominent engineers in the nation were brought to the Sault to oversee its design and construction. This was an engineering marvel; the only larger power plant in the United States was at Niagara Falls.

The huge hyrdoelectric plant never achieved the builders' dream of turning Sault Ste. Marie into a bustling metropolis.

Build it and they shall come.

They built it – but no one came.

It ended up being a colossal failure. Right from the start, the plant had grave technical problems; serious defects in the foundation prevented the plant from operating at design capacity. Only one industry was attracted to the area by the plant. The power plant did not produce enough revenue to prevent the facility from becoming a financial disaster. Both the owners and the engineers, fearing bad publicity "generated" by its technical and financial failures let the plant slide into obscurity.

Even though the hydroelectric plant appeared to be a failure, it had durability. Most power plants built at the turn of the century are either obsolete or have been demolished. The Sault hydroelectric plant, with its whopping 80 turbines whirring away, still generates enough power for 60% of the eastern third of the Upper Peninsula.

Many looked upon the monolith as a blunder, a grandiose idea that had no chance of succeeding. It did not turn the Sault into a burgeoning metropolis with all the up-scale accruements that accompany economic growth; instead, the Sault remained for years a community of less than 20,000 population, with only modest growth.

The quarter-mile length of the Edison Sault hydroelectric plant is apparent in this 1950s aerial photograph.

Today, many Sault residents burrow comfortably in their homes during the long cold winters, smugly delighted that their quaint and historically charming city on the river never succeeded in becoming a big city with all the blight of contemporary urban sprawl. From this perspective, the Sault hydroelectric plant was a success.

GATEWAY TO THE ATLANTIC

SAULT STE. MARIE LOCKS

A new lock costing over $400 million is scheduled to be built in the first decade of the twenty-first century.

The St. Mary's River, connecting Lake Superior with Lake Huron and Lake Michigan, is only 15 miles long, yet it is one of the most important rivers in the world. The waterway connects the vast resources of the upper Midwest with the industrial heartland of America. Iron ore extracted from the bowels of the earth in the Upper Peninsula and ripe grain from brimming Dakota silos are loaded into huge cargo-carrying vessels that journey eastward across the vast expanse of Lake Superior to the Soo Locks. The locks, located at Sault Ste. Marie, are the strategic conduits that make the Great Lakes a connecting river to the Atlantic Ocean.

Until 1797, the St. Mary's was just a beautiful, descending rapids teaming with whitefish and trout. These fish were a primary source of food for the Ojibwa Indians who inhabited the lush, forested riverbanks. As a pristine waterway, it was resplendent; as a navigable river it was a nightmare. The problem is the St. Mary's River descends 21 feet from Lake Superior to Lake Huron. This descending water creates turbulent rapids – a severe hindrance to boat navigation. Small boats or canoes with skillful navigators could matriculate the rapids, but large ships had to unload their cargo at the north end of the St. Mary's, load it on wagons, haul it down Portage Avenue, (a street that parallels the waterway) and then reload the cargo on a waiting boat at the South end of the St. Mary's River: a costly and time-consuming process. The first lock was built on the St. Mary's in 1797 by the Northwest Trading Company. It was only 38 feet long, small by today's standards, and built on the Canadian side of the river. The War of 1812 made short work of this lock. It was destroyed

The locks are an inevitable outgrowth of 20th century progress, but a way of life was extinguished in the process.

during the war after only 15 years of operation. Again, freight had to be transported around the rapids. It would be another 43 years before another lock was built.

By the mid-19th century, the volume of commerce on the St. Mary's was rapidly increasing. The acceleration in traffic was primarily due to the iron ore and copper discoveries in the 1840s in the central and western Upper Peninsula. This new mineral resource needed cheap transportation to the iron and copper smelters in the lower Midwest. Shipping the ore via the Great Lakes was the most cost effective way; this mandated that locks be built on the St. Mary's River to accommodate the ships transporting Upper Peninsula "gold" to ports south.

A Sault Ste. Marie Lock as it appeared in the 1880s. Charles Harvey built the first locks on the St. Mary's River in the 1850s.

This increased ore traffic, coupled with an alarming concern that the country may be drifting toward civil war, prompted the U.S. Congress to take swift action. The government knew a lock system at Sault Ste. Marie was vital and would ensure the industrial north an abundant supply of iron ore, an essential ingredient in making war weapons. As a result, a congressional act in 1852 granted 750,000 acres to the State of Michigan as compensation to the company that would build a lock.

The Fairbanks Scale Company was awarded the lock contract in 1853, with Charles T. Harvey, a traveling salesman and resourceful accountant for the company, as the on-site manager responsible for building the locks. Harvey had been thinking for some time about the need for locks. In the early 1850s he was in the Sault recovering from typhoid fever when he looked at the possibility of locks on the St. Mary's. Rambling about the remote settlement during his recuperation, it occurred to him that the way to facilitate travel between Lake Superior and Lake Huron was to build a canal, about a mile long, with locks at one end that would enable ships to negotiate the St. Mary's rapids.

Harvey was only 24 when he started to build the locks, and ironically, he was not an engineer. However, this did not bother the confident Harvey. With 400-immigrant workers in tow from the East Coast, Harvey set out for the Sault to build the world's largest lock system. He was unable to get local fur trappers to work on the canal project because the trappers viewed ditch digging beneath their more lofty station in life.

A viewing stand (top right) gives visitors a closer look at freighters as they journey through a lock. A new lock costing $427 million will be built in the early years of the 21st century.

Harvey was a no-nonsense employer. He was industrious and had a facile mind that was geared to common sense solutions to difficult problems. He fought the bitter cold in winter and overcame a cholera epidemic that swept through the 1,000-employee village. Afraid the epidemic would panic the workers and they would flee, Harvey, in the dark of night, surreptitiously buried the cholera victims in the deep forest that surrounded the Sault.

Harvey desperately tried to keep the working conditions as bearable as possible during the long, cold winter months. He built huge bonfires at the work site where the frozen, beleaguered workers could periodically warm their shivering bodies. Frostbite was a constant enemy of the hard-working immigrants during the winter. To combat this, Harvey assigned men to watch for frostbite on fellow workers. Snow rubs, a primitive but somewhat effective way of treating frostbite, would be immediately applied to those in need of medical attention.

Severe winters were not the only problems that Harvey had to deal with. Fear of an Indian uprising made the workers

The most recently built lock, the MacArthur, named after the famed World War II general, Douglas MacArthur, was built in 1943 and is beginning to show its age. The MacArthur Lock is the closest to the tourist-viewing stand, where observers are nearly able to shake hands with the seamen on board ship.

uneasy, and some workers fearfully deserted. The problems never ended for Harvey. Unhappy workers grumbled about working conditions and went on a short strike. In spite of all these calamities, Harvey endured. While exhausted workers at a day's end fell into their beds drained of all life, Harvey roamed the unfinished lock excavation, taking sightings for the next day's dig and using only the glow of the Northern Lights to illuminate his nocturnal wanderings.

Finally, after two long and grueling years (1853-1855), Harvey finished his grand locks (now known as the State Locks). The 350-foot locks were the largest built in the United States. Critics scoffed, saying they were "too big." Time, however, would prove Harvey right when a need for even larger locks became evident just 25 years later.

For the rest of his life, Harvey would continue to be a force in large scale building projects, the New York elevated train being his most notable achievement after the Soo Locks. Harvey – the traveling salesman who made his mark on America in a most unlikely manner.

In the early 1870s it was apparent that the State of Michigan didn't have the financial resources to expand the locks. In 1871 the Federal Government took ownership of the locks, and they in turn handed over the responsibility of the Locks to the U.S. Army Corps of Engineers.

In 1881 the Weitzel lock was built. The 550-foot lock was considered the last word in lock construction – but it wasn't. Only seventeen years later, in 1898, it was apparent that the Weitzel was insufficient in size with new and larger vessels plying the Great Lakes. A new lock was needed – and built – the five-million dollar Poe Lock came on-line in 1891. It was 850-feet long and large enough to accommodate the ever increasing size of the ships being built. The draft of the new Poe was 20 feet. There wasn't a need to build a lock with a deeper draft than Lake St. Clair's 20-foot draft capacity. Many ships using the locks traversed Lake St. Clair (near Detroit) on their Great Lakes journey.

At the turn of the century, the iron and copper mines in the central and western Upper Peninsula were prospering beyond what anyone would have imagined. They were supplying the necessary iron ore and copper that drove the economic engines of the United States. The increasing demands for the raw mineral wealth resulted in ever-increasing ship traffic at the Sault Locks. Again, more – and bigger – locks were needed.

To meet that need, the Davis Lock was constructed in 1914, and a few short years later in 1919, the Sabin Lock was completed. These behemoth locks were 1,350 feet in length; nearly double the length of the previously built Poe Lock. The Sabin lock is now closed. Both the Sabin and Davis Locks will be replaced with a new lock once funding is established.

Today, the U.S. Corps of Engineers is searching for

congressional funding that would build yet another lock. Two-thirds of the Great Lakes vessels can't use the locks today because of the insufficient size of the locks. Repairing them won't solve the problem. With much of the nation's iron ore passing through the locks, military officials are concerned that U.S. steel making capacity – vital to our national defense – could be impaired if a new lock is not built. The estimated cost of a new lock is $400 million, a far cry from the five million the Poe Lock cost one hundred years earlier.

The Soo Locks are an indispensable Great Lakes connection – a gateway for raw materials to flow from the upper Midwest to the industrial heartland. The Sault Ste. Marie locks are the primary underpinning of the city's economy. It is the principal tourist attraction in the eastern Upper Peninsula and the revenue it generates for the local economy is essential to the Sault's economic health.

Building the locks called for a great sacrifice: it decimated the St. Mary's natural beauty. The rapids have been tamed, and masses of concrete and steel now impregnate the once majestic river site. The unfettered rhythm of the river is a footnote in history as are the Ojibwa Indians that huddled on the river's shores, living in harmony with the ebb and flow of the rushing water.

Charles T. Harvey

162

THE UPPER PENINSULA'S
"Old Faithful"

VICTORIA

The blow-off from the air compressor sprayed water 100 feet in the air – creating a magical wintertime ice sculpture.

Copper was king in the Rockland area until the turn of the century. By 1900, the once prosperous Victoria mine in Rockland languished as the mining company's ledger books were written in red. One of primary reasons for the financial difficulty of the mine was the cost in getting coal to the copper lode. The steam boiler that powered the mining equipment needed coal and it was twenty miles away. In addition, the road to the Victoria Mine was treacherous, often impassable. The road was steep and strewn with rocks and boulders that made transporting the coal to the mine difficult – and expensive. The deepening of the mineshafts and the exorbitant price of coal energy was financially draining the investors; the end of the Victoria Mine was close at hand by 1899.

One of several houses restored in the Victoria settlement near Rockland. The small community provided housing for the miners who worked at the Victoria Copper Mine. Miners walked to the nearby mine for a dollar-a-day wage.

One man refused to accept the end of the Victoria Mine: Captain Thomas Hooper, a mine manager with a considerable reputation, was appointed superintendent by a new group of owners in 1899. Hooper was a visionary and not about to let Old Victoria slide into oblivion, but even he felt only divine intervention would save the mine.

Saving the mine looked hopeless, but Hooper was not to be denied. He heard about a Canadian engineer, Charles Taylor, who had constructed hydraulic (water) driven air compressors. Hooper thought this might work, if it did, it would be a cheap source of energy for the Victoria Mine. Reports stated the air compressor needed a dependable source of water and a location from which the water could descend. With these two conditions present, Taylor said he could supply an unlimited amount of pneumatic (air) pressure with a system that had no moving parts. This sounded too good to be true to the desperate Hooper, but anything was worth investigating.

Victoria's Old Faithful last spewed water 100 feet in the air in 1931.

Hooper went to Norwich, Connecticut, to see one of Taylor's compressors at work. Impressed, but still skeptical, Hooper, secured a contract with Taylor in 1903 and the building of the air compressor began. So confident was Taylor of his engineering skills that he agreed to accept $1,000 less for each three percent the compressor efficiency fell below the targeted 70 percent. Taylor said the system would produce 4,000 horsepower, more than the mine would ever need.

Work began on the project in 1903. The most difficult of the tasks was the creation of a 26-foot high by 170-foot long chamber of solid rock – 300 feet below the earth's surface. To create the chamber, they created a drift (horizontal tunnel) at the base of the river and bore into the rock; the huge chamber was dank and putrid, making working conditions miserable. Even under these appalling conditions, the cavernous chamber and the rest of the compressor infrastructure was completed by 1904. The investors watched the progress both with trepidation and anticipation. They saw the miners working long hours, yet not producing one ounce of copper. They were worried.

The day finally arrived; the air compressor was finished and ready for its initial test run. It was 1904; a gala ceremonial crowd gathered at the mine site all eager to see the new compressor begin its long awaited mission – providing cheap energy for the mine. The investors nervously awaited the start-up, realizing that a failure of the new compressor would not only be a financial disaster, but that the Victoria Mine would have to close.

The gates were opened and water rushed into the feed channel and then into the vertical tubes. The system was started. Hours passed but nothing happened! Time ebbed away, spectators became doubtful – and more hours passed away – still nothing happened.

Finally a gurgling sound was heard near the end of the blow-off pipe. Within moments, a shaft of water gushed out of the pipe, reaching high above the river to a delighted and awed crowd. With a confident wave of his hand, Taylor, beaming, looked at Captain Hooper and said, "Sir, your compressor is ready to go to work."

The system is quite simple, yet ingenious. Water cascades down an intake pipe creating bubbles of air. The descending water produces a large amount of air as it descends to the large chamber. The air-laden water travels vertically in the chamber forcing the air to the top of the chamber where it is compressed into a smaller tube and brought to the surface with tremendous force.

This hydroelectric dam in Victoria, built in 1931, replaced the older dam that created the 100-foot blow-off.

The compressed air is channeled to the mine where it provides power to run the hoist, railroad engine, and the pumps – and still has energy left. The unused or excess air is channeled into a "blow-off" pipe that spews air and water into the atmosphere at a high velocity, creating a geyser – the Upper Peninsula's answer to Wyoming's "Old Faithful." In the wintertime, the geyser would freeze, creating a magical winter sculpture – the predecessor and perhaps inspiration for Michigan Tech's Ice Carnival.

For the next 20 years, the Taylor hydraulic air compressor faithfully performed its task of providing cheap energy for the Victoria Mine. By 1923, with years of low copper prices, Victoria was no longer economically sustainable and was forced to shut down.

However, this did not spell the end for the giant air compressor; it was granted a reprieve on life when the owners decided that it could serve the public as a tourist attraction. For the next 10 years, tourists delighted in seeing the old geyser expel spraying water 100 feet in the air. The death knell finally arrived in 1931 when the new hydroelectric Victoria Dam went on-line.

This was the end of an era. With the tremendous cost of fossil fuels and ever-escalating inflation, perhaps it is time to re-visit Taylor's hydraulic air compressor as a cheap source of energy; the genius of Taylor's system is as applicable today as it was 100 years ago.

WATER
Everywhere

THE CORNISH PUMP

The largest steam pump ever built in the United States extracted water from the Chapin Mine in Iron Mountain.

The Cornish Pump and Mining Museum houses the largest steam pump ever built. The building is located at the intersection of Kent and Carpenter avenues in Iron Mountain.

The Chapin Mine in Iron Mountain was one of the wettest mines in the world and mining officials were alarmed at a series of cave-ins due to the wet conditions. The Chapin mine had one of the richest iron ore veins in the Upper Peninsula, and mine owners were not about to let a water problem stop them from harvesting the underground wealth.

As a result, in 1890, mine officials purchased a pump that was similar to the ones used in Cornwall, England. Hence, the Iron Mountain pump became known as the "Cornish Pump." The huge, fifty-four-foot-tall pump went on-line in 1893. It did the job of extracting water out of the lower shafts at the rate of 3,400 gallons per minute.

A line of connecting steel rods extending 1,500 feet below the surface were attached to a series of pumps at varying intervals; the pumps pushed the water to the next level, eventually forcing it to the surface.

The pump cost over a quarter-of-a-million dollars (an astronomical expense in 1893) to construct, and weighed over 155,000 pounds. This behemoth helped make the Chapin Mine the largest ore-producing mine in the Menominee Range.

The enormous pump began operating in 1893 and was in use until 1914, except for an interval period from 1898 to 1908 when the earth shifted and forced the pump out of alignment. When the pump went back on-line in 1908 it was moved to the Ludington Mine, not far from its present location. Nineteen fourteen is the final year of the pump's operation; new electric pumps became the state of the art and the old Cornish steam-driven pump, unable to adapt to the new power source, headed for the moth-ball sanctuary of out-dated equipment.

The 54-foot tall pump went on-line in 1893. At full capacity it pumped water at the rate of 3,400 gallons-per-minute.

The pump sat idle until 1934 when the Chapin Mine was shut down forever. Owners of the pump, the Oliver Mining Company, deeded the pump to Dickinson County. The pump is now housed in the Dickinson Cornish Pumping Engine and Mining Museum located on a hilltop at the intersection of Kent and Carpenter avenues in Iron Mountain.

The pump and the museum skirted disaster in 1999 when a 1,000-foot cave-in (sink hole) occurred adjacent to the building. The area beneath the museum is honeycombed with mine shafts, making a sink hole a possibility (however rare) that could occur at any time. The 30-foot wide hole butted the foundation of the museum and placed the building in danger. This forced the museum to close its doors for a two-year period. This closing financially strapped the privately-funded museum that relied heavily on tourist dollars for its income.

The gaping and dangerous hole next to the building was capped with 35-foot rebarred cement. This allowed the Cornish Pump Museum to re-open its doors in June of 2001. Ironically, the museum is experiencing a water problem with excessive water draining into the recessed footings of the pump. Temporary water pumps were needed to extract water from the base of the huge

Cornish pump until engineers solved the problem. A twist of fate: the largest water pump built in the United States sits inactive in water while smaller and much inferior pumps extract water surrounding it.

This monumental pump is a top tourist attraction in Iron Mountain and a must-see exhibit for anyone interested in Upper Peninsula mining.

In 1999, a 1,000-foot cave-in left a huge hole next to the pump museum. Officials closed the Cornish Pump and Mining Museum until the gaping hole was capped. The facility re-opened in 2001.

WHEN SIZE Mattered

QUINCY MINE HOIST

The world's largest hoist is located just north of Hancock.

Who said that size doesn't matter? It mattered to the owners of the Quincy Mine nearly 90 years ago. They wanted – and needed – the largest steam-driven hoist in the world.

At the top of Quincy Hill are the mine buildings that house the huge mine hoist, as well as a mining gift shop.

A rich vein of copper, stretching thread-like from Copper Harbor to Ontonagon, could only be dislodged from the earth's deep recesses with an enormous hoist. Extracting copper from a depth of nearly two miles (on the incline) below the surface would require a hoist not yet available. With this in mind, the Quincy Mine officials embarked on building a behemoth hoist. Just two miles north of Downtown Hancock, they built the oversized hoist at a cost of $187,000. It had one mission – to raise ten tons of copper in one haul from the bowels of the earth. The newly created hoist was to accomplish that mission with ease.

Construction on the monstrous hoist by Bruno Norberg began prior to World War I, but completion was delayed until after the war. When finished, the unit was so heavy that it demanded a concrete foundation that contained enough cement to build a mile-long, two-lane highway.

The gigantic hoist, housed in a cavernous four-story

building, dominated the hoist-house with an intimidating feeling of unbridled power. Part of the hoist is a huge drum with 10,000 feet of 1-5/8" coiled rope tethered to a 10,000 pound skip that the miners filled with the copper country "gold." The skip hauled the precious ore to the surface.

The Quincy Mine Hoist is so heavy that it needed a floor that had enough concrete to build a mile-long, two-lane highway.

A Corliss-type steam-air engine provided power for the hoist and generated over 25,000 horsepower. Also housed in the hoist building was a Norberg air compressor that delivered 5,000 cubic feet of free air per minute at 100 pounds per square inch above atmospheric pressure. These statistics verify the power and capability of the mine hoist.

The hoist became operational in 1920 and faithfully served the copper miners until 1931 when the Quincy mine closed. In the 1960s it was recognized that the hoist had historical significance and must be saved and restored. Yalmer Matilla Contracting Inc. was given the job of restoring the historic mining hoist. Ted Huhta, a Matilla employee, was given the specific task of recreating authentic reproductions of parts of the hoist that were not available. Huhta spent untold hours finding and making parts for the landmark hoist.

The Quincy Mine Hoist Association, a non-profit organization, owns the hoist. It includes representatives of the Quincy Mining Company, the Norberg Manufacturing Company and Michigan Technological University.

Today, this top-notch tourist attraction draws people from all walks of life and every corner of the United States. Interestingly, the largest hoist prior to the completion of the Quincy hoist was a Bruno Norberg hoist at the Tamarack Mining Company in Calumet. Norberg installed 37 hoists throughout the Upper Peninsula, a testimony to his engineering genius.

A JOURNEY TO THE SMITHSONIAN

THE GREAT ONTONAGON BOULDER

Moving the 3,700-pound copper boulder in 1843 was no easy task – it took 21 men a week to move the boulder up a 50-foot hill.

It was only worth about $600.
It was near impossible to move.
Men drew guns over it.
Royalty in Europe talked about it.
It was the Great Ontonagon Boulder!

In 1843, the famed boulder nestled on the bank of the Ontonagon River, approximately 21 miles from the mouth of the river, and close to the site that eventually became the village of Ontonagon. The solid copper slab weighed 3,700 pounds and measured roughly two feet by three feet. Not particularly large by boulder standards (whatever that is), but extremely heavy for its size. Copper is a dense mineral (14 percent heavier than iron).

After its discovery in 1765 by an English fur trader, Alexander Henry, it became a prize that men feuded over. It was believed to be the largest single piece of copper ever discovered. The Ojibwa Indians living near the Ontonagon River believed it had mystical properties and called it "Manitou." The sacred boulder was a gift from Manitou, the mediator between them and the Great Spirit. Legend has it that the location of the copper boulder was not to be revealed to the white man. Divulging its location would mean certain trouble for the perpetrator, and in all likelihood, the poor wretch would suffer the wrath of Manitou.

Apparently, White Pigeon, an Ojibwa in the Ontonagon area, did not believe in the Manitou legacy, or didn't see a need to live by the spiritual mores of his native culture. White Pigeon violated the Indian code in 1821 by leading early explorers Lewis Cass and Henry Schoolcraft to the boulder's resting place on the

In today's market, copper is selling for one dollar a pound. This makes the Great Ontonagon Boulder worth $3,700. Good question for Trivial Pursuit.

Ontonagon River.

Sure enough, White Pigeon got his comeuppance from the great Manitou. Six years later, in 1826, a scrawny, emaciated White Pigeon turned up at a treaty meeting in Fond du Lac looking like death warmed-over. Manitou had extracted his revenge on the once proud and robust Chippewa. Hanging from White Pigeon's spindly neck, and resting on his bony rib cage, was a medallion that he received from Lewis Cass for his effort in guiding him to the boulder location. White Pigeon found out it doesn't pay to anger the Indian spirits.

Lewis Cass attempted to move the boulder, but all he could do was advance the huge rock 4 to 5 feet from the riverbank. Two years later an expedition from the Sault tried their luck at moving the boulder – they were no more successful than Cass.

In 1841 came an unabashed fortune hunter, Juluis Eldred, a Detroit entrepreneur and hardware merchant. Eldred was a disciplined and determined man. He heard about the "immovable" boulder and was determined that he would be the one to get it. Eldred was no geologist or metallurgist – and could have cared less about its mineral content. Nor was he an ardent Indian artifact collector, interested in preserving a spiritual relic for posterity. Eldred, above all else, was a capitalist. He was out to see how much money he could make by owning the boulder. Eldred's plan was simple: get the boulder from the Ontonagon River bank, bring it to Detroit where he would charge admission to the curious who wanted to see the exotic rock that had spiritual powers.

A paper-mache replica of the Great Ontonagon Boulder is housed in the Ontonagon County Historical Museum.

Eldred set out on his boulder mission in 1841 and arrived at the mouth of the Ontonagon River later that year. He quickly struck a purchasing agreement with the Native Indians. Eldred made no attempt to remove the boulder in '41 but came back in 1843 to dislodge his find. He was unsuccessful. The job was more difficult than he thought. Not to be denied, Eldred came back in 1843, this time with a ton of equipment (block and tackle, chains, cart wheels, etc.) to remove the copper mass.

All did not go well on Eldred's third visit to the boulder site. When he got to the location, two men, Jim Paul and Nick Myraclur had taken possession of the celebrated boulder. Both

Elred and Paul produced legal documents giving them ownership of the precious boulder. Paul, an illiterate, tough woodsman, was determined to keep the rock in his possession. The previous winter, Paul built a cabin next to the boulder – just to guard it from other would-be poachers.

When Paul and Eldred confronted each other over rock ownership, legend has it that Paul, in frustration, brandished his pistols about and said to Eldred. "I don't give two hoots in hell for your orders, I got a couple of orders here (sticking his weapon in Eldred's face) that are a lot better."

Not only was Eldred facing a hostile and armed Paul, but also the United States Government which got into the act when a Major Cunningham showed up with an order from the Secretary of War to take possession of the boulder for the government. To top it off, a Colonel Hammond and twenty miners entered the fray, waving a Secretary of War authorization that entitled them to procure the rock for the government. It literally turned into a three (four?) ring circus.

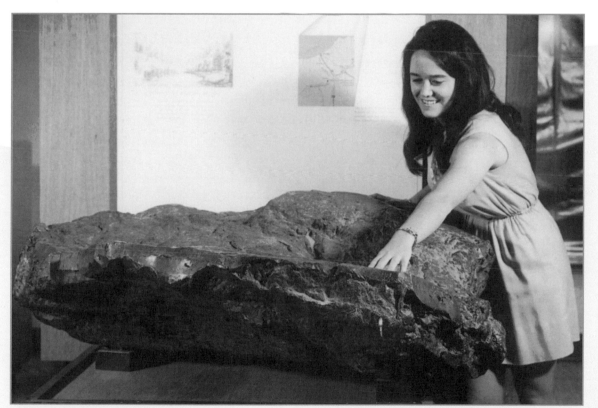

History is murky as to what happened next, but the best judgment is that the entrepreneurial Eldred bought off Hammond and Paul (for $1,365 or $1,800) and gained possession of the boulder. The saga of the boulder owner-ship does not end here; Eldred would later do battle with the government.

The Great Ontonagon Boulder, weighing 3,700 pounds, is the property of the Smithsonian. In 1971, the famed boulder was moved to the Smithsonian's Museum of Natural History.

For the next 41 days Eldred and his battalion of workers would grunt, groan and curse the boulder while moving it four-and-a-half miles to the mouth of the Ontonagon River. Up and down steep terrain the exhausted cadre would push, prod, and shove the prized rock along an ingenious, jerry-rigged rail track that Eldred brought with him from Detroit. They finally reached the mouth of the Ontonagon River on August 14th, 1843. The hard won prize was then loaded on a ship and taken to Detroit. Eldred could smell the cash coming in.

How could one boulder be so important? No one knows for sure, but the drama and the legend that surround the Great Ontonagon Copper Boulder add to the rich history of the Upper Peninsula.

But, again, all was not well. History is not clear on this, but either at the mouth of the Ontonagon River or when the Boulder arrived in Detroit, the long arm of the Federal agents accosted an exasperated Eldred. Major Cunningham, again, claimed the boulder for the government, but this time he offered Eldred $700 for his trophy rock. The beleaguered Eldred was distraught; he had already invested several thousand in the project and still had nothing to show for it.

Eldred then struck a deal with the government: he said the Smithsonian (government museum) could have the boulder if he were allowed to keep it in Detroit for three years, where he would charge 25 cents a customer to view his sacred stone. Eldred was confident he could recoup his investment in the three-year period.

After only a week or two of showing the boulder, Eldred, for whatever reason, gave up on his long-range plan and turned the boulder over to Cunningham and the government – with the stipulation that he would get future remuneration. In addition, Eldred was granted the privilege of escorting the boulder to Washington, D.C. He delighted in being the attendant for his boulder and basked at the attention he received for being its personal escort to the Capital City. Eventually, the 28th Congress provided Eldred with a check for $5,664.98 for his trouble in getting the boulder to the Smithsonian. Elred would die four years later – dead broke.

Jim Paul, who once claimed the boulder and was bought off by Eldred, took to selling whiskey and spinning yarns about the copper boulder in his Ontonagon tavern. Paul is considered the founder of Ontonagon and is still revered by area residents. He is buried in the village cemetery.

In 1971, the famed boulder was moved to its present location in the National Museum of Natural History's "Our Restless Earth" display in the Physical Geology Hall.

The Great Ontonagon Boulder is not the last word in pure copper chunks. In 2001, a 34,000-pound slab of pure copper (over nine times the size of Ontonagon Boulder) was retrieved from the bottom of Lake Superior near Eagle Harbor in the Keweenaw Peninsula. It is one of the world's largest specimens of pure copper. No, the Federal Government didn't get – nor want – this chunk of copper; the state and federal governments are content to let Michigan Technological University (MTU) house the "rock" at the University's Seaman Mineral Museum. MTU, be on guard – Manitou may not like his new residence.

BEEHIVES IN THE WOODS

ROCK RIVER KILNS

The stone remnants of the beehive-shaped charcoal kilns protrude from the thick growth deep in the Rock River woodland in the Hiawatha National Forest. Built by the Union Fuel Company in the late 1870s and early 1880s, they provided charcoal for the smelters in the Marquette Iron Range. It took eight masons three-and-a-half days to build one kiln. These skilled artisans made 30 cents an hour – considered a decent wage at the time.

Remnants of a charcoal kiln in Rock River nestled against a lone birch tree. This stone residue is one of twelve kilns that were on this site in the early 1880s.

Cords of hardwood were layered in the bottom of the kiln and subjected to a weeklong controlled burn. What remained after the burn was charcoal. The charcoal residue was scooped out of the kiln bottom and loaded on railroad boxcars and sent to Marquette. The charcoal was the fuel for the blast furnaces that turned iron ore into pig iron. At peak production there were 12 kilns in the Rock River area (including the communities of Onota and Whitefish) producing 45 carloads of charcoal a month.

By 1896, the hardwood in the area was depleted and the production at the Rock River kilns ceased. After sixteen years of operating, the small community of Rock River, with a population of 200, disappeared. No evidence of any community life exists at the site; all that remains are the foundations of the old kilns.

GOD'S LITTLE ACRE

ROCK RIVER GRAVES

One can only imagine the anguish the parents suffered at losing three children in one month.

Three neatly lettered wooden grave markers protrude from a thick, emerald green ground cover of myrtle; the markers bear the names Libbie, Amanda and Abbey, all children ranging in age from three months to nine years. The three died in a diphtheria epidemic in December of 1885.

For over a hundred years, the stoic aspen and maple trees, and a lone lilac shrub, have embraced the children's small burial ground. The trees stand as vigilant sentinels, guarding the hallowed ground. These are the only graves in the small cemetery deep in the Hiawatha National Forest.

Embedded in a thick green cover of myrtle are the graves of the Trudell children who died from diptheria in 1885.

Kiln employee Charles Trudell was the father of the children. They are buried close to what used to be the small community of Rock River. Although there is no evidence of the hamlet, the site is dotted with the foundations of wood-burning kilns that were used to make charcoal in the late 1870s to mid 1890s. The kiln employees made up the settlement of Rock River.

The Alger County Historical Society restored the gravesites after a power line built in the area disturbed the original site. The gray, weathered, wood markers with indented black lettering are produced with such accuracy that it is difficult to detect that they are not the original grave markers.

MUNCHKINS
ON SUPERIOR'S SHORE

THE PICKLE BARREL IN GRAND MARAIS

The fictional characters, "The Teenie Weenies," capture the heart of Chicago readers and then become real life munchkins in Grand Marais.

Imagine: Leprechauns, in elfin costumes, gaily prancing about a miniature pickle barrel house, deep in an Upper Peninsula forest. It happened back in 1926, when elfin people were transformed from static cartoon characters to flesh and blood imps that danced their way into the heart of Mary Donahey. These miniature people were spawned from the creative pen of Mary's husband, William Donahey, a Chicago cartoonist and writer. The make-believe leprechauns were called the Teenie Weenies. The Teenie Weenies first appeared in the 1914 edition of the Sunday *Chicago Tribune*. These charismatic miniature people delivered delightful tales to enamored readers of the *Chicago Tribune* from their inception until Donahey's death in 1970. The journalistic success of the Teenies led to publications in other papers and books, much to the satisfaction of the reading public. But it was in Grand Marais that the Teenie Weenies came to life.

William Donahey was also an illustrator for a canned food company, The Reid, Murdock & Company. The cartoon illustrator and the corporation joined forces and began a successful venture in launching corporate products with the Teenie Weenie people as advertising agents. The Teenie Weenie cartoon characters were incorporated into Teenie Weenie Peanut Butter, Peas, Sardines, but most importantly, Teenie Weenie Pickles. These tasty, small, sweet pickled cucumbers were sold in attractive little pickle barrels as well as in glass jars. This cooperative effort between Reid, Murdock & Company, and Bill Donahey, lasted only until a copyright problem with another company resulted in the Teenie Weenies being dropped as a marketing tool for the food corporation.

The local county commission is presently evaluating the status of the old icon, hoping in some way that the old house can be saved.

In 1926, William and Mary Donahey met with friends S.P. Stevens and his wife from Evanston, Illinois. William owned land in the Upper Peninsula and suggested that the Stevens join them on a trip to the remote Upper Peninsula. The Stevens agreed and together the couples journeyed to the Upper Peninsula. Their destination: Grand Marais. They traveled for two days to reach Grand Marais; the last 26 miles to the isolated Lake Superior village was on a two-rut road.

William and Mary Donahey at their Pickle Barrel home on Grand Sable Lake near Grand Marais. (circa 1927)

After their arrival, the foursome went for a walk to Grand Sable Lake, a picturesque lake not far from the village. Beautiful, four mile-long, Grand Sable Lake was bordered with a thick growth of hemlocks, pine, white birch and maples. It was an idyllic setting.

They walked the shoreline of Grand Sable Lake until dusk. In the twilight hours, they came upon what appeared to be a shack in the woods, but after a closer inspection they discovered the building was not a shack, but a life-size replica of the Pickle Barrel House, the same house that Donahey had created for his Teenie Weenie people in his illustrations for Reid, Murdock & Company.

Mary Donahey was enthralled when she saw the Pickle Barrel house; but the best was yet to come. Within no time a host of Teenie Weenie people came gaily marching out of the barrel house and surrounded the miniature residence in their bright Teenie Weenie costumes. Leading the band of leprechauns was the Teenie Weenie General, all decked out in his red coat and colorful plumed hat. The General made a gracious bow to the Donaheys and then presented them with a huge golden key – the key to the barrel house. He then welcomed his guests with a well-rehearsed verse.

The Pickle Barrel House in downtown Grand Marais. Descendants of William Donahey who live in Grand Marais are concerned about the deterioration of the Barrel House.

The plumed General and the other Teenie Weenies were children from the local school who dressed up as the fictional characters. The Stevenses and William had prepared the surprise welcoming for Mary. She was awestruck and could not believe that her husband's Teenie Weenie fairyland people had become a reality; a storybook fantasy had taken on life in the isolated Upper Michigan village of Grand Marais.

Bill Donahey knew in advance of the existence of the barrel house that was assembled in Grand Marais, but kept it a secret from his writer wife Mary. He and the Stevenses had planned this surprise for Mary long before they left Chicago.

Stevens, along with Harold Cunliff, the proprietor of the company that made the barrels for the Monarch Teenie Weenie Sweet Pickles, built the Pickle Barrel House in Chicago. After its completion, the Barrel House was disassembled and trucked to Grand Marais where it then journeyed four more miles to Grand Sable Lake where it was reassembled on William Donahey's lake property.

It took two weeks to reconstruct the Barrel House on the Donahey site. When it was finally completed it was a work of art; the "house" was completed with beds made, floors scrubbed and flowers carefully arranged in the cozy barrel interior. Finishing the Pickle Barrel House was not an easy task; windows had to be cut on a curved surface, and the bunk bed had to be constructed for a curved interior; eventually all carpentry problems were solved and the quaint little house was ready for occupancy. The second floor of the Barrel House is a 16-foot diameter bedroom complete with four curved windows and awnings. A niche on the second floor, underneath one of the four awning windows, provided a comfortable space for the writers to type out their Teenie Weenie manuscripts.

The Stevenses and Donaheys resided in the Teenie Weenie Pickle Barrel House for several months. Word of the curious little dwelling spread throughout the region and visitors (as many as 200 a day) came to examine the odd spectacle, all hoping to see the diminutive people they imagined lived in the fairy tale pickle barrel. Adults were just as inquisitive as children about the oddity, but probably deferred to their children as the reason they were viewing the house. This was long before it was fashionable to recognize the legitimacy of the playful and inquisitive child that resides in all adults.

All the attention that the Pickle House was drawing was exciting for Mary Donahey, but after a while it became tedious and the Donaheys stopped using the Pickle House as a summer writing retreat.

In the late 1930s the Donaheys moved the Pickle Barrel House to a prominent location in Grand Marais. The house was given to the village (although there was no deed transaction) and placed on property adjacent to Hill's store. In the 1950s, the Hills, facing financial difficulty, were forced to sell the store, and the Pickle Barrel House, sitting on store property, was included in the sale.

Over the next decade, the Pickle Barrel House served the community in varying capacities. A welcoming center and a small store were two of the businesses that operated the old barrel house. Janet Ogden, a niece to William Donahey and a resident of Grand Marais, recalls childhood days when the Pickle Barrel House was unoccupied and unlocked. She and her friends frequently played in the pickle house in those innocent growing-up years. Janet said, "It was a delightful playhouse, it's the dream of every child to have an authentic playhouse – we had one in Grand Marais."

Today, the white Pickle Barrel House sits on a downtown corner, unoccupied and showing signs of its age. The absentee owner of the barrel house resides in a nursing home in Lower Michigan. Mary Dempsy, Grand Marais resident, and great niece to William Donahey, was unsuccessful in her effort to buy the Pickle Barrel House. Dempsy views the quaint building as a village landmark and would like to see it restored and preserved for community heritage.

The Teenie Weenies and Grand Marais are inexorably linked; the Pickle Barrel House and the courtly elves are part of the community's heritage; it is imperative this legacy be preserved.

A HAUGHTY HOTEL

BREITUNG HOTEL

Negaunee's grand hotel burned to the ground in 1988.

Residents said that it was a high-class hotel, and they marveled at its opulence. It had plush, red velvet curtains, a billiard room, a barbershop, a bar and even a maid's personal living quarters. The famed Breitung Hotel, built in downtown Negaunee in 1879, was an illustrious hotel that catered to upper-echelon mining executives and traveling salesmen.

Andrew Seass, a cigar manufacturer and the first owner, was the driving force behind the building of the hotel. Seass built the upscale hotel to accommodate the many mining, engineering, geology and railroad officials who were coming to Negaunee to do business. In the early years, the hotel bristled with activity when the iron ore mines were flourishing.

The new community bandshell is on the old Breitung Hotel site in downtown Negaunee. Landscaping in the summer of 2002 will complete the bandshell project.

Seass made it easy for traveling salesmen. They were given a special room where they could set up their merchandise, and they had a special landing at the side of the hotel where they could drop off their commodities.

Everyone who arrived in the city by train could get a horse and buggy ride to the Breitung for their night's stay. It was rumored that the horse took so many trips to the train depot that it frequently went by itself to pick up potential customers. (Current hotels at this time do not have driverless courtesy vans.)

The Breitung Hotel stayed in the Seass family until 1952. Afterward, it had several owners until Orvall and Helga Sutton bought the hotel in 1966. Owner Helga Sutton said, "It was a wonderful place."

In 1879, cigar manufacturer Andrew Seass built the elegant Breitung Hotel. Complete with plush, red velvet curtains, it was considered high-class at the turn of the century.

Many notables stayed at the hotel, the most famous being Teddy Roosevelt.

By 1979, the glory years of the hotel had passed and the structure had only a 50 percent occupancy, most of them being retired people who had no relatives or any other place to live.

In 1986, the aging lady was in such bad shape that the State of Michigan Police and Fire Marshall Division closed down the venerable hotel, citing several fire code violations. Fourteen residents were removed from the building at that time.

Further examination of the building revealed several roof leaks, faulty wiring, supporting timber structural damage and a need for steel reinforcement of the tower.

After the condemnation, the Breitung remained empty for two years until 1988 when a local, private non-profit committee was formed to save the old hostel. Early efforts garnered a $20,000 grant to begin restoration. The committee was hopeful that the old hotel could be saved and returned to her grandeur.

But, it was not to be.

On January 15th, 1988, the hotel went up in flames. It was completely destroyed. Only charred, smoldering timbers and twisted steel remained where the grand hotel once stood. A vagrant who settled in the empty hotel had lit a fire in the building to get warm; the drunken trespasser then left the building, leaving the fire unattended. Within 25 minutes the entire structure was in flames. With the Breitung now a charred memory, the hope of rejuvenating the downtown with the hotel as the centerpiece, literally went up in smoke.

City officials, however, did not abandon the dream of resurrecting the downtown. Fifteen years later, Negaunee built an impressive band shell on the site. While not as majestic as a restored old hotel, the prominent site at the end of Iron Street in downtown Negaunee is now occupied by a building that will serve the community as a gathering site for musical entertainment.

HENRY FORD'S
HOME AWAY FROM HOME

THUNDER BAY INN

The 1957 movie classic, **Anatomy of a Murder,**
was filmed at the historic inn.

The gracious, elegantly appointed suite has an exquisite mahogany bedroom set commanding center stage. A distinctive art nouveau green chaise lounge obliquely placed draws your eye to the far corner of the room. This chamber could be a movie set for a tasteful period movie or a center spread in a Martha Stewart fashion magazine.

But it's neither.

It was Henry Ford's suite during the 1940s at his company hotel, the picturesque Thunder Bay Inn in Big Bay. Ford often stayed here when visiting Big Bay. He had financial interests in the small community located 30 miles north of Marquette.

A sawmill a short distance from the hotel on nearby Lake Independence was Ford's bustling enterprise. The mill manufactured wood siding for Ford's popular station wagons (Woodys) during the 1940s and 1950s. The close proximity of the company hotel afforded him the ability to actively monitor the mill. In addition, Ford was a member of the exclusive Huron Mountain Club, a remote retreat adjacent to Big Bay, where Ford often entertained other industrial giants.

What transpired in the quiet moments when Ford rambled about the room in solitude? Did nation-shaping ideas germinate in the serene ambiance of this lovely chamber? Ideas that would transcend the boundaries of the quiet hotel and eventually affect the lives of millions of Americans? The walls may well have witnessed defining moments in history, but they stand in stoic silence, never yielding the murmurs or whispers of what one of America's greatest tycoons said in his reflective moments.

The likable Smalls are receptive and friendly; their geniality at the historically rich Thunder Bay Inn makes your stay a pleasant experience.

183

The Thunder Bay Inn had a rich history prior to Henry Ford acquiring it in 1940. Built in 1911, the building first served as a combination store, post office, barbershop, and livery. The huge two-story structure supplied the local lumberjacks and trappers with the necessary supplies needed to survive the long cold winters in the northern woods. Later it was renovated into a hotel to accommodate the rugged woodsmen and trappers who came to Big Bay seeking respite and revelry after hard months of labor in the wilderness.

Nineteen fifty-nine was a momentous year for the Thunder Bay Inn. The glamour and glitz of Hollywood's elite arrived at the little town on the lake to make a movie; not just any movie, but one based on a murder that occurred in the quaint village just a few years earlier. The Thunder Bay Inn was used to film selected scenes for the movie. This was a cinema production with marquee names: Jimmy Stewart, Lee Remick and Ben Gazarra were a few of the larger-than-life Tinsel Town celebrities who put Big Bay and the Thunder Bay Inn on the map. The movie, *Anatomy of a Murder*, written by local attorney, John Voelker, and directed by the legendary Otto Preminger, went on to garner seven Academy Award nominations. Although it received more nominations in 1959 than any other film, it failed to capture the elusive Oscar.

The spacious knotty pine bar was added to the Thunder Bay Inn for the filming of the movie *Anatomy of a Murder*.

In order to accommodate a bar scene in the movie, a new pub was added on to the south end of the Inn. This addition provided the needed room to film the tavern scenes, and today still serves food and drink for hungry and thirsty travelers who visit the remote village. A display board in the Inn's dining room is packed with newspaper articles about the movie filming at the Thunder Bay Inn; this board, along with a scrapbook of pictures in the dining area, acquaints guests with the role the movie played in the history of the old hotel.

The Inn's expansive front porch looks like it's straight out of an advertisement for a gracious southern mansion. The pillared veranda's entry doors lead to an ample-sized, French-door vestibule that empties into a spacious dining/lounge area. A huge, 15-panel, segmented window that generously sprays light into the dining area dominates the front of the room. In addition, it gives guests an opportunity to soak in a panoramic view of Lake Independence.

Owners Darryl and Eileen Small relax in a chase lounge in the Henry Ford room at the Thunder Bay Inn.

The Thunder Bay Inn, built in 1911, was once a post office, barbershop and livery. The elegant inn now serves guests in a restored, historic setting.

Soft light spills through smaller windowpanes at the north end of the dining room. The casual light sheds unobtrusively across the room where its fading illumination casts a dwindling glow on an impressive stone fireplace. The hearth, replete with white wicker chairs wrapped cozily around the perimeter, provides the room with a snug ambiance. Nearby, an old Victrola sits forlornly on a table, as if it were waiting for someone to place an old vinyl disc on its dusty turntable. One could imagine the cavernous room filling with the sweet sounds of a melody from a bygone era. The Great Gatsby would have felt at home here.

Darryl and Eileen Small, the present owners, bought the financially troubled Inn for $75,000 in 1986 after the previous owners declared bankruptcy. The Smalls were determined to turn the historic old hotel into an elegant but comfortable bed and breakfast hostel; a destination place for global travelers.

The industrious Smalls toiled unrelentingly over the next 14 years in upgrading the 12-room hotel. The renovations were numerous: all rooms were done with different wallpaper imported form England; antique period pieces were placed in each room, contributing to a vintage ambiance; the kitchen was modernized and the menu expanded. Hotel guests have the luxury of sauntering out to a spacious second floor balcony where on clear summer days they are greeted by a breathtaking view of the early morning sun peeking out over Lake Independence.

The inn caters to snowmobilers in the winter and tourists in the summer. In addition, periodically provided entertainment is in the dining area. The inn can easily accommodate groups that need a quiet place for a seminar. Travelers who are seeking a quiet and historic, but off-the-beaten-path, place to stay may find the Thunder Bay Inn an ideal location.

THE LADY
ON THE LAKE

HOUSE OF LUDINGTON

"New Ludington Hotel – The largest and only hotel in the city having baths, steam heat and electric call bells. $2.00 per day."

Michigan Gazetteer and Business Directory 1893.

This ad, just prior to the turn of the century, touted the new Ludington Hotel in Escanaba as the only place to stay when visiting the city. The Queen Anne style hotel is nestled near the edge of Bay de Noc at the east end of the main thoroughfare. It was built in 1883 by John Christie and named after local lumber baron John Ludington. The new brick building replaced the old wood-framed Gaynor Hotel that had occupied the site for the previous twelve years.

Not content with its size because of a demand for more room space, Christie enlarged the hotel by adding an east wing in 1903 and a west wing in 1910. He could now confidently boast that he had a 100-room hotel.

John Christie died in 1919, leaving the hotel to his son, James Thomas Christie. The Christie descendants owned the hotel for the next 29 years, eventually selling it in 1939 to Pat Hayes for $50,000. Hayes was a shrewd businessman. After making a down payment of $20,000, he refused to make any more payments, and then declared bankruptcy. The clever Hayes, knowing it was to his legal advantage, moved into the hotel. The Christies, attempting to get the rest of their money, took Hayes

Ornate and segmented French doors and a massive fireplace dominate the well-appointed dining room in the House of Ludington.

to court. The local judge, noting that the hotel was Hayes' residence, let him retain the hotel with no additional payments. If Hayes had pursued other employment opportunities – like political fund raising – he could have plied his skills without fear of repercussion.

Seventy-three-year-old Hayes ran the hotel for thirty years until his death in 1969. These were the prosperous decades for the flourishing hotel. It catered to celebrities as well as to traveling salesmen. The cuisine at the hotel was gaining in reputation by serving sumptuous dinners at reasonable prices.

The Ludington House was named after lumberman Nelson Ludington. The hotel exemplifies Queen Anne resort architecture, popular in the late 1880s and 1890s.

Rumors that Hoffa is buried in cement in a corner of the basement were never proven.

Hayes did some modernizing of the hotel. Many of the renovations were in keeping with the elegant Queen Anne architecture; others were grossly out of place. One ill-advised change he made was adding a modern external glass elevator to the front facade of the building. This tortuous extension of a glass wall on the front of the building clashed with the Ludington's quaint, brick-arched windows. The contemporary glass elevator, in juxtaposition to the vintage octagonal red-shingled turret, jars aesthetic sensibilities. During elevator construction, the Escanaba city council was unhappy with the modernistic elevator and voiced a disapproval of the addition.

After Hayes' death the hotel fell upon hard times. Loyal employees kept the hotel open for the next eight years, until finally mounting debt and the Internal Revenue Service closed it down. It appeared the golden years were a thing of the past and but a fading memory for the Ludington.

New life was given to the hotel in 1982 when Gerald and Vernice Lancour purchased the Ludington at a bargain price. John Christie had seen the Ludington at its best; the Lancours saw it at its worst. The building had suffered the indignities of time and was in severe need of renovation. The Lancours added a new roof, re-plumbed, rewired and refurbished the aging hotel, but all their efforts were not enough to keep the hotel solvent.

By 1996 the hotel again fell upon hard financial times. In an attempt to keep the hotel afloat, Lancour sometimes paid the employees in cash. The Internal Revenue Service, not well known for its compassion, did not look kindly upon wage earners not paying taxes. As a result, the hotel closed again and Lancour took up residency in a penal institution for the better part of a year.

The lien holders, MFC First National Bank, were forced to foreclose on the hotel; they became the reluctant, but temporary proprietors.

In May of 1998, new owners, Edwaed and Suzell Eisenberger, bought the financially troubled hotel. Within a few short months the Eisenbergers had refurbished it and once again opened its doors for business.

The interior of the turn-of-the-century hotel still has vestiges of elegance. A cozy lounge with curtained booths occasionally features easy listening music – an ideal place to sip a cocktail in comfort. The courtly King George dining room, featuring ornate hand-carved cherry wood cabinets, houses antique silver and a valuable large gold punch bowl. Michigan's first governor, Lewis Cass, was once the proud owner of these exquisite cabinets. A huge fireplace dominates one wall and gives warmth to the stately dining room.

Over the years, the rich and famous have been guests at the venerable hotel. John Sousa, Randy Travis, Henry Ford, Cornelius Vanderbilt Jr., Jimmy Hoffa and Johnny Cash were a few of the famed who temporarily lodged at the Ludington.

Today, the grand old lady of east Ludington Avenue is still receiving guests; for 117 years she has provided respite for weary travelers. Like many imposing old buildings, she has suffered humiliation during her life, but has endured the hardships, and continues to provide the community with a regal hostel where an exhausted wayfarer can bed down in first-class comfort.

Built in 1883, The Ludington Hotel, shown here, replaced the wood-framed Gaynor Hotel that occupied the site for the previous twelve years.

THE MAGNIFICENT MANOR

LAURIUM MANOR

Laurium's Cornelia Hoatson received a 45-room mansion for a wedding present.

Cornelia Hoatson was enjoying a pleasant Sunday afternoon ride with her husband when they came across an impressive, nearly completed mansion on a nearby street. Cornelia looked longingly at the elegant house. Her husband, Captain Thomas Hoatson, asked her, "Would you like a tour of the home?" Cornelia declined, saying, "It wouldn't be proper etiquette to barge in, unannounced, into someone's home even though it wasn't finished." Thomas Hoatson then eagerly revealed, to her unbelievable delight, that indeed it was proper, because the house was hers as a wedding present.

This is how the largest mansion in western Upper Michigan came into being at the turn of the century. It was 1908, and the pretentious 45-room home was built by banking, railroad and mining tycoon, Captain Thomas Hoatson. With no expense spared, he built the impressive 13,000 square-foot, $50,000, art nouveau home just blocks off Highway U.S. 41 in Laurium.

Art nouveau was a popular architectural movement from 1880 to 1910 and is characterized by curving undulated lines often referred to as whiplash lines. In the United States, Louis Tiffany was a promoter of art nouveau. The famed stained glass Tiffany lamps are representative of this style and are popular with today's antique consumers. The interior of the home with its uncommon shades of green, plum and lavender, while considered garish by today's standards, was on the cutting edge of interior design at the turn of the century. These colors, however, do give the home a true art nouveau feel. Although somewhat resurrected today, art nouveau was eventually replaced by the art deco movement of the 1920s and 1930s.

The restored Laurium Manor is one of the priceless historic jewels that adds to the rich heritage not only of the Copper Country, but also of all the Upper Peninsula.

The neoclassic facade, with its expansive 17 Corinthian cedar columns, supports the elegant two-leveled front portico. Hand-laid porcelain tile and sandstone (from the nearby Jacobsville Quarry) provide the flooring for the imposing and spacious 1,000-foot entry.

The mansion has had several owners in its 92-year existence. Some treated her with dignity and loving care, as Captain Hoatson and Cornelia did; others avariciously plundered the elegant home, removing irreplaceable and priceless chandeliers and stained glass windows. When Thomas Hoatson died in 1929, Cornelia continued to live in the Manor for another eighteen years, until her death in 1947. The home remained in the Hoatson family for two more years and then was sold to new owners who kept possession of the home for the next thirty years. Their tragic murder-suicide deaths in 1979 put the house back on the market.

Thomas Hoatson built this elegant mansion for his wife as a wedding present. The pretentious 45-room, 13,000 square-foot manor cost $50,000 in 1908.

From 1979 to 1989 the grand old mansion had five owners. It was during this period that the Laurium Manor was pillaged for profit by rapacious owners who cared little for the significance of the historic home. The residence was so neglected and savagely raped that the next owners (and present) were almost deterred from buying the house – believing that it was beyond recovery.

David and Julie Sprenger, both Michigan Tech graduates, are the present owners and have been for the past ten years. They are painstakingly restoring the manor to its former grandeur. It has not been an easy task.

Many of the tasks the Sprengers lovingly worked on over the ten-year restoration period were exhaustingly labor-intensive. One such task was removing the linoleum and glued-down carpeting, which resulted in exposing well-preserved wood floors. The canvas wall paintings and friezes, once cleaned, were restored to their original luster.

The Manor's carriage house was used to shelter Captain Hoatson's sleek, beloved Pierce Arrow. A unique feature of the carriage house is the turntable. When used effectively, it easily fits the car in its designated space by rotating the car 90 degrees. Also, early cars did not have reverse so a turntable was a necessity if you had a garage.

The kitchen was updated out of necessity. However, it retained its turn of the century flavor with its small floor tiles and an attached butler's pantry with its dark-stained oak. The kitchen has a huge 80-cubic-foot icebox. It was designed with owner convenience in mind; the iceman never had to enter the kitchen proper; he deposited the ice blocks in the cubicle from the backside of the refrigerator.

Unique to the home is the elephant hide wall coverings in the formal dining room. It is doubtful today that one could cover their walls with an animal fabric without eliciting howls of protest by animal rights groups. However, at the turn of the century this was not considered offensive.

The dining room also has a push-button switch, located in the middle of the room under a rug. When activated by the foot, it summons the waiter in the kitchen to serve the prepared dinner. It appears that informally eating a snack while standing over the kitchen sink was not a frequent dinning style by the Hoatsons.

The Laurium Manor takes on a special Christmas charm when the Sprengers and many of their friends spend an evening lovingly gracing the mansion with holiday decorations. This does not go unappreciated by Laurium villagers who stream by the Manor and admiringly gaze at the enormous wreath and twinkling lights that so elegantly adorn the front porch.

Restoring and preserving what was once grand enhances the attractiveness of a community, not only as a place to visit but also as a place to live.

The neoclassic facade of the Laurium Manor's two-level front portico is supported by elegant Corinthian columns. Hand-laid porcelain tile and sandstone provide the flooring for the imposing 1,000-square-foot entrance.

A SUPERIOR VIEW

THE LANDMARK INN

Louis Armstong; Peter, Paul and Mary; Don Hutson; Bud Abbott and Lou Costello were some of the notable celebrities who stayed at the historic inn.

For fifteen years, bitter cold winds swept off the frozen lake and howled through the silent, empty corridors. No chatter of guests, no rattle of pots and pans, and no tinkling of glasses in the bar. The Northland sat shrouded in solitude from 1982 to 1995, a shabby reminder of the earlier years when it enjoyed the reputation of being the best hotel in the Upper Peninsula.

That all changed in 1995 when Bruce and Christine Pesola – Team Landmark – purchased the derelict building and spent nineteen months returning it to its original splendor. Spending upwards of $5 million, the Pesolas created a restoration that is a work of art.

The original Northland was just an idea until George Shiras II approached the Rotary Club about the possibility of a new hotel, a first-class hotel of which the city would be proud. Initial plans called for the sale of $300,000 in stock. Enough money was raised to begin working on the foundation, which was completed in 1920. Then the money ran out. For the next nine years, the basement, capped with wood, sat waiting for something to happen. Children used the surface as a playground and police routinely chased them away.

George Shiras raised two-thirds of the required capital through Kawbawgam Hotel Company to continue the project in 1929. Upon completion on January 8, 1930, thirteen years after its inception, the Northland had cost $350,000.

Frank Russell, owner of *The Mining Journal* and WDMJ Radio, bought the hotel in 1950. He added murals of outdoor scenes by photographer Ebb Warren to the Northland Bar.

The 1960s began a series of changes in ownership. Russell sold the hotel to Edward L. Pearce who, after five years, turned it over to Lincoln Frazier and Max Reynolds. They donated the Northland to St. Luke's Hospital to be used in a fund-raising drive. The hospital immediately put the hotel on the market.

Dick Lutey, Ted Gaspar and Don Pearce bought the hotel in 1970 for $250,000 and changed the name to the Heritage House. The aristocratic dining room was henceforth to be called The Tin Lizzie after the 1911 Ford decorating the entrance. In 1975, Lutey, Pearce and Gaspar sold their interests to Jane Lightner, but when she defaulted on loans a year later, the hotel passed into the hands of the First of America Bank. Kenneth Hogg briefly operated the hotel for the bank.

The lobby of the Northland Hotel (Landmark Inn) was so badly deteriorated that an entire new lobby had to be constructed. The new lobby was based on the original architecture and includes 1920s and 1930s period furnishings.

In 1978, Ted Bogdan, previous owner of the local Holiday Inn, bought the hotel for $412,000 plus back taxes and renamed it the "Old Marquette Inn." He added Dirty Annie's Saloon and made the Crow's Nest restaurant on the sixth floor, the city's premier place for dining. In December 1982, the Old Marquette Inn was closed and Bogdan filed for bankruptcy. The hotel ended up back in the lap of the First of America Bank.

Ed Havlic, president of a Chicago investment firm, attempted to resurrect the hotel from 1984 to 1995 with scant success. Funding tied to various schemes involving federal and state grants failed to materialize. Havlic did, however, gut the interior of the hotel and replace the wooden windows with modern metal ones.

The Pesolas purchased a mere shell of a building, rolled up their sleeves and got to work. The finished product includes 62 guestrooms, each with a different décor, and a penthouse suite. On the sixth floor, the Sky Room gourmet restaurant offers diners a view of the sky through the windows and on the painted ceiling mural. A club-like, cozy Executive Lounge across the hallway overlooks the harbor and the rooftops of the historic district. The main dining room was returned to its original place on the east side of the building, and the former saloon became an English pub with a mezzanine level balcony.

Louis Armstrong and the musical trio Peter, Paul and

Mary stayed at the Northland Hotel (Landmark Inn) after local gigs. Bud Abbott and Lou Costello, famous comedy duo in the '30s and '40s, drew a crowd of 5,000 at the high school stadium in 1942 and held the audience captive when they entertained at the Marquette Branch Prison.

Green Bay Packer and football icon Don Hutson sued the hotel for $100,000 in 1949. He claimed that he had sustained a severe cut on the palm of his hand because of a bathroom faucet. He complained that he had not been "warned of the dangers lurking in the bathroom." The suit was settled amicably, with no monetary award.

The Landmark Inn (formerly the Northland Hotel) was built in 1930 and renovated in 1997 at a cost of $5 million. This hotel is the most opulent in Upper Michigan.

The silent derelict sitting vacant-eyed at the top of Front Street hill has been restored to the elegant hostelry envisioned by George Shiras II and the Kawbawgam Hotel Company seventy years ago.

MINING MEMORABILIA

MICHIGAN IRON INDUSTRY MUSEUM

A small, but classy museum is nestled in the pines just east of Negaunee.

Visitor Pat Goldsworthy treks through a recreated mine drift in the Michigan Iron Industry Museum. It is one of the many presentations that tell the story of mining in Michigan's Upper Peninsula.

Nestled in the woods two miles east of Negaunee is one of the state's best kept secrets; cloistered in the maples and pines, between U.S. 41 and County Road 492, is one of the state's smallest, but one of the classiest museums to be found anywhere.

This is Michigan's Iron Industry Museum.

Located on the site of the first iron ore blast furnaces is a 4,000 square foot museum artistically woven into the landscape. Since this jewel in the Upper Peninsula opened its doors in 1987, thousands of iron mining buffs and curious visitors have trekked through the history of Michigan's three iron ranges.

The museum narrates by static and interactive displays, artifacts and audio-visual programs. They tell the history of iron ore mining and the people who labored in the deep, underground mines. It is the miner's story and the museum relates the history of how hardworking miners altered the land and shaped the culture of Upper Michigan. A unique feature of the museum is a block-long interpretive trail that leads from the parking lot to the museum. The pleasant boardwalk is marked with placards that tell the mining story. This tree-lined trail is an enjoyable walk as well as an educational one; it is also the primary entryway for visitors.

Adjacent to the museum parking lot is a memorial dedicated to the 51 miners that lost their lives in the infamous Barnes-Heckers mine disaster in 1926. The granite memorial, with the miners' names engraved, was placed a considerable distance from the museum, thus allowing it special consideration by visitors.

Frank Matthews, a retired miner from Negaunee, is more responsible than anyone for this prestigious little museum in the woods. In 1972, a bearded Matthews led state officials to a site on the Carp River where the first forge was constructed. Matthews, a local legend, and keeper of his own museum on U.S. 41, had visions that someday a museum would be built to properly honor the mining industry. Matthews's effort to have a museum to honor the mining industry was listened to attentively by state officials. They left agreeing with Matthews that an iron museum should be built on the site of the first forge. Even after its approval by state officials, it would take years before it became a reality.

Finally, in 1985, Matthews's dream would be realized and ground broken for the new facility. During the long and arduous 15-year period of planning, and attempts to get funding, Matthews worked closely with the organizing committee. He never did see the completed project; he died two months after the groundbreaking ceremony, but he died knowing that his dream of an iron mine museum was going to be a reality. The museum opened its doors in 1987.

Though the museum is somewhat off the main thoroughfare, it is well worth taking the extra time to visit this historic site. The museum is open from May through October and there is no admission fee.

The Michigan Iron Industry Museum is nestled in a forested ravine near the Carp River not far from Negaunee. This jewel in the woods is small by museum standards, but is first-rate in quality.

THE UPPER PENINSULA'S NATIONAL MUSEUM

U.S. NATIONAL SKI HALL OF FAME AND MUSEUM

Ishpeming fought to keep the Ski Hall of Fame in the Upper Peninsula.

Cooperstown, New York.
Canton, Ohio.
Ishpeming, Michigan.
Most sports enthusiasts would recognize the first two as the locations of the National Baseball Hall of Fame and the National Football Hall of Fame, but few would recognize the third as being the home of the National Ski Hall of Fame.

They're missing something.

The $1.7 million frame building is unique among its contemporaries. Architecturally, more than any other hall of fame, the building reflects the sport. Its roof, a tapered soaring pinnacle, shaped like a ski hill, invites one to visualize a graceful skier descending the precipitous roof on a snowy winter day.

The new Ski Hall of Fame building was built in 1989 when the old structure had long outlived its usefulness. If Ishpeming were to continue as the location of the National Ski Hall of Fame, they would have to build a new facility.

An effort was underway by outside forces to move the facility to another location – outside of Ishpeming. A new building would ensure the Hall of Fame remained in Ishpeming.

At that time, other areas of the country (Lake Placid, New York, and several Colorado sites) were actively seeking to be the location of the hall of fame.

Ishpeming was considered too remote and inaccessible. Even Chicago was once suggested. The Ishpeming ski enthusiasts did not back down; under tremendous pressure they continually emphasized that Ishpeming was the birthplace of skiing in the

SKI HALL OF FAME UPPER PENINSULA MEMBERS

Paul Bietila
Ralph Bietila
Walter Bietila
Burton Boyum
E.O. "Buck" Erickson
Barbara Ferries
Charles Ferries
Henry Hall
Clarence "Coy" Hill
John Hostvedt
George A. Newett
Paul Joseph Perrault
Wilbert Rasmussen
Carl Tellefsen

United States and the rightful claimant to the Hall of Fame. Ishpeming had the oldest active ski club in America and residents felt their community was the legitimate place for the ski hall of fame. After Ishpeming obtained approval and built the new facility, other cities ceased to actively solicit a location change.

The driving force behind the new Ski Hall of Fame building was skiing enthusiast and community activist Burt Boyum. The Board Chairman of the National Ski Hall of Fame, John Pontti, said, "Without Burt's determination and leadership, the Hall of Fame building would have never become a reality."

The old National Ski Hall of Fame building located in Ishpeming was abandoned in 1989 when the new facility on U.S. 41 was completed.

Prior to the new structure, the Hall of Fame was located in a house-like building nestled in the corner of a residential section in Ishpeming's 8th addition. Construction on the first hall of fame building began in 1953 and was dedicated in 1954. Cleveland Cliffs donated the land for the original site and made the land available for the new facility at a modest fee. "Cliffs," the local mining company, has been a strong supporter of skiing ever since its inception.

The projected cost for the new frame building was near $2-million. Local organizers in 1989 anticipated a long fund-raising period. However, things were about to take a dramatic turn. Local State Representative Dominic "The Godfather" Jacobetti jumped in and promised the committee in May of that year, that by December he would have a half-million dollars from the state treasury for the project. This caught the organizers off guard; they were not financially ready for ground breaking. Although the state money would have given them a good start, other funding was needed. Jacobetti then promised the committee another half-million the following year. With these incentives in place, the committee felt they could proceed with construction. The first installment of $400,000 arrived in December – close to the half million that was promised. The remaining half-million, due the following year, never materialized. Representative Jacobetti died, and with him went any chance for additional state funds. However, the resourceful organizers from Ishpeming found other funding sources at the midnight hour, and the building became a reality in 1989.

The new facility is first-class. The spacious entry is distinguished by the largest stained glass piece in the Upper

Peninsula. A birch and pine tree glass collage with an underlayment of an Upper Peninsula map dominates the 18 square-foot lobby. The huge creation was donated to the museum by Marquette General Hospital. The hospital gave the mammoth piece to the Ski Hall when a hospital expansion could no longer accommodate a wall hanging of its proportion.

In addition, a well-stocked gift shop with an ample supply of memorabilia occupies the lobby area.

The Roland Palmedo Ski Library is one of the largest in the United States. Researchers from around the world come to Ishpeming to have the opportunity to use the facility's rich resource of materials. The building houses a large auditorium that is frequently used to show visitors a 20-minute orientation on the history of skiing.

The architecture of the $1.7-million National Ski Hall of Fame reflects the sport, with a glass insert in the steep roof that is reminiscent of a ski jump.

The "Great Room" is most impressive: it is the heart of the museum. Tastefully arranged in the room are artifacts from the earliest records of skiing (would you believe 4,000 years?) to contemporary remembrances. Pictures of 350 inducted hall of fame members with biographical sketches are honored in this hallowed room.

A staff of 12 paid and volunteer employees maintain the $200,000-a-year private facility. A substantial amount of the yearly maintenance costs comes from the revenue of the 8,000 annual visitors who admiringly trek through the ski shrine.

Visitors from every state in the union as well as from 35 foreign countries have delighted in seeing the hall of fame. The Upper Peninsula is proud of its skiing history and feels privileged that the Upper Peninsula is home to the museum that honors its heritage.

APPARITIONS
On A Cliff

BIG BAY LIGHTHOUSE

Haunted? Does the ghost of the first lighthouse keeper, William Pryor, roam the old watchtower?

He was a strange man, a perfectionist – and a whiner; he was not well liked. One day he disappeared, and for a year and a half, his whereabouts were unknown – that is, until hunters in the isolated wilderness of Northern Marquette County found his corpse. Time had taken its toll – his head, severed from his body, was hanging in a noose from a tree, while the remaining human carcass on the forest floor was badly decomposed, and had suffered from the ravages of time and feasting wild animals.

This was William Pryor, the first light keeper at the Big Bay Lighthouse. No one knows for sure why Pryor took his life, but it was speculated that he felt tremendous guilt about the death of his son. Pryor was a hard taskmaster and his 21-year-old son bore the brunt of his pettiness. In 1901, the young Pryor injured himself with an ax, but William, not believing the injury to be serious, refused to take his son to a doctor. As a result, gangrene set in and the youthful Pryor died. The death of his son may well have precipitated Pryor's suicide, but no one knows for certain.

It was 1896 when Pryor began his duties as the lighthouse keeper in Big Bay. Now, more than one hundred years later, owners of the old lighthouse say Pryor is still around – this time, however, it is his tortured spirit that roams the old lighthouse, occasionally and mystically appearing to the guests. Rumor has it that he will not rest until the renovation of the lighthouse is complete.

Linda Gamble, owner of the bed and breakfast lighthouse, was a witness to one of Pryor's nocturnal visits. In 1996, Linda was awakened by noisy guests coming in late one evening from one of the local watering holes in Big Bay. Investigating the

In the early years, a cistern (an underground water tank of rainwater) provided water for everyday chores. Drinking water was laboriously hauled up from Lake Superior, 60 feet below the lighthouse.

noise, Gamble found the late evening arrivals bedded down for the evening and not responsible for the clatter that emanated from the kitchen. She went to the kitchen, only to discover that all of the kitchen cabinet doors were open. At this point she suspected it was a late night visit from a perturbed William Pryor. Linda closed the kitchen cabinet doors and went to bed. Early the next morning, before any of the guests awoke, she returned to the kitchen, only to again find several of the kitchen cabinet doors ajar. She was now certain that a mischievous and upset Pryor was on the prowl the previous evening.

The Big Bay Lighthouse, built just before the turn of the century, and the fourth lighthouse constructed in Marquette County, is perched precariously on a sixty-foot cliff that scans Lake Superior's "dead spot." This dead spot is an area between Granite Island and the Huron Islands, a span of some 33 miles without navigational aids. The Big Bay point was the ideal place for a lighthouse; located halfway between Granite and Huron islands. A lighthouse on the point would conveniently bridge the dead spot between the islands. The government approved the lighthouse plan in 1893. Construction was completed on the $25,000 structure in 1896.

The Big Bay Lighthouse, built in 1896 at a cost of $25,000, is rumored to be haunted by William Pryor, the first keeper at the lighthouse.

It was an imposing lighthouse, dominated by a majestic turret rising from a grassy promontory, giving the lighthouse a castle-like appearance. The tower, 125 feet above Lake Superior, held a third order Fresnel lens that cast a brilliant illumination 18 miles into Superior, providing sea mariners with a pin of light, enough brightness to guide their vessels safely along the dangerous shoals of the Big Bay point.

The lighthouse is as spacious as it is impressive. It housed a duplex with 17 rooms that easily provided ample living space for the light keeper and assistant light keeper's families. Each duplex contained a kitchen, a parlor and three bedrooms. A roomy dining area and a well-appointed living room with a brick fireplace occupy the first floor. The living and the dining rooms are joined by a cavernous entryway that provides an ideal place for lighthouse guests to lounge.

The library has two doors, with access from either duplex.

A door from the library leads to a circular iron staircase that provides passage to the light-tower; this made easy entry to the tower for either the keeper or assistant keeper.

A third-order Fresnel lens that guided sailors around Big Bay Point was installed in 1896 and served the mariners until 1961. The massive and heavy lens, valued at $500,000, was removed by the Army Corps of Engineers in 1961 and stored in various locations (Marquette, Chicago, Traverse City); at times its ownership and location were uncertain. In 1988, lighthouse owner "Buck" Gotschall located the missing lens in Traverse City, Michigan and brought it back "home." After a 27-year absence, the 64-prism lens is back, now on display in an out-building adjacent to the lighthouse. Gotschall said, "The lens combines history and art, it's something everyone should see."

A third-order Fresnel lens guided mariners around Big Bay Point for 65 years. The heavy, 64-prism light is now on display in a building adjacent to the lighthouse.

Owned by the U.S. Coast Guard and operated as a lighthouse for 65 years, it became a victim of technology; new, efficient, and compact navigation devices made the Big Bay Lighthouse an anachronism; a relic from the past with little use in a modern world. The Coast Guard sold the 4,500-foot lakefront property and lighthouse in 1961 to a Chicago physician who used it as a vacation home. He retained the lighthouse for 17 years, and then sold it to a Traverse City businessman, who in 1986, sold it to Buck Gotschall. Gotschall converted the venerable old lighthouse into a bed and breakfast hostel, and for the next five years he was the keeper of the Big Bay Lighthouse.

Nineteen-ninety-one saw another change in ownership with Linda and Jeff Gamble acquiring the lighthouse from Gotschall. Prior to coming to Big Bay, Linda was the facility manager at the Frank Lloyd Wright Museum in Chicago and Jeff was a tour guide for the museum. The Gambles continue to operate the old lighthouse as a bed and breakfast establishment. Attempting to generate more business, the Gambles converted the lighthouse from a seasonal establishment to a year-round inn. Reduced rates were adopted for the winter months as an incentive to stay at the historic lighthouse during the off-season.

The lighthouse on a cliff continues to intrigue and lure travelers who love the idea of a "sleepover" in a haunted "castle lighthouse." Set in the rugged Huron Mountains, the lighthouse location offers the adventurous traveler an unparalleled panorama of Lake Superior's vastness, whether it is in its awesome fury on a cold November day, or on a peacefully shimmering, warm August afternoon.

"THE ROCK"

GRANITE ISLAND LIGHTHOUSE

Scott Holman, owner of the lighthouse, has sponsored several charitable events at the historic landmark.

A bitter cold, north wind sweeps across the vast, open water, provoking the sea from a quiet solitude into a convulsive, angry turbulence – unleashing its raw force on the steep, naked cliffs of Granite Island, a defenseless rock outcropping located in Lake Superior, 10 miles from Marquette. Seeking refuge from the searing winds, the sparse shoots of the stunted island evergreens burrow protectively into rock crevasses, probing for any refuge from the incessant, taunting winds that sweep the tiny island in the long winter months.

Sound inhospitable? Scot Holman didn't think so – at least not during the more inviting summer months. And he put his money where his mouth is. Holman bought the remote Island for $86,000 in 2000. Ever since he took ownership, Scott has been busy restoring the sturdy, old lighthouse, making it a livable and attractive jewel in the sea.

In spite of its small size – slightly over two acres – it has a population in the thousands: summertime seagulls who blanket the remote island in white and for years were the island's only occupants.

The United States Government established Granite Island as a lighthouse in 1868. Its location was ideal. A lighthouse was needed between the Huron Islands and Marquette to safely guide east-bound ships to the Marquette Harbor. In addition, the 60-foot rock outcropping itself was a shipping hazard and needed marking.

Granite Island is well named; the solid igneous formation rises perpendicular to the lake and is more of a "protruding rock" than an island. Prior to a lighthouse being established on the small island, very few ever trespassed it. A landing site had to be

The steel-grated circular staircase before restoration; it spirals to the lighthouse tower.

carved out just to make the island accessible by lighthouse keepers. The sheer, straight rock walls are formidable and make any landing, other than at the prepared site, near impossible. The south approach to the island, prior to 1902, required building a wood platform with a compound derrick. It was inadequate and was replaced with a concrete elevated platform with a boom-type derrick, and built high enough to avoid superior's wicked storms.

The quaint, yet sturdy, Granite Island Lighthouse has been patiently and meticulously restored by owners Scott and Martine Holman.

The lighthouse dwelling and tower are sturdily constructed of cut granite. The granite used in the light station may have come from the Huron Islands located 15 miles to the west, or it may be stone residue from the top of Granite Island. Scott believes the granite in the light station is leftover rock from the site preparation. He noted that the light station rock more closely resembles the Granite Island rock than the Huron Island rock. White limestone bordering the corners, windows and towers is visually pleasing and adds to the dwelling's quaintness.

As a ship navigation aid, lighthouses have become obsolete. Granite Island lighthouse is no exception. Radar and other sophisticated communication systems (such as Global Positioning Systems) have relegated lighthouses as relics of a bygone era when mariners depended on the faint glimmer of a distant light to guide them safely through a perilous sea. In spite of all the modern technology, a solar-powered light on a fabricated tower still emanates light to vessels plying the frigid Lake Superior waters. The Coast Guard Aid to Navigation maintains the light.

The United States Coast Guard, responsible for the lighthouse since 1939, abandoned the outmoded, old sentinel when the new technology became available. With limited financial resources, the Coast Guard found it difficult to maintain Granite Island (and other lighthouses). As a result, the lighthouse had little maintenance over the past decades, and time and the elements slowly eroded the watchtower.

The Coast Guard's policy of selling abandoned lighthouses to private parties (three others in the Upper Peninsula have been sold: Big Bay, Mendota, and Sands Hill) is subject to argument. Many believe the old lighthouses should be restored by the government and available for public use. The government however, with its financial constraints, found maintaining inactive lighthouses to be a difficult task. As a result, many fell into a state of irrevocable disrepair. By selling the lighthouses, the Coast Guard maintains that it's removing an expensive taxpayer burden as well as turning the structure over to parties with a vested interest, and who are more likely to preserve the historic dwellings.

After Scott Holman purchased the Lighthouse, he and his wife, Martine, rolled up their sleeves and began the arduous task of restoring the "grand lady in the sea." One of the first tasks that the Holmans faced in restoring the dwelling was to repair a hole in the roof. With the roof repaired, Scott and Martine then renovated the entire interior that had fallen into a state of ruin; time and vandals were unwanted visitors that were not kind to the old lighthouse. The Holmans have continued restoring and improving the lighthouse dwelling.

A warm, soft light captures the coziness of the beautifully restored dining room in the Granite Island Lighthouse.

Thousands of hours of labor have updated the lighthouse with the latest in creature comforts. Multiple sources of power were installed: Four solar panels, two wind generators, storage batteries and a back-up power generator ensure guests enjoy the island in contentment. Computers monitor the island's systems. Four video cameras and a microwave dish monitor the heating, lighting and other functions with an on-shore computer.

Entrepreneur Holman provides support for community activities by sponsoring charitable events at the lighthouse. The Lake Superior Theater and the Great Lakes Shipwreck Society have had successful promotional events at the "Rock."

Holman plans to continue using the Rock for charitable events as well as for hosting retreats for his business associates. It's an ideal place to hold a meeting for busy executives who more than likely would enjoy a weekend of quiet solitude on a remote island in Lake Superior.

Unlike the infamous Alcatraz "Rock," the Granite Island Rock allows you to come and go at your own choosing (weather and waves permitting).

Scott, reflecting on his island said, "It is unique to go to bed at night, looking out the windows to see the lights of Marquette in the distance – that is a view nobody else has, and you realize how remotely situated you really are on the rock."

Waking up on Granite Island, one is afforded the delicious opportunity to see the soft, early-morning sun invitingly bathe the peninsula shoreline with a delicate sunrise glow. The Upper Peninsula awakens to yet another day.

A WAYFARER'S Refuge

MARQUETTE LIGHTHOUSE

It is speculated that Father Marquette stopped at Lighthouse Point when he traversed Lake Superior.

Enshrined by photographers and artists, the lighthouse has become an icon for the city: a nostalgic relic of days when sailboats and schooners struggled through Lake Superior gales seeking refuge behind the breakwall in the harbor.

The necessity for a lighthouse on the rugged out-cropping that jutted into the lake was apparent from the beginning when Marquette became a shipping port for newly-discovered iron ore in the late 1840s. After the first Sault Ste. Marie lock was opened in the early 1850s, the need became more pressing.

The first lighthouse was built in 1853. By 1866, its condition had so deteriorated that the United States Congress appropriated $13,000 for reconstruction. The tower that stands today is still essentially that same construction.

The nearest lifesaving station was at Portage Entry in the Copper Country. During a crisis, the crew, along with their equipment, hastened to Marquette – usually by hopping aboard the next train. In a particularly vicious 1886 storm, two ships in the harbor were at the mercy of the wind and waves and two others were grounded at the mouth of the Chocolay River. The Portage Entry crew arrived in time, but the necessity of a station in Marquette had become indisputable.

The United States Government had purchased 980 feet of lakeshore property from the city in 1874 for $500. By 1891, a lightkeeper's house, which also furnished room and board for members of a lifesaving crew, had been constructed.

In 1887, a fourth-order Fresnel lens that was lit by kerosene was installed in the lighthouse. The state-of-the-art light projected light over a 19-mile radius. When it became obsolete, it was replaced by an electric light.

Today, a Westinghouse 36-inch Airway Beacon, rated at 703,000 candlepower, sends a powerful beam over the lake, guiding mariners into the harbor.

The 1887 Fresnel lens is on display at the Marquette Maritime Museum, a short walk from the lighthouse where it once served.

Air horns, referred to locally as foghorns, warned ships of land ahead when the lighthouse beacon could not penetrate the fog. The mournful two-syllable tones droning monotonously throughout the night and morning are familiar – and for some – comforting sounds. In 1970, they were replaced by new electric models and moved from Lighthouse Point to the ends of the two harbor breakwaters.

In 1983, two outdated signal towers were removed from the lighthouse site by a Chinook helicopter, and an adjacent building was demolished by dynamite. The city took exception, citing a municipal ordinance requiring prior approval before using explosives within city limits. The Coast Guard maintained that the property belonged to the Federal Government, and as such was exempt from city jurisdiction. The issue died a natural death.

The first lighthouse in Marquette was built in 1853 and remodeled in 1886. In 1906, a second floor was added to the lightkeeper's house.

Joseph Gannon, Marquette resident and European traveler, reported that Marquette's lighthouse was, in fact, a replica of a friary monastery at LaRabida, Spain. Gannon reported that while visiting the Spanish seaport city, he had run into an employee of the United States Government who had been sent to LaRabida to look over the tower and to plan changes to the lighthouse in Gannon's hometown back in Michigan.

Captain Robert Harris, a lighthouse historian, investigated the claim and declared it to be false. Harris observed that the Marquette lighthouse was typical of many governmentally designed lighthouses in that era. The monastery theory was thus debunked.

The imaginary connection had romanticized the lighthouse's ancestry. Some in the community were disappointed in having to give up this small illustrious link to the old world.

A United States Congress bent on cutting the national debt sounded the death knell for the Marquette Lighthouse and

Coast Guard Station in the early 1990s. Funding was cut, generating local outrage. After many to-dos, the funds were restored in 1995. The historic Marquette lighthouse station still stands, sending out a beam of light to guide sailors and boaters toward the comfort and security of the Marquette Harbor.

In 2002, The United States Coast Guard turned the lighthouse over to the Marquette Maritime Museum. After some renovation, the museum plans on opening the lighthouse to the public.

A LIGHTHOUSE METAMORPHOSIS

THE SAND POINT LIGHTHOUSE

The Delta County Historical Society rolled up its sleeves and restored the old lighthouse to its 1860s look.

Not many buildings, much less a lighthouse, get a chance for a complete makeover – an opportunity to regain a look it had a hundred years earlier. The Sand Point Lighthouse, located at the end of Ludington Street in Escanaba, was afforded that luxury in the 1980s. Over the preceding century the lighthouse was drastically altered – so much that it was not recognizable as a lighthouse. The worst destruction to the lighthouse occurred in 1939 when the Coast Guard, with the best intentions in mind, converted the lighthouse into a family residence for the officer-in-charge of the new Aids to Navigation Team.

This misguided, but well intended, effort by the Coast Guard was the final act of desecration to the historic landmark. Only an arduous effort by Delta County Historical Society could resurrect the old lighthouse and restore it to its authentic 1860s, simple, but elegant look.

The cast-iron lantern tower at the Sand Point Lighthouse was retrieved from Poverty Island and houses a Fresnel lens that the historical society obtained from Menominee.

During the 1860s, Escanaba was a busy port city with schooners and steamers transporting iron ore and lumber from Upper Michigan's heartland to points south. The high level of port activity dictated that a lighthouse be built to alert seafarers of a dangerous sand reef that jutted out from Sand Point Harbor into Bay de Noc. With concerns for harbor safety in mind, the story-and-a-half Sand Point Lighthouse was built in 1867 at a cost of $11,000. The lighthouse's beacon sent a shaft of light 18 miles into the darkness of Lake Michigan for the next 72 years.

Tragedy struck the lighthouse in 1886 when a fire engulfed the dwelling, killing Mary Terry, an 18-year veteran lighthouse keeper and one of the Great Lake's first woman light keepers.

The Sand Point Lighthouse, built in 1867, sent a shaft of light 18 miles into Lake Michigan for the next 72 years. The completely renovated lighthouse was opened to the public in 1990.

Dredging and filling the harbor over the years altered the shoreline, eventually leaving the lighthouse inland and far removed from the water hazards to which it had been designed to alert ships. To correct this problem, the Coast Guard built a crib light just off shore; this new crib light relegated the Sand Point lighthouse to the bone yard. It had no further use.

The tower that housed the lens and lanterns was removed as well as the distinctive circular metal staircase that wound up the tower to the beacon. In addition, the original story-and-a-half lighthouse was raised four feet, thus turning the stately old lighthouse into a comfortable two-story home. The addition of aluminum siding was the final architectural blow – the death knell for the old lighthouse. History was obliterated.

By 1985, the Coast Guard no longer had use for the dwelling and was considering razing the old landmark. Alerted to the possible destruction of the lighthouse, the Delta County Historical Society stepped in, knowing that a historic gem was beneath the aluminum cladding. With the goal of restoring the lighthouse, the Society obtained a lease from the Coast Guard and began the formidable task of renovating the old dwelling.

Using the historic 1887 blueprints, the Historical Society began the restoration. Adding ten feet to the top of the tower and lowering the roof four feet were major and costly structural changes that were necessary to get the lighthouse back to its original appearance.

The most difficult task the reconstruction faced was replacing the lantern tower. The old tower was nowhere to be found. Perseverance paid off, however, when they discovered a cast-iron lantern room on Poverty Island (an isolated island in Big Bay de Noc) that was suited for the Sand Point Lighthouse. A Fresnel lens, located in Menominee, was placed in the lantern room, the final touch in re-crowning the Sand Point Lighthouse.

The task was complete and one of the oldest historic jewels in Delta County was now opened to the public in 1990. Preserving the past at times is difficult, but the Delta County Historical Society clearly demonstrated that determination could preserve history – thus providing enjoyment for future generations.

THE GRAVEYARD
OF LAKE SUPERIOR

The Whitefish Point Lighthouse just celebrated its 150th year. Its beacon is still guiding the mariners of the night safely through the dangerous waters off Whitefish Point.

WHITEFISH POINT LIGHTHOUSE

Three hundred and twenty mariners lost their lives off treacherous Whitefish Point.

The 80-mile stretch of barren shore and open sea that extends from Munising east to Whitefish Point is a deadly place on Lake Superior and has rightly earned the reputation as the "Lake Superior graveyard." Since the early days of navigation, this isolated stretch of Lake Superior has devoured or shattered over 550 ships and claimed the lives of 320 seamen: the most shipwrecks for any area on Lake Superior.

Treacherous northwest storms generate vicious seas on the open, 200-mile expanse causing many maritime wrecks. As unbelievable as it may seem, collisions are also responsible for many sunken boats in the graveyard.

The lake is so large, it would appear unlikely that collisions would occur; however, the narrowing of the lake at the east end makes for boat congestion and increases the possibilities of accidents. This was particularly true in the 1880s when over 3,000 boats plied this dangerous area. This, along with fog, makes the journey particularly hazardous. Collisions are less likely to occur today, with only 200 larger vessels navigating the lake, and with the advent of modern technology (radar, etc.) that keeps ships at a safe distance from each other.

Early on, Congress was aware of the need for a lighthouse on this foreboding stretch but was reluctant to spend the money. Horace Greeley, a New York columnist and prominent anti-slavery speaker, sailed Lake Superior in 1846 and expressed concern about navigating the perilous waters at Whitefish Point. He recognized the need for a lighthouse in the region and pleaded his case in the papers, saying, "...each month's delay is virtual manslaughter." The prominent

The iron-pile skeletal tower at Whitefish Point was commissioned by Abraham Lincoln in 1861. Lincoln was concerned about getting the necessary iron ore to sustain the North's war effort.

Greeley (presidential candidate in 1872) influenced Congress, and in 1847 the legislative body passed an appropriation of $5,000 for a lighthouse. Construction was underway shortly after the approval.

The Shipwreck Museum at Whitefish Point is one of several buildings at the lighthouse complex. The bell from the *Edmund Fitzgerald*, along with other nautical artifacts, are housed in the museum.

The Edmund Fitzgerald sank in one of the worst storms on Superior, in 1975. It claimed 29 lives and is the most notable of ships sunk off Whitefish Point. Singer/song-writer Gordon Lightfoot immortalized the wreck with his famous recording, "The Wreck of the Edmund Fitzgerald."

By 1859 the Whitefish Point Lighthouse and keeper's residence was completed. It was one of the first lighthouse on Lake Superior. The 65-foot tower was constructed of split stone and brick with a base diameter of 25 feet. Thirteen Winslow lamps in an octagon shape with 14-inch reflectors cast a life-saving light 17 miles off Whitefish point; it was a comforting pinnacle of light to seafarers traversing the great lake.

The stone lighthouse tower did not remain in service long; after a decade of use the tower began to deteriorate and a new one was needed. With the country in a civil war in the 1860s, the need for iron ore was more critical then ever. The government didn't want delays in getting the ore to the steel-producing smelters. Steel was essential for producing weapons for the Northern Army.

With that in mind, Lincoln ordered a replacement for the old stone tower. The new lighthouse tower was an iron-pile skeletal tower – the same one that stands on the site today. Detour and the Manitou Islands had similar steel-framed towers built at the same time as the Whitefish Point Lighthouse.

Between 1848 and 1903, eleven light-keepers manned the isolated outpost. In 1903, Robert Carlson of Marquette tended the lighthouse for the next 31 years – the longest tenure of any keeper in the lighthouse's history. The granddaughter of Carlson, Bertha Rollo, who lived at the remote lighthouse and now resides in Sault Ste. Marie, said, "We cooked on a wood and coal stove and polished it once a week. For washing, you pumped water from the hand pump in the kitchen and scrubbed your clothes in a galvanized tub. You got a bath in the same tub on Saturday night." Playing cards and reading books from a traveling Marine Library were the only forms of entertainment during the long, cold winters.

During Carlson's tenure, a new and experimental system was used to alert boats that they were near Whitefish Point. This was the hydrophone system; a communication process that was used for 13 years (1912-1925). The hydrophone was an instrument used for detecting and registering the distance and direction of sound transmitted through water. The new system was simple but ingenious. A submarine bell was located in 180 feet of water and electrically controlled through a cable that ran from the signal building to the submerged bell. Ship personnel would listen with a hydrophone for bell sounds that provided them with a geographical bearing. By 1925, the hydrophone became obsolete and was replaced with an AM directional radio. It was the first directional radio on Lake Superior.

With increased automation and technology, the lighthouse keeper's job became expendable. As a result, by 1950 the Coast Guard Life Station at Whitefish Point was no longer deemed necessary and the life station was abandoned. By 1971 the light, fog signal, and radio beacon were all fully automated and operated from Sault Ste. Marie.

The massive girded and plated light tower at Whitefish Point is in remarkably good shape after 141 years in the elements.

With limited human occupation of the lighthouse site, vandalism – and time – slowly eroded the old buildings. The Whitefish Township board was concerned with the conditions of the lighthouse site and sought out the assistance of the Great Lakes Historical Society (GLHS), hoping they could aid in preserving and restoring the historic site. The GLHS obtained a 25-year lease with the Coast Guard and restoration was underway. The Coast Guard was equally pleased with the cooperative venture as they were divesting themselves from an outdated lighthouse and life-saving station. Completing the transfer in 1996, the government ceded permanent ownership of the property to the GLHS.

Whitefish Point is more than just a restored lighthouse; it is an entire seafaring complex. It has one of the few renovated light keeper's quarters and an impressive museum gallery that houses the bell from the *Edmund Fitzgerald*. In addition, the site has a shipwreck theater, a boardwalk, and a well-stocked Museum Store. Presently a $4-million expansion project is underway. The money will go for continued restoration of the present facilities as well as adding two new wings to the museum gallery.

Making Whitefish Point even more attractive to tourists is the migration of hawks, eagles, vultures, and falcons (raptors) in the spring. The Great Lakes shoreline is used as a guide to their northern breeding grounds. The bird observatory, one of the leading in the country, offers a unique glimpse of this breath-taking migration. Since 1979, 15,000 to 23,000 raptors annually migrate through Whitefish Point.

THE LOG CABIN
Castle

GRANOT LOMA

A cozy cabin with 70 rooms was built on the shore of Lake Superior by Louis Kaufman in 1922.

Movie stars Fred Astaire, Mary Pickford and Lionel Barrymore, along with heavyweight fighters Max Schmeling and Gene Tunney, and musical geniuses George Gershwin and Cole Porter at one time were all houseguests at the famed "log cabin castle" – Granot Loma.

The sprawling 40,000-acre estate nestled on the rocky shores of Lake Superior, fifteen miles north of Marquette, was built by Marquette banking multi-millionaire Louis Kaufman in the early 1920s. The $5 million construction cost of the main lodge and the thirteen out-buildings was considered astronomical even at that time.

How Marquette's "Versailles" came into being is intriguing. Louis Kaufman, builder of the grand edifice, created the palatial estate largely because he was denied entrance to the exclusive Huron Mountain Club, located just fifteen miles north of Granot Loma.

Why Louis Kaufman was denied entry into this illustrious conglomerate of wealth is not known for sure, but speculation centered on several possible factors. When Kaufman made application for membership, the Club insiders, not so subtly stated, "Kaufman will gain entry as soon as hell freezes over." The purveyor of that statement could not have realized he was in the Upper Peninsula and the likelihood of that occurring was very possible.

Gossip at the time speculated that Kaufman's membership was denied because his wife was part Native American and he was Jewish. Kaufman was Episcopalian while in Marquette, but

Louis Kaufman spent $5 million building Granot Loma. The Marquette banker and entrepreneur died in 1942.

third-generation family members asked the local historical society to eliminate any mention of the family origins. Being a "king maker," Kaufman offended many in his rise to power and wealth, the Huron Mountain Club President apparently was one of them.

At any rate, the rejection by the private club embarked Kaufman on the building of his own grand estate – Granot Loma – an estate that made the Huron Mountain Club look like a needy stepsister.

The curious name for the family complex, Granot Loma, was arrived at from using the first two letters in the names of five of his eight children: Graveraet, Ann, Otto, Louis, and Marie.

Kaufman began his grand log castle construction in 1919 with 80 workers. He used mostly local craftsmen for the building, believing they were the best around at their specialized trades. For the next three-and-a-half years, the massive work force toiled daily until the Lodge was finally completed in 1922.

The exterior log construction conceals the solid steel frame infrastructure. Its "woodsy appearance" belies the fact that steel supports give the lodge a fortress-like strength, a desirable feature when the December Lake Superior waves thrust their awesome force at the promontory-perched residence.

Huron Mountain Club members were snobbish and rich, thus only the very select could enter this elitist domain. Henry Ford himself was put on a waiting list until an opening occurred.

Twenty-two architects and eighty construction workers created and built Granot Loma. It took 38 fireplaces to take the winter chill out of the lodge.

Twenty-two architects intensively labored to build the 70-room, 30-bathroom, isolated "Taj Mahal." To take the chill out of the winter, 38 fireplaces, all of different design, are located in each bedroom, as well as the behemoth main living room 25-foot fireplace that can comfortably accommodate eight-foot logs. Of the 25 servants needed to care for the pricey lodge, one had the sole responsibility of tending the fires during the long and cold winters.

Louis Kaufman was a man of vision. With Prohibition the name of the game in the 1920s, Louis adequately prepared his estate for the nationwide drought by buying a New York liquor store and sending its inventory to Granot Loma. Always one to execute in style, Louis neatly stored the contraband in "his and hers" vaults in the basement of the main lodge. Elliot Ness never did discover this cache of forbidden treasure.

After Kaufman's death in 1942, Granot Loma was little used.

His wife, now tired of counting deer, remarried and went off to explore the casinos of Europe. She would die in style in 1956 in Monte Carlo on the French Riviera.

An aerial shot of the 70-room log mansion at Granot Loma.

Louis Kaufman's daughter, Joan, eventually would take control of Granot Loma. With little hesitancy to repeating wedding nuptials, the much-married Joan wed the estate's hog attendant, Jack Martin, for her fifth and final marriage. (Any resemblance to the D.H. Lawrence novel, *Lady Chatterly's Lover* is accidental.)

Joan Kaufman died in 1976, leaving the estate to Jack Martin. Although land-rich he was cash poor and had to sell off much of the property to keep the costly estate running. Over the Martin years, the size of the estate went from its original 40,000 acres down to its present 5,000 acres.

When Martin died, Granot Loma became the property of his heirs. They retained the estate until 1987 when it was sold to 34-year-old Chicago financier, Tom Baldwin, for over $4 million dollars. Baldwin immediately began a $5 million dollar renovation that included an updated commercial-size kitchen as well as an elaborate "paver" driveway. There is speculation that the grand old estate is up for sale. If you're looking for a cozy hideaway for yourself and a few friends – this might be the place you've been looking for. However, before you move in, check your bank account to see if you have the required millions needed to purchase the entry keys. Imagine your fingers dancing down the ivory on the same piano that George Gerswhin once played while your houseguests listen attentively to your sweet notes of harmony that softly float in the air in the log cabin castle.

THE TRAVELING MANSION

THE LONGYEAR HOME

In 1890, John Longyear built the largest residence in the Upper Peninsula. But all was not well, and unforseen events would force Longyear to dismantle his sandstone palace.

The story has been repeated for almost a hundred years: While they were riding in a carriage down the Champs Elysées in Paris, John Longyear suggested to his wife, Mary Beecher Longyear, that they disassemble their 60-room mansion in Marquette and move it elsewhere. She greeted his idea, by all accounts, with great enthusiasm.

The Longyear mansion had been built in 1890 at a cost of $250,000 – a substantial amount even by today's standards; an astronomical amount at the turn of the century. Leaded glass windows adorned the magnificent building, which was outfitted with parquet floors and elaborately carved woodwork. The octagonal entry rose two floors to be capped by a genuine Tiffany stained glass dome. A library, music room, drawing room and sitting room were situated off of the entry. The basement housed a bowling alley, billiard parlor and servant's quarters. The mansion, built of Lake Superior sandstone, reflected the height of Victorian opulence and style.

What prompted Longyear to undertake such a huge and costly endeavor, just ten years after the house was completed?

The view of Lake Superior and Presque Isle from the window of the master bedroom was a constant and painful reminder of their son Howard's death. On July 12, 1900, Howard, who was home for the summer from Cornell University, and his friend, Hugh Allen, had decided to canoe to the Huron Mountains. They paddled from the calm harbor to the Black Rocks where they encountered stiff winds. The canoe capsized. Their bodies were recovered four days later. It was reported that

John and Mary Longyear had walked the entire shore from the Huron Mountains to Presque Isle, hoping to find their son alive.

Longyear owned a flat shoreland that extended from the base of the bluff, on which their house was built, to Lake Superior. After Howard's untimely death, they wanted to deed the property to the city for a park to be named after their son. The Marquette and Southwestern Railroad had other plans for that same piece of lakeside property: a railway that would benefit the local economy. Longyear had his own survey done, suggesting an alternate route. The dispute was put into the hands of the legal system.

The Longyears left for Europe in June 1901. Mary vowed that if the railroad prevailed, she would never return to Marquette. They were in Paris when they heard that the blasting of the rail bed through their property had already commenced.

So began the long and historic move of the largest, most elegant dwelling in Marquette to Brookline, Massachusetts (a suburb of Boston.)

The awesome task began in January 1903. By June of the first year, enough of the pieces, wrapped in burlap and straw, had arrived to begin reassembling the house, but it took three years to complete the job. The entire house was loaded onto two trains with a total of 190 cars and traveled 1,300 miles to its destination.

The 60-room Longyear Mansion was disassembled in 1903 and reassembled three years later in Brookline, Massachusetts. It took 190 railroad cars to transport the mansion.

The Longyear mansion still stands in its Brookline reincarnation. After the death of Mary Longyear in 1931, the house was bequeathed to the Mary Baker Eddy Foundation as a museum. The Longyears were Christian Scientists, the religion founded by Eddy.

Because of the large expense incurred in maintaining the museum, the house was sold to a developer in 1996 for a reported $6.5 million. Plans were announced to turn the now one-hundred-room building into luxury condominiums selling for $1 million. Once again, the house would revert to its original purpose – a home.

Mary Beecher Longyear was true to her word: she never returned to Marquette.

THE SISTERS' PALACE

HARBOUR HOUSE

A charming house that was made into a museum captures Crystal Falls at the turn of the century.

Perched on the crest of a hill overlooking Crystal Falls and adjacent to the business district is a charming Queen Anne/Colonial Revival house built in 1895 that now serves the community as a quaint and exemplary museum.

This first-class little museum was purchased for the city of Crystal Falls by Howard Koob for $10,000 in 1982. Hard labor and unselfish contributions by the citizens of Crystal Falls restored the once distinguished home to its original stately appearance.

The wrap-around porches on the first and second floor are the most distinguishing features of the celebrated house. The white balustrade porches give the house a depth and dignity that the cold, stone masonry alone could never achieve.

Local attorney and state legislator Michael Moriarty built the "steamboat" style house in 1900. Ironically, he occupied only two rooms on the second-floor, where he both lived and worked. Moriarty was known as "Merciful Mike" because of his pleasant disposition.

Curiously, Moriarty deeded the house to his secretary, Mary Ellen Harbour, who, along with six other family members (her parents, three sisters and one brother), lived in the elegant home. Mary Ellen and her three sisters were a Crystal Falls class act. With intriguing eyes and long black hair, the flaunting foursome were the village trendsetters.

Eventually, the sisters all left Crystal Falls, each seeking their own way in the world outside of their small but prosperous community. Later in life, Mary Ellen and her sister Lucette returned to Crystal Falls and reoccupied the second-floor of the house.

The Harbour House provides a delightful trip into the past, and anyone with the slightest curiosity about local history should put it on their must-see list.

When Moriarty and the sisters passed away, the handsome home was sold several times before the First National Bank finally took possession. Koob then bought the house for the Crystal Falls Historical Society.

The Harbour House in Crystal Falls, built in 1895, typifies Queen Anne/Colonial architecture. Today the mansion serves the community as a museum.

The interior of the home has been painstakingly restored and reflects what an opulent dwelling looked like at the turn of the century. The main floor living area is decorated with Victorian furniture and is dominated by a cozy fireplace.

Characteristic of the time, many wealthy homes had a music room. The Harbour house reflects that grandeur with a well-appointed music room complete with a piano and phonograph.

A handsomely carved banister leads to the second floor with its unique four "theme rooms": sports, women, veterans, and Native Americans. The rooms, all trimmed with artifacts from the turn of the century, give an insightful glimpse into what Crystal Falls looked like one hundred years ago.

THE SHRINE OF THE SNOWSHOE PRIEST

FREDERIC BARAGA

The thirty-five foot statue dominates the skyline on the red rock cliffs that overlook Keweenaw Bay.

Praised as one of the most significant historical-religious shrines in the Midwest, Father Frederic Baraga's shrine sits on top of red rock cliffs overlooking Keweenaw Bay. The impressive monument stands in testimony to the priest who labored untiringly for 25 years teaching the gospel to the Chippewa Indians. In his nomadic, evangelical journey, Baraga converted 25,000 Native Americans to Christianity.

The shrine is located adjacent to U.S. 41 just west of L'Anse. Its location is most fitting, situated on a prominent rock outcropping that once was a site where the Chippewa Indians met, and where they viewed their canoes plying the waters on the southern part of the Keweenaw Bay.

The shrine is an architectural gem. The 35-foot brass figure of Bishop Baraga is holding a cross in his right hand and a pair of snowshoes in his left hand, the two items that are most closely identified with his life. The sculpture rests on a stainless steel "cloud" that is supported by five laminated parabolic wood beams, anchored into five, concrete, 9-1/2 foot teepees. Each supportive beam represents a mission established by Bishop Baraga. The statue, with its heavy center and slender supportive arches, looks as though it will cave-in at any moment – it doesn't – a testimony to the engineering geniuses of Jack Anderson and Arthur Chaput, the designers and builders of the marvelous monument.

The movement to honor Baraga began in 1969 and culminated with completion of the statue in 1972. The $50,000 shrine was made out of indigenous material whenever possible; the brass shell of the figure was hammered out of copper from Ontonagon.

The Bishop Baraga Shrine with Baraga's trademark cross and snowshoes.

Sculptor Jack Anderson and co-sculptor Arthur Chaput were the creative artisans that fabricated a remarkable likeness of Baraga into a massive bronze figure. The Ellico family of L'Anse generously donated land for the site.

The Bishop Baraga Shrine in L'Anse is located on a rock cliff at the southern end of Keweenaw Bay.

In May of 1972, Anderson and Chaput had completed their masterpiece, and made ready for its 50-mile journey from Lake Linden to L'Anse. The statue was cradled in a special trailer and very carefully guided through the streets of Houghton and Hancock to its final destination at the red cliffs. Another trailer and a pickup truck loaded with statue accessories followed the lead trailer.

Upon arrival at the site, the snowshoes and cross were welded to the figure. The impressive sculpture, now in an upright position, was for the first time seen in its regal splendor. Suspended upright, above the base, it was now ready to be gently mounted on its pedestal.

But a near tragedy was close at hand. As the statue was lowered into position, a portion of the hemline caught on one of the beams. To dislodge the figure from the beam an acetylene torch was used. During this operation the torch ignited the polyurethane lining within the statue, causing smoke, and then fire, to engulf the sculpture. The crowd that gathered to witness this grand occasion was stunned; an outburst of crying, and then prayers, occurred as the shocked crowd hovered around the beleaguered statue. The bronze monolith, spewing dark clouds of smoke, was gently lowered to the ground before a now silent and stunned crowd. A quick inspection of the sacred icon revealed there was no serious damage, in spite of what had appeared to be a near catastrophe. Two weeks later, after some minimal repair work was completed, a resurrected and healthy Baraga statue was placed on his pedestal on June 14, 1972.

Today, 30,000 to 40,000 people annually visit the well-known shrine; some on a religious pilgrimage and others just to enjoy the simplistic beauty of the shrine. Frederick Baraga would have been pleased to know that his work was honored by this impressive shrine, but would have taken even greater joy in knowing that the descendants of many Chippewa Native Americans were now practicing Christians.

JACKSON MINE MONUMENT

*A*djacent to Highway U.S. 41 on Negaunee's east side is a small city park. In the park, and easy to see from the highway, is a pyramid monument on the ground's perimeter. This is the Jackson Mine Monument.

It marks the discovery of iron ore in 1844. The monument is one-and-a-half miles northeast of the actual site, but it was moved to its present location in 1974, the new site being more tourist-friendly.

The Jackson Monument in Negaunee commemorates the discovery of iron ore in the Lake Superior region. The stone pyramid was erected in 1904 and moved to its present site in 1974.

In 1844, William Burt, a surveyor, was delineating boundaries for the U.S. government when his magnetic compass began to give suspect readings. The men in his party went on a short foray into the adjacent woods and found pieces of iron ore under a fallen tree. On that day, they discovered the largest iron ore deposit in the United States.

The following year, Philo Everett and a small group of explorers from Jackson, Michigan, came to the Negaunee area to follow-up Burt's discovery. Chippewa Chief Marji-Gesick led Everett and his band to the iron ore rock outcropping that Burt discovered.

Everett formed the Jackson Mining Company and began extracting ore in 1847. This was the beginning of the great Lake Superior area iron ore mining industry – an industry that would eventually produce $49 billion of wealth.

THE MONUMENT
VANDALS LOVE

"OLD ISH"

The marvelous monument survived a beheading over 40 years ago.

The vigilant Indian warrior proudly stands on his pedestal in downtown Ishpeming with bow in hand and eyes fixed steadily on the horizon. The armed sentry, in his stoic stance, is ready to alert the citizenry of any impending danger. This regal Indian warrior is affectionately called Old Ish and has been standing in the city center since 1884. The sleek gladiator, with the finely chiseled body, is ready to defend Ishpeming from his lofty perch, be it against any adversary: the Huns, the Vikings or the Hessians.

But, only one foe strikes fear into the heart of Old Ish – the vandals. When Old Ish scans the horizon, he's not looking for barbaric invaders, he's gazing for marauding monument molesters.

Landmark desecraters over the years have taunted, tormented and toppled the Ishpeming icon. At times, Old Ish's defiled body has been anything but pretty – marred and maimed many times, he is put back together, placed back on his pedestal and ready to do battle again. In spite of all the abuse he has taken, he still stands tall in the main intersection of downtown Ishpeming.

Over the years, Old Ish has been the recipient of other slings and arrows. The cast iron arrows on his back have been replaced many times, eventually forcing city employees to make his arrows out of car antennas. The quiver that once housed his arrow arsenal is gone. The city grew tired of replacing the arrows and the quiver; as a result Old Ish is arrowless and quiverless; he is a defenseless warrior with no serious weapon to ward off village plunderers.

On more than one occasion, mutilators have disturbed his solitude.

In the late 1950s, Old Ish was painted a garish pink by Marquette High School pranksters. The mischievous miscreants who did the dirty deed were intent on painting the historic monument the Marquette School colors – red and white. However, the impetuous youths ended up blending the red and white paint and Old Ish was garnished in a delicate shade of pink. It appeared that the Indian sculpture was making more of a fashion statement than provoking a high school football rivalry.

Over the years, "Old Ish" has been battered and beaten by vandals. Yet today, he still stands proudly in Ishpeming's downtown.

The vandals were distraught when they found out their devilish deed had not produced the intended results. Nobody got the message. The disappointed Marquette pranksters (Ishpeming residents called them felons) who painted the statue were caught. At their arraignment they were hardly apologetic; they expressed more concern about their errant message than about the possibility of spending a few days in the slammer.

The Marquette vandals, however, were outdone in 1963 when a K.I. Sawyer Air Force Base man yanked Old Ish off his pedestal, sending him ignominiously to the pavement, where he was humiliatingly decapitated in the wicked assault. Old Ish, like Humpty Dumpty, had to be pieced back together – again. Where are all the king's horses and all the king's men when you need them?

In spite of the abuse, he has endured over three centuries and still stands proud, ready to take on all comers who are intent on his destruction. Vandals come and go, but Old Ish still dominates his domain – the city square.

TOWER OF HISTORY

SAULT STE. MARIE TOWER OF HISTORY

Monument honors early Catholic Missionaries.

Rising 210 feet above the swift-flowing St. Mary's River is the Sault Ste. Marie Tower of History, the tallest building in the Upper Peninsula, and a memorial to the early Catholic Missionaries. The 21-story cement monolith scrapes the blue sky with its ethereal-bound towers. The monument is built near the spot where one of the early missionaries, Father Marquette, built his first mission in 1668.

The shrine, built in 1969, is dedicated to Father Marquette and all the Catholic apostles who played a significant role in disseminating the Catholic religion in the Great Lakes and upper Midwest. Father Jacques Marquette was the most notable of the early evangelists, but there were others who preceded him on the mission to convert the Native Americans to Catholicism.

Father Issac Jogues was the first missionary to set foot on Manhattan Island and the first priest to penetrate the wilds in the Sault Ste. Marie area. Father Jogues explored the St. Mary's River area in the 1640s. It was on the banks of the St. Mary's that Jogues gave the first mass in the territory that is now the United States and north of what were then Spanish land holdings.

Not all the native population was enamored with the evangelical priests. The Iroquois Indians in New York captured Jogues, severed his fingers, and kept him as a slave for 13 months. Eventually rescued, Jogues returned to France where he recovered, only to insist one year later that he be returned to complete his missionary work in North America. Father Jogues was not as lucky his second time around; a hatchet to the head provided him a martyr's death in the new world. The Catholic Church declared him a saint in 1930.

The impressive shrine is composed of three vertical, rectangular-shaped, columns that soar into the heavens. The pinnacle of the columns supports five viewing platforms placed at various levels, each platform facing a different compass direction. A spectacular 360-degree panoramic vista greets those who journey to the top. On a clear day a spectator can scan the blue sky for a distance of 25 miles in all directions.

This awesome viewing sight is even more impressive at night when the lights on the ships, weaving their way up the St. Mary's River, illuminate the water with tapering reflections that disappear into the darkness at the water's edge.

The three vertical columns each house a system for getting to the top of the structure. One column holds an elevator which can whisk a rider to the top in 26 seconds, while the other two columns have staircases that are suitable for those who are in good physical shape – or think they are in good physical shape.

The early missionaries, Fathers Jogues, Raymbault, Allouez, Marquette and Baraga, would be pleased to know that their missionary work was not forgotten, and would be delighted that a memorial was built on a site where the Indians had an encampment; the fur traders bartered their pelts; and priests spread the gospel.

The 21-story Tower of History in Sault Ste. Marie stands as a monument to early Catholic Missionaries in the Midwest. On a clear day a visitor has a 25-mile panoramic view.

HIAWATHA'S RIVER

TAHQUAMENON FALLS

Other than the Niagara Falls, there are none larger east of the Mississippi.

The Tahquamenon Falls are the most visited attraction in the Upper Peninsula, with 360,000 visitors a year viewing their majestic power and beauty. Not only a U.P. attraction, they are considered one of the top attractions in the State of Michigan.

Interestingly, the Upper Falls are in Luce County while the Lower Falls are in Chippewa County; both, however, are part of the 40,000-acre Tahquamenon Falls State Park. The Falls are in two separate locations on the river.

The Upper Falls, located 21 miles northeast of Newberry, are the more spectacular of the two. A precipitous 50-foot drop sends water crashing off submerged rocks at the base of the cliff, creating gossamer-like clouds of mist that float ephemerally from the spray generated by the 50,000 gallons of water-per-second that hurtle off the rock ledge.

The Upper Falls are easy to access in either the summer or winter by taking Michigan Highway 123 north from Newberry. To those more adventurous, trekking to the falls in the winter holds a special treat; the ornate ice sculptures created by the falls are majestic. Set against a surreal white landscape, the falls beckon the nimble fingers of a talented artist to capture its winter enchantment. This is a journey well worth braving the frigid temperatures on a clear and cold January day.

Four miles down river, heading toward the mouth of the Tahqamenon, are the Lower Falls. Not nearly as sensational, the Lower Falls are a series of five cascades that surround an Island. The total drop of the cascades is 22 feet, insignificant when compared to the 50-foot drop of the Upper Falls. A neat dimension, however,

Longfellow, with his powerful poetry, etched the Tahquamenon River into American literary immortality.

to the Lower Falls is the river island in the midst of the cascading falls. Accessible by a rented rowboat, the island can be a great viewing site for the Lower Falls.

Historically, the Falls became an important tourist attraction in the late 1920s when Captain Joe Beach decided to use his narrow gauge railroad for transporting visitors from Soo Junction to the falls. Originally, the railroad transported logs from the Hunter's Mill on the river to Soo Junction. The 1920s witnessed the declining importance of logging in the area and as a result, the railroad and the sawmill became relics of the past.

Beach thought that using the old railroad as transportation to the falls would induce more tourists to visit the spectacular waterfall. His vision was "on the money." The old railroad did increase the fall attendance.

The shores of the Tahquamenon River were once inhabited by the Chippewa Indians who fished and trapped the river's bountiful resources.

To make the operation work, Captain Beach needed a boat to ferry the tourists upstream to the falls from the railroad terminal site at Hutter's Mill. The Hutter Mill, once a thriving sawmill, became the loading site for Beach's new boat.

The new boat (*Betty B*) was built in Saginaw in 1937 and brought to the Tahquamenon River. After the tourists had taken the trolley (the now famed Toonerville Trolley) from Soo Junction to Hunter's Mill on the river, they boarded the *Betty B* for a pleasant ride to the falls.

Prior to the rail trolley and the ferryboat, the only way to get to the falls was to walk upriver on a trail that led to the river's edge and then make your way through the dense forest to the falls. It was the same trail the Indians and fur traders used to portage their canoes.

In the 1930s, the state of Michigan was busy acquiring the land around the falls in an effort to make the pristine area a state park. By 1947, it became the Tahquamenon Falls State Park, the second largest in the state of Michigan.

Joe Beach's son, R.J. Beach, took over the trolley and riverboat rides complex and operated it until 1983. The famed "Toonerville Trolley" is still in operation, carrying thousands of sightseers to the falls every year.

Geologically, the falls came into existence some 8,000 years ago when the last retreating glacier exposed some old Cambrian sandstone. This left a rocky escarpment, which the water flows over; this rocky crust extends 200 feet across the river. One of the oldest beech-maple climax forests (300-400 years old) in Michigan surrounds the falls, creating a picturesque, amphitheater-like setting.

The Tahquamenon Upper Falls with its precipitous 50-foot drop enchants thousands of yearly visitors.

Prior to the falls becoming a tourist mecca, the Chippewa Indians fished and trapped along the river's bountiful resources. In the latter part of the last century, the river served as conduit for loggers to float logs to mills downstream.

The pleasing amber color of the water is caused by tannin leached from the cedar, spruce and hemlock in the swamps that surround the river. It is not caused by rust or muddiness.

The drainage area of the Tahquamenon is tremendous in size. Eight hundred and twenty square miles, much of it swamp, provide the voluminous water for the 94-mile meandering river. The headwaters of the river are just north of McMillan, where small springs are the genesis of the waterway.

Henry Wadsworth Longfellow immortalized the Tahquamenon River in his epic poem, *Song of Hiawatha*, by describing how Hiawatha built a canoe, "by the rushing Tahquamenon," which means, "marsh of blueberries."

HUMONGOUS FUNGUS

CRYSTAL FALLS' MUSHROOM

*The world's largest mushroom is located
10 miles from Crystal Falls.*

If you expect to see one large, edible mushroom, located in a picturesque forest near Crystal Falls, forget it – you won't; this large mushroom, or fungus, is mostly below the ground, and detecting its exact location is difficult. Only the small umbrella-shaped head of the mushroom pierces the forest floor; this protrusion provides the only testimony to the existence of the larger subterranean fungus that parents this succulent off-spring. This fungus covers 37 acres and weighs 600 pounds per acre. The common name for the mushroom from this giant fungus is the "honey mushroom;" but those with a snobbish scientific bent refer to this illustrious plant as *Armillaria bulbosa*. The honey mushroom prefers hardwoods and warm temperatures. (Wouldn't they have been better off to set up housekeeping in Florida?) The Crystal Falls' mushroom is at least 1,500 years old, and possibly much older.

The *Armillaria bulbosa* produces normal-sized mushrooms that grow above the ground on stumps, or on the ground adjacent to decaying wood. Harvested every autumn, these tasty morsels are scattered over the entire area of the fungus' surface; and unlike many mushrooms, it does not grow in fairy rings,* but is scattered unevenly throughout its massive surface.

Now, if your community has something that is one-of-a-kind in its midst, even if it as odd as a large mushroom, what do you do about it? The only honorable thing to do – arrange a gala fest around its glorious existence. In the long tradition of American entrepreneurialism, Crystal Falls did just that; and every August they celebrate the fungal growth with a grand community celebration, replete with mushroom culinary delights concocted specifically for the festivity. Mushroom burgers, mushroom pizza, and mushroom omelets are a few of the many menu delights that tease the palate of residents and visitors alike. To augment this celebration, the city has a flea market, a horse pull, a pancake breakfast, duck race, and the compulsory ice-cream social.

Other large mushrooms have been located since the Crystal Falls discovery, each claiming to be larger than the last. The obnoxious bragging by other overzealous communities claiming they possess the world's largest mushroom has not affected the citizenry of Crystal Falls. Be it the world's largest, second largest – or whatever – the Crystal Fall denizens continue to have their Fungus Fest; and with calendar punctuality, celebrate its birthday each August with a rip-roaring community coronation.

A fairy ring is lighter grass growing on a lawn or meadow. The mythical genesis of the ring is said to be from fairies who left the telltale rings behind after dancing all night on the meadow. However, now that we are more enlightened, we know the lighter areas of grass are not related to fairy dance overtures. Only in rare cases are fairies responsible for these ring phenomena.

Crystal Falls erected a mushroom greeting sign at a village portal. The town turned the mushroom discovery into a rip-roaring August summer fest.

THE
ENIGMATIC
Light

THE PAULDING LIGHT

"Ripley's Believe It or Not" once offered $100,000 to anyone who could identify the source of the mysterious light near Watersmeet.

"There it is!" shrieked a thrilled elderly lady from St. Paul. Sure enough, on the horizon miles away, cradled in a hilly recess, a small, sharply-focused white light flickered in a small hollow. The diminutive circular sphere playfully danced on the horizon. It looked like a distant car or train light. The light was present for a minute and then faded away only to return several minutes later; this pattern repeated itself for several hours.

Some spectators observed the light having a color range, from red to green, but not all of the onlookers could see the multi-colors in the light. A young couple from Minnesota walked down a nearby grade in an attempt to get nearer to the light, hoping that a closer inspection would unlock its mysterious origin. However, after a several-block journey they realized the futility of their mission and returned to the viewing site, no wiser in detecting its secret origins.

Mystery light(s) are interesting phenomena that have intrigued and beguiled humans for centuries. The Paulding Light near Watersmeet is one of those mystery lights that residents and tourists alike have jawboned about for decades in area coffee shops, each expressing an authoritative opinion as to the source of the mysterious light.

Getting to the Paulding Light is easy. The site is located between Watersmeet and Paulding on Highway U.S. 45. Approximately four miles north of Watersmeet, go east for one mile on Robbins Pond Road. At the end of the mile on Robbins Pond Road is the light observation site. From here a moderate incline descends in a northern direction; the incline is parallel to a power line that heads toward the light source.

Amenities here are nonexistant: no picnic tables, toilets, barbecue grills, or any other creature comforts. It is not uncommon to see beer cans strewn about the site, and the only trash receptacle overflowing with litter. Apparently the recent emphasis on personal responsibility in taking care of the environment has not penetrated some levels of society. Other than the guardrail, the only other man-made object at the site is a federal forest sign that makes a brief statement about the light. The road is partially plowed during the winter, making the site only accessible by snowmobiles.

Tourists from Minnesota reading information about the Paulding Light. The inexplicable light intrigues all who visit the site near Watersmeet.

Ghost lights are not limited to the Upper Peninsula; it is a phenomenon that occurs across the United States with more sightings in the Southwest and West. Earth Light Resources lists 25 ghost lights across the United States. All of the mystery lights are accompanied by explanations both scientific and mythological. Rigid and complex scientific explanations don't have the same appeal to the public as a fascinating legend.

Ghost lights have also been called will o' wisps, spook-lights and earthlights. The lights are usually fixed to a specific location and are fairly reliable in the regularity of their appearance. The Paulding Light is this kind of light. Some ghost lights have disappeared with encroaching urban sprawl; this would be supportive of those who argue that some of these lights may have a natural explanation. But for the most part, the ghost lights remain a mystery – and the Paulding Light is no exception.

The television series, "Unsolved Mysteries," visited the sight and failed to solve the riddle of the inexplicable light. Ripley's Believe It or Not offered $100,000 to anyone who could accurately identify the light source. The prize money remains uncollected.

Theories on the Paulding Light are plentiful, ranging from pseudo-scientific to engaging folk tales. The legend most associated with the Paulding Light is the appealing story that the light is the waving signal lantern of a decapitated railroad brakeman, whose ghost is destined to remain forever at the sight where he met his untimely death.

Another legend suggests that the light is the responsibility of an angry Native American chief upset about the power lines, while still another speculates that it is the light of a mail carrier who was killed while crossing the swamp.

More scientific, but no less provable, are theories that sound believable, yet lack documentation. One theory popularly circulated is that the light is merely reflected light from passing cars. The plausibility of this explanation is called into question when the light was purported to have been seen at the turn of the century, long before the existence of cars in the Upper Peninsula.

Leaking radioactivity is another theory. Seismologists point out that small earthquakes left minute cracks in the earth's surface, which result in the leaking of radioactive gasses into the air. The radioactive gas in turn causes the illumination. Again, there is no evidence to support this theory.

Another great scientific explanation suggests that it is reflected light generated from swamp gas. If this were so, then why is the light visible during the winter months when the land-scape is covered with snow?

One more theory that has not held up against scientific scrutiny is that the mysterious light is related to the Northern Lights. Again no supportive evidence suggests that the two are related.

The Paulding Light mystery will probably remain just that – a mystery, but speculation by area resident, tourists, and armchair scientists as to the origin of the light will continue. Meanwhile, the curious will continually trek to Paulding to see the enigmatic light.

AN ITALIANATE
MASTERPIECE

THE CHURCH OF THE IMMACULATE CONCEPTION

A beautiful Italianate church built for $13,000 in 1902.

Driving east up a gentle rise on Blaine Street in Iron Mountain, just three blocks off U.S. 41, is a delightful surprise; it's the impressive Italianate, Immaculate Conception Catholic Church.

Its Italianate architecture makes it one of a kind. There are no traditional symmetrical gothic spires reaching to the sky, but instead, a church with a "Wright-like" horizontal presentation that binds the church more to the earth than to the heavens.

Italian immigrants came to Iron Mountain in hope of working the rich veins of iron ore near Millie Hill. The Italians brought with them their customs, strong work ethics, and of course, their Catholic faith. As with any new immigrant group, they formed their own enclave, as did the Swedes, "Cousin Jacks," and others as they arrived in the mining community. Each ethnic group would build their own church. Until the Italians were able to build their church, they worshiped at St. Joseph's, the French parish in downtown Iron Mountain.

By 1890 they solicited enough money to build the wooden-framed Holy Rosary Church; it was constructed on a site close to the present Immaculate Conception Church. Tragedy struck three years later when a fire severely damaged the church. Father Cavicchi, the parish priest living on the second floor of the church, was seriously burned on his face and arms while trying to rescue some money and valuable church papers from the fire. The papers were lost, but Father Cavicchi did recover some of the money. The damage was estimated at $4,000, with insurance covering half that amount. The resourceful parishioners repaired the church and once again it served as a spiritual sanctuary.

Within a decade, the population of the church soon reached its physical limits, and it became apparent that a new church was needed. Out of this need was born the historic and beautiful Italian Renaissance church of the Immaculate Conception. Italian miner parishioners and their gifted parish priest, Father Sinopoli, painstakingly built the historic landmark.

The first task in building a church was to obtain the desired property. The parishioners purchased fourteen lots around the site of their old Holy Rosary church for the sum of $1,000. A local merchant, Carmine Gaudio, contributed $500 of the $1,000. To augment Gaudio's generosity, the industrious parishioners raised over $5,000 in six days for the new building. This was largely done with church members making pledges for the new house of worship. The church constituency was large enough to divide the population into geographical districts named after the provinces of Italy. This geographical organization facilitated the pledging process.

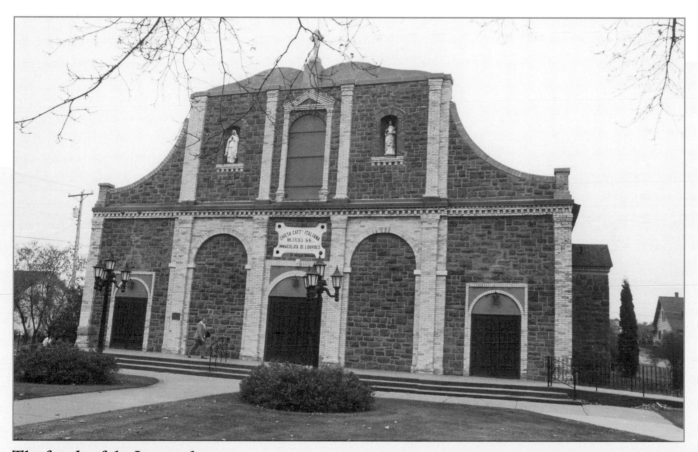

The facade of the Immaculate Conception Church is classic Italian Renaissance with its tall, arched, stained-glass windows framed by elongated pilasters. The two recesses on the upper level house the statues of the church's patronesses.

Ground was broken for the new church in June of 1902. Most of the construction workers were men of the parish, who labored on the church after an exhausting 10-hour day in the mine. Many dog-tired miners donated a day of work on the weekend – just to see their church completed. The sandstone for the church was quarried and hauled by horse and wagon from a quarry a mile south of the church. Timber trusses were used to support the barrel vault ceiling and the wooden roof.

The impressive and distinctive facade of the church is classic Italian Renaissance. Tall, arched, stained glass windows framed by elongated pilasters dominate the upper register of the church front. Adjacent to the upper window are two recesses that lodge the statues of the church patronesses, Mary of Lourdes and Saint Barbara, the patron saint for miners.

The traditional locations for spires and bell towers at the front of the church are noticeably absent from this unique structure. Instead, a singular bell tower majestically rises from the rear of the church. The tapered, three-segmented tower is topped by a belfry with arcade openings. A hexagonal dome with a cross sits on top of the belfry.

Americanized Italian architecture was in vogue in the United States in the early 1900s. In support of this vernacular construction were the budgetary limitations that prevented the church from having elaborate carved stone decorations that were characteristically Italian Renaissance.

The exterior of the church looks much the same as it did in 1904; however, the interior has undergone changes over the century. A showpiece altar made of unusual minerals and stones from the local Chapin Mine was removed and replaced by a more contemporary one. The stones from the Chapin mine form the backdrop for the recessed grotto at the front of the nave (main floor of the church). Candles surround a statue of the Virgin Mary in the grotto. The original ceiling in the nave was a work of art, oil painted upon metal, depicting the glorification of the Immaculate Conception. Surrounding the Virgin were angels genuflecting and holding a ribbon that said, "pray for the church." The impressive oil painting was painted over during restorations.

The Menominee Stained Glass Works made three of the stained glass windows. One is the impressive stained glass window above the choir loft. Its colorful glass casts a soft light on the choir as their melodic voices cascade to the appreciative parishioners in the nave.

The church was built for the grand sum of $13,000 (valued at $40,000 at the time). The relatively modest cost of the church was possible because most of the labor was supplied from the sweat of the members. Unbelievably, the church was built in less than a year, a remarkable feat when considering the modest construction equipment that was available at the turn of the century. Upon its completion, the parishioners looked with great pride upon the magnificent edifice they built.

Church officials pondered what to do with the old Holy Rosary church located next to the new Italianate masterpiece. The parish decided to turn it over to the Society of Christopher Columbus to be used for entertainment. In keeping with the Victorian and Catholic moral code, it was clearly stated that the

The church is more vernacular (indigenous to the area) Italian Renaissance than American Italian Renaissance.

pastor had the right to preview any scripts or plays before they were permitted to use the facility. If anything was done contrary to good morals and good custom, the parish priest had the right to close it down. Eventually the old church was torn down.

In 1989, the church celebrated its 100th birthday. Parishioner Ray Mariucci and others searched for the cornerstone that Father Sinopoli buried a century earlier. Many efforts failed to locate the hidden Sinopoli documents. Mariucci, in one last attempt, drilled into stone in search of the elusive document. As luck would have it, he hit a vertical opening capped with a cement cork. Inside was a tattered parchment put there by Father Sinopli ten decades earlier. The fragmented parchment is now in a glass showcase in the nave of the church.

A $400,000 renovation of the Church is underway, which includes a new roof and stone repair. Today, the thriving Immaculate Conception Church serves 800 families in the Iron Mountain area. No longer a spiritual refuge for Italians only, it provides religious comfort for a variety of ethnic groups and continues to faithfully serve the people of Iron Mountain.

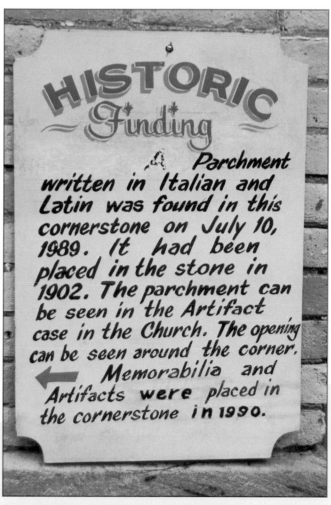

Ray Mariucci and other parishioners found the cornerstone after a number of failed explorations.

A JEWISH House Of Worship

TEMPLE JACOB

A small but stately Jewish Temple in Hancock is one of only two synagogues in the Upper Peninsula.

You can't help but notice it as you drive north across the Houghton-Hancock Bridge, nestled in the hillside is a building with a distinctive copper dome topped by a pointed Jewish star. This is the Temple Jacob, a Jewish Synagogue that greets all those crossing the Portage Channel heading north on the Keweenaw Peninsula. From its lofty perch on the hillside, Temple Jacob impassively observes the vessels making their way on the Portage Canal, a ribbon of water that divides the Keweenaw Peninsula.

Since its establishment in 1912, the synagogue has not changed much. The original entryway carpet, threadworn from age, still provides sure footing for the Temple worshippers. The congregation, however, has diminished in size. Today, the Temple has 12 dues-paying members and forty households in the community. At its peak attendance, in 1910, there were 100 to 150 Jewish families in the Houghton, Hancock and Calumet area who attended Temple Jacob, most having immigrated to the Copper Country from eastern Europe during the late 1800s.

The Upper Peninsula has never had a large Jewish population, but the small numbers didn't deter them from playing a significant – if unnoticed – role in the development of many of the small lumbering and mining communities in the Upper Peninsula.

Unlike early Finnish and Italian immigrants who created a work force for the flourishing copper and iron mines, the Jews established themselves as peddlers and retailers in the small communities scattered throughout the Upper Peninsula. Durable clothing, kitchen utensils and children's toys were a few of the many goods the Jewish peddlers provided for the families of the

A lit menorah casts a soft glow in the interior of the synagogue.

hard-working miners and loggers.

While Finnish, Italian, and other ethnic groups settled in homogeneous enclaves in mining or lumbering towns, the Jews were scattered throughout the community. The scattering of the population presented problems, the foremost being the constant struggle against gravitating toward – and the absorption by – the larger culture in which they found themselves. They succeeded quite well; today the Jewish population remains relatively small, but the religious and cultural traditions remain intact and are being passed on to the future generations.

The first thing Jews did in establishing a new community was to authorize a cemetery; the second was the creation of a synagogue that had a Sunday school and a ladies club. With the population of the Copper Country in the early 1900s large enough to support a synagogue, it became imperative that a house of worship be built.

Jacob Gartner, a Hancock Jewish merchant, was one of the driving forces behind the building of Temple Jacob in Hancock. With his capable leadership in 1910, the Quincy Mining Company donated a building site on the busy intersection of U.S. 41 and Michigan 26. Next came the difficult task of raising the $10,000 needed to build the synagogue. Entrepreneurial Gartner raised the money, and construction began on the Temple. His untiring efforts culminated in the completion of the finest synagogue in the Upper Peninsula. Gartner, however, did not live to see his edifice completed; he died shortly after the ground breaking. Thankful Copper Country Jews rewarded his labor and named the Temple "Jacob" after him.

Large, arched, stained glass windows dominate the sanctuary in Temple Jacob. The wooden pews are unpretentious but functional.

Selecting an architect for the building was no easy matter. Although there are no specific documents that prove Henry L. Ottenheimer of Chicago is the architect of the Temple Jacob, he is generally given credit for the design. Ottenheimer was known in Chicago as the "Dainty Designer of Beautiful Homes," largely because he designed houses with a baroque influence for wealthy German-Jewish businessmen on Chicago's near-south side.

In addition to Temple Jacob, Ottenheimer designed Houghton's Shelden-Dee block and the Douglass House Hotel. Ottenheimer trained under world-famous architect Louis Sullivan,

and the Houghton buildings reflect the influences of the famed Chicago skyline architect.

The Temple Jacob has elegance about it even though its symmetry is simple and unadorned – a square brick building, resting on Jacobsville sandstone. The entry door surround has a Tudor look and is inscribed with "*Adat Yisrae*," meaning "Congregation of Israel." The door is flanked by two sconces and a Grecian pediment roof (a low-pitched gable on the front of a building) that caps the entry appendage. Adjacent to the front doors (inside the sconces) are unique vertical columns of slightly raised brick ends (zipper brickwork). This architectural touch gives the building front a subtle definition and adds character to the entry-way facade. A hipped roof with gables provides a covering for the house of worship. The pinnacle of the roof is crowned with a distinguishing copper dome, a Jewish reflection of its ties to the Keweenaw Peninsula.

The interior of the synagogue is plain but in good taste. A kitchen and social hall are downstairs, while the upper level is occupied by the sanctuary and balcony. Large, arched, stained glass windows on the sides and rear of the synagogue dominate the interior.

The balcony, facing west at the rear of the sanctuary, was the seating for the women at a time when orthodoxy was prevalent; however, over the years, the synagogue drifted toward the contemporary Reform Movement, and the practice of segregating the congregation by gender slipped quietly into the history books. The wooden pews are unpretentious, but functional and comfortable. A number of smaller, arched, stained glass windows are scattered through the sanctuary that depict scenes from the *Old Testament* (e.g. the burning bush, Noah's Ark, etc.). These windows circle the interior and give it a visual as well as spiritual unanimity.

The Five Books of Moses, which constitute the *Torah*, are sacred Jewish religious scriptures. Temple Jacob houses five of these essential and expensive documents that are hand-copied on parchment by a scribe (a year's work). In order to preserve the *Torah*, a yad, or pointer, is used during a reading; this prevents oil from hands from contaminating the parchment. The Temple Jacob Torahs came from Europe at the turn of the century and are in excellent condition for their age.

For a brief time, Temple Jacob had a large enough population to have a full-time Rabbi. Over the decades, however, the Jewish population dwindled, and they could no longer maintain these services. As a result, student rabbis serve the Temple from the Hebrew Union College in Cincinnati, Ohio for the High Holy Days. Local Jewish families host the visiting rabbis for these periodic visits.

Because they have no permanent rabbi, the synagogue leaders provide leadership for religious services. This makes the remote temple somewhat self-sufficient and requires the synagogue leaders to provide religious training for the youth of the congregation. Without temple members providing volunteer religious instructors, synagogues like Temple Jacob would have a difficult time surviving. Upper Peninsula Judaism is not a spectator sport – everybody has to take part.

Norbert Kahn, a Jewish immigrant, came to the Copper Country from Germany in the 1920s, eventually ending up in Houghton where he married the daughter of Isidore Gartner (Jacob Gartner's son). He assumed a position at the Gartner clothing store in Hancock. Kahn, having lived in Germany, was more aware than most of the critical situation Jews faced in the Nazi country in the 1930s. Concerned about his relatives' safety in Hitler's anti-Semitic dictatorship, Kahn managed to get 35 relatives out of Germany to the safety of the United States.

A small but distinctive Jewish synagogue on a Hancock hillside overlooking the Portage Canal. The roof of Temple Jacob is crowned with a unique copper dome and topped with a star.

Judaism has survived in the Upper Peninsula in spite of the declining numbers. Today, only a small number of Jews move to the Upper Peninsula, and those who do have difficulty finding a suitable Jewish mate. Many Jews of the current generation have married non-Jewish spouses. Temple Jacob, however, stands proudly as a reminder of the Jewish contributions to the early development of the Keweenaw Peninsula; its ever-present golden dome a symbolic representation of the Jewish presence in the Copper Country. The small synagogue and its members are woven into the rich historical tapestry that makes Upper Michigan what it is today.

A SANDSTONE Edifice

ST. PETER CATHEDRAL

The largest church in the Upper Peninsula is the Diocese of the Catholic Church.

New York has St. Patrick's, London has St. Paul's, both grand churches of the first order. But the Upper Peninsula has its own impressive house of worship – St. Peter Cathedral. It may not be as large as the others, and perhaps not as grand, but to Upper Peninsula Catholics it is a cherished place of prayer and has basilica stature.

The beginning of St. Peter was inauspicious. Bishop Frederic Baraga visited Marquette on October 1853, confirmed 30 people and selected a site for the town's first Catholic church, on the corner of Fourth and Superior streets.

Three years later, Father Sebastian Duroc began the construction of a two-story frame building on the site. When it was finished, he held services on the first floor and lived on the second floor.

Father Thiele, who arrived in 1864, was prepared to begin construction of a larger church, a frame structure of Gothic design with a stone foundation. Bishop Baraga laid the cornerstone and dedicated it to St. Peter. The insulation under the siding was omitted to save money. As a result, during bitter winter weather, the wood furnace had to be fired up three days and nights in advance to enable the congregation to attend.

On September 14, 1879, the Right Reverend John Vertin was consecrated as Bishop and removed the pastor, Father John C. Kenny. When Rev. Vertin returned home from Negaunee the night of October 2, he was greeted by the sight of the burning cathedral. The widely circulated story was that some of the parishioners, angered by Kenny's dismissal, set the fire as an act of vengeance against the

In this photograph, the spires of St. Peter's appear to be heaven-bound.

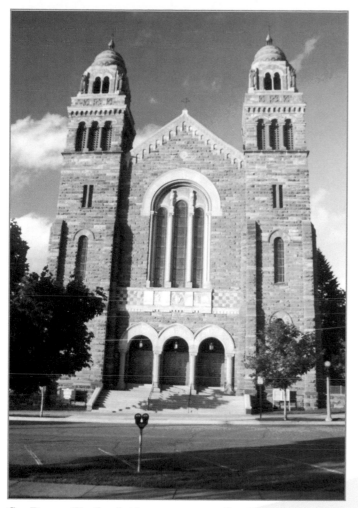

St. Peter Cathedral, consecrated in 1890, is built with Marquette sandstone. The roof is supported by 24 marble-faced Romanesque pillars.

bishop. Vertin reinstated Kenny as the pastor of the church, now a pile of blackened ruins.

The homeless congregation attended services at the "French Church", St. John the Baptist, until the foundation of the new cathedral was completed on Christmas Eve, 1883. It would be seven years before St. Peter was consecrated and the Mass was moved upstairs.

A second fire razed the cathedral again in November 1935. Father Francis Scheringer and the custodian, Rock Beauchamp, masked against the smoke and linked with a rope, fought the flames and smoke to the main altar to bring out the Sacred Vessels. Seconds after they exited the burning building, the roof caved in and the floor collapsed.

Mass was celebrated in the auditorium of Bishop Baraga School, across the street, until the new cathedral was completed in September, 1938.

The new St. Peter Cathedral was bigger and better in every way. The steeples were higher and roofed with blue and red domes capped with gold-leafed crosses. The nave was longer and the ceiling was higher, supported by huge, marble, Romanesque columns. Altars and a bishop's throne of marble were added. New stained glass windows were installed. Intricate mosaics outlined in marble framed the Stations of the Cross.

In 1947, the cathedral was completely redecorated at a cost of $25,000, and in the 1960s, changes were made to accommodate the dictums of the Vatican II Council. The cathedral was given a face-lift and updated in the 1980s at a cost of $300,000. The beauty of St. Peter Cathedral has justly been recognized: in 1996, the *Chicago Tribune* praised it as "the most beautiful sandstone structure in the world."

The rebuilding of St. Peter Cathedral after the disasterous 1935 fire. The fire, believed to have been started by spontaneous combustion in the coal bin, destroyed the largest and most expensive church in Marquette. Hundreds of men, women and children watched the blazing inferno as many wept.

A DESCENT OF TERROR

COPPER PEAK

The world's largest artificial ski slide.

Poised precariously on the edge of a towering 18-story structure, a helmeted skier endures the penetrating sub-zero winds and prepares for takeoff down a precipitous 469-foot chute (in-run) that will catapult him on a 500-foot airborne journey over a cliff-like embankment, hopefully, landing gracefully and upright at the bottom of the mountain – a 1,700-foot journey of terror.

If you can do this, you are one of a select 100 skiers in the world who have the skill and courage to descend this mountain on a pair of eight-foot fiberglass skis. This is Copper Peak in Ironwood, one of six ski-flying, 120-meter jumps in the world and the only one in the western hemisphere.

The world's largest artificial ski slide is located a short five miles from Lake Superior. The massive, steel-girded superstructure sits on top of a 365-foot rock outcropping known as "Chippewa Hill." It was also known at one time as "Chippewa Bluff" or "Old Peak."

The site was explored for valuable copper as early as 1850. No significant amount of copper was ever unearthed, but remnants of the early mining operations are evident. Excavations left a 100-foot tunnel in the hillside and rock residue in four neighboring pits. Because of its rich copper mining history, the Michigan Historical Commission declared the area a historical site in 1974.

The immense, cantilevered steel structure rises 241 feet above the rock outcropping, providing an unparalleled 360-degree vista, the highest unobstructed view in the Midwest. From its apex, one can drink in a 40-mile panorama that includes the Apostle Islands, Porcupine Mountain, and under ideal conditions you might be fortunate enough to see faint light emanating from

Thunder Bay, Canada, over 100 miles away.

During the summer months and the fall color season, the top of the ski scaffold is open to the public. Climb it if you dare!

To ascend the ski hill, an 800-foot chair lift ride to the crest of the landing is first. This is a pleasant ride, but can be somewhat intimidating to those not used to riding lifts. Downhill skiers will have no problems with the lift ride.

The skyward journey continues by entering an elevator at the base of the steel structure that soars an additional 18 stories. The elevator ride whisks you up to a platform that is 1,700 feet above sea level. Scanning the horizon from this height, you may wonder if indeed you expired and are now experiencing an unexpected celestial journey.

Like an appendage of a giant mantis, the Copper Peak scaffolding penetrates the Ironwood forest.

At this elevation there are the ever-present strong winds that sway the mammoth structure – as it was designed to do. This does little to alleviate your anxiety. Your ascent is still not complete! Now, only the fearless or foolhardy will climb the remaining 60 feet to the pinnacle of the jump. Tourists (and cowardly authors) have been known to crawl the last 60 feet to the starting gate. Crawling, however, is not recommended for competitive skiers, it does little to impress the judges – and only encourages delightful barbs from your colleagues.

If you do make the summit, the phenomenal view that unfolds before you is breathtaking; your audacity is well-rewarded. In addition, you have bragging rights for the next century; your friends will no longer be able to tolerate you.

The first competition on Copper Peak was held in 1970. Since then nine other tournaments have been held, the last in 1994. Copper Peak Inc., a Michigan non-profit organization, owns the million-dollar hill. The site can accommodate 50,000 spectators.

In 1970 the hill record was established at 440 feet. This has been eclipsed 11 times, with the current record of 518 feet set in 1994 by Austrian skiers Mathias Wallner and Werner Shuster.

Ski flying is not an Olympic sport; the smaller 90 and 120-meter hills are used in the Olympics. Jumps on the 120-meter hills are usually in the 300-350 foot range; they are in the 400-500 foot range on a ski-flying hill. Style points are more important in the 90 and 120 meter, while in ski flying, distance is the primary consideration.

Copper Peak was required to modify its landing because of skiers increasing the length of their jumps. Without this correction skiers risked the danger of "out-jumping" the landing and chancing serious injury. Improved skis, tight-fitting flight suits, and the aerodynamic "V" flying form are responsible for increasing hill distances. Updating at the site has included flattening the landing, building snow-making capabilities, constructing new judges' stands and rock stabilization. Cost for the update was one-quarter-of-a-million dollars.

Copper Peak's 18-story steel superstructure sits majestically on top of Chippewa Hill in Ironwood. Although it has not been the site of ski-flying tournaments in recent years, it still attracts summertime tourists who dare to climb the monolith.

THE HOME
OF
"Old Main"

SUOMI COLLEGE
NOW: FINLANDIA UNIVERSITY

The only Finnish institution of higher education in the United States.

Tucked away in the Keweenaw Peninsula in the city of Hancock is a small college (university) with national prominence. It is Suomi College, now known as Finlandia University – the only Finnish college in the United States.

In 1999, the Suomi Board of Control made a major decision – to change the college's name from Suomi (meaning Finland) to Finlandia University. School officials reasoned that the name change was necessary to recruit new students. When school representatives attended university recruiting conferences, perspective students often thought the Suomi recruiting booth was a foreign nation or a Native American institution. With student recruiting the name of the game at the college level, it was imperative that Suomi explore all avenues to maintain – or hopefully increase – its enrollment. As a result, the Suomi board, after expressing mixed feeling, renamed the venerable institution Finlandia University (hereon referred to as Finlandia University). School officials felt the new name would have a much broader appeal to young, college-bound students.

Finlandia University was founded in 1896 by Reverend John Nikander, a deeply religious Lutheran minister with a mission to create a Finnish seminary in Hancock. Finnish miners living in scattered Copper Country enclaves worked the prosperous copper mines and provided a natural base for locating and training young men for the ministry.

Finlandia University had a quiet beginning. From 1896 to 1900 the school operated out of a sandstone building near the Hancock Cemetery. By 1899, it was apparent that a larger facility was needed. As a result, Rev. Nikander embarked on a mission to construct Finlandia's first building. A lot was bought on Quincy Street for $4,000. With a v-plow and a team of horses, the site was leveled and the construction of the building was underway.

The laying of the cornerstone in May of 1899 was a momentous occasion as 2,000 excited well-wishers witnessed the gala event. A special train fare enabled 300 people from Calumet to come for the grand occasion. A cornerstone rock from Finland was planned, but the rock never arrived. As a result, the determined founders hastily procured a stone from a Keweenaw quarry. With little time or money the stone was never engraved properly, but Finlandia had a cornerstone, inauspicious as it was.

Construction of "Old Main" began in 1899 and was completed in 1900. The $20,500 building was constructed with Portage Entry sandstone.

In 1900, the $20,500 building was completed; later to be affectionately dubbed "Old Main." The massive castle-like structure, with Portage Entry sandstone walls and a citadel demeanor, reflects the power and fortitude of the early Finnish settlers in the Keweenaw Peninsula.

For nearly 40 years Old Main was the only campus building; it was the chapel, classroom, dormitory, office and library, all in one. A century later, the revered old sandstone building stands proudly on Quincy Street as an administrative building for the University.

In 1906, Finlandia valued its property at $53,000 and its debts at $27,000. Enrollment in the early years slowly inched forward; after the first decade, Finlandia had 72 students enrolled in its seminary school, with the first missionary graduating class in 1906.

The second major building at Suomi was Nikander Hall, built north of Old Main in 1937. Nikander Hall houses the music/theater, business, and art departments and provides the school with a chapel and classrooms.

Finlandia achieved junior college status in 1922 and expanded its curriculum in liberal arts, with emphasis on business. In meeting student needs, the school's thrust became more secular and less religious. Continuing to enlarge, Finlandia, in 1950, offered a two-year graphic arts program. In 1972, criminal justice and data processing courses were added to the curriculum. Finlandia has always considered its strength to be commerce and liberal arts.

As Finlandia continued to expand, more buildings were constructed; a Student Center was built in 1963, and the Paavo Nurmi Center was completed in 1969. The Paavo Nurmi Center houses the school gymnasium, swimming pool and other physical education facilities. Wargelin Hall, constructed in 1965, houses the campus library and the biology and chemistry departments as well as the criminal justice and photography departments.

Today, Finlandia has over 11 major buildings and houses 102 of its 422 students. Sixty percent of the student body is from Houghton County. The expanding University has 140-150 employees with a faculty of 44. Finlandia has an annual budget of nearly eight million and a $10-30 million impact on the area economy. Beyond providing a rich cultural addition for the people of Houghton County, it is a vital economic underpinning of the Keweenaw Peninsula. Today, Finlandia is a community college, not a private institution, yet it still maintains its religious affiliation with the Evangelical Lutheran Church of America (ELCA).

Finland recognizes Finlandia as a worthy stepchild and participates in a foreign student exchange program with its sister school in Kuopio, Finland. The Prime Minister of Finland and the Finnish Speaker of the House raise funds for the Suomi College foundation.

Sports programs at Finlandia continue to play a role in the university's growth. Finlandia has a strong intramural program, and now a competitive program of intercollegiate competition. In the 1920s Finlandia had a competitive hockey program as well as men's and women's basketball. With a tightening budget and a limited enrollment, all intercollegiate sports were eventually dropped, except for men's basketball. From the 1950s to the 1980s Finlandia had a quality men's roundball program. In 1957, pulling a surprise upset, they beat highly touted, and much larger Northern Michigan University (NMU). Finally, the '80s saw the basketball program, the only remaining intercollegiate sport, fall to the financial ax.

The Finnish-American Heritage Center was completed in 1990. The Center houses a museum, art gallery, theater, and the Finnish-American archives.

The sports programs received new life when in the late 1990s, the university decided to once again re-enter competitive intercollegiate programs. The hardwood game was first reinstated for both men and women in 1999. This was followed by the introduction of an intercollegiate hockey program and a girls' volleyball schedule. Success came quickly in men's basketball as Finlandia again dispatched NMU (enrollment 8,000) in the second year of the new basketball program. In 1989, Detroit businessman

Early Forsyth gave one of the largest individual gifts ever to Finlandia, a $3 million bequest. Curiously, Forsyth never attended Finlandia. The only connection Forsyth had with the university was through his mother who was born in Calumet and taught school in Painesdale for a year. Previously, Forsyth had made gifts to Finlandia in memory of his mother's family.

The 1990s saw more change. Finlandia expanded from granting two-year associate degrees to awarding four-year baccalaureate degrees. Art and Design, Human Services, and Business are now four-year degree programs.

When Finlandia opened its doors in 1896, it had 12 students and a mission to provide an education for the Finnish children of the mining community, as well as prepare young men for the Lutheran ministry. From this humble, inauspicious beginning, Finlandia evolved into a secular institution that provides 422 students with the skills needed to meet the demands of an increasingly technological society.

"Old Main," the first building at Finlandia University, is now the campus administration offices.

HOME OF THE Helpful Ghosts

CALUMET THEATRE

In 1900, the jubilant residents of Calumet celebrated the opening of one of the first municipal theaters in the United States.

Haunted?

It may be. Even if one is not inclined to believe in hauntings, or ghosts, it is not advisable to aggravate them – just in case you're wrong. However, the ghosts that reside in the old, but illustrious Calumet Theatre are purported friendly.

The first reported "ghost experience" occurred in 1958 when actress Addyce Lane began a long monologue about the proper role of women in Shakespeare's *The Taming of the Shrew.* During her lengthy discourse, she went blank – not a word of carefully rehearsed dialogue was at her command. The audience, sensing this lapse, became restless and irritated. Lane, in desperation, glanced up to the balcony section where an apparition miraculously occurred. There, in the balcony, was Madame Helena Modjeska (a world famous actress at the turn of the century who performed at the Calumet Theatre on three different occasions), mouthing the words that Lane could not remember. Actress Lane gracefully flowed back into the script, and the production was a success – thanks to the haunting of a helpful ghost.

It is not often that a community has a surplus of money and is looking for a place to spend it. However, this was the case in Calumet in 1898. By most standards, the town of 50,000 was prospering. The municipality had a beautiful park, paved and lighted streets, and excellent village fire and police departments. The city fathers were concerned now about the town being cultureless. One city councilman was alleged to have remarked, "This isn't a Klondike town. What Calumet really needs is an opera house."

The grand, 100-plus-year-old Calumet Theatre is the sovereign of sandstone in the Copper Country.

253

The city had $50,000 in surplus funds, this with an augmentation of $25,000, provided Calumet with the funding necessary to build a grand opera house. Although few theaters built at that time were actually opera houses, it had a nice ring to it and allowed community leaders to proudly declare their city had cultural significance.

Although the new building was called the Calumet Opera House, the town itself, up to 1929, was called Red Jacket.

The interior of the Calumet Theatre in the 1950s. Misguided restorations in 1934 and 1945 obliterated the theater's original interior. It took a quarter-of-a-million dollars to restore the damage done in the earlier restorations.

The new opera house, completed in 1900, was grand by any standards. Italian Renaissance was the architectural style of choice, a popular building form at the turn of the century. The first floor of the building is Portage Entry sandstone, a common and readily available building material in Calumet at the time. (Calumet can imperiously boast of having more sandstone structures than any other Upper Peninsula town.) However, of all the grand sandstone buildings in Calumet, the Opera House is the crown jewel.

The second floor of the edifice is a light yellow-brown brick, while the roof and cornices are of native copper. The pinnacle of the building is a square clock tower that originally was crowned with a cupola; the octagonal cupola, lamentably, was destroyed in the 1930s. The clock tower remains.

The imposing front entrance has a sandstone-pillared porte cochere. The entry leads into an impressive marble-tiled foyer. The foyer leads to a 1,200-seat theater with a 28-foot-high proscenium (stage arch). Two symmetrical balconies provide patrons with unobstructed views of the play. The stage is flanked by four box seats – two on each side. The price of a box seat on opening night was $25 – considered an outrageous amount at that time. Willing benefactors however, paid the outlandish rate, being fully aware that those of lesser economic means in the 25-cent seats could cast an enviable gaze upon them in their well-appointed cubicles.

The Calumet Theatre was a happening: after the turn of the century anybody who was important played the grand theater. Traveling Broadway shows with original casts came to Calumet to the delight of residents. Sarah Bernhardt, Lillian Russell, John Philip Sousa, and Douglas Fairbanks Sr. were a few of the marquee names who performed at the theater. Prominent social activists Eugene V. Debs and women's rights advocate Jane Addams lectured to eager Keweenaw citizens.

Debs was a five-time U.S. presidential candidate and the only person to run for president while in prison. (Debs garnered one-million votes in 1920 while incarcerated). Boxing great John L. Sullivan, a nationally renowned pugilist, gave a boxing lesson to male patrons at the theater. Strapping young miners were not averse to acquiring skills they thought would impress the fair maidens of the community.

In spite of the sophistication the theater brought to Calumet, not all those in attendance shared in that urbanity; copper miners were tough, hardy men who lacked the refinement of some of the more upscale patrons. This became evident only one month after the theater opened when the manager had to place a burly guard in the balcony to prevent the young toughs from spitting on the elegant clothing of the guests below.

The theater had difficult years as well.

The Calumet Theatre, one of the first municipal theaters in the United States, opened its doors in 1900 replete with an elegant interior and an electrified copper chandelier.

The great copper strike of 1913 brought famed lawyer Clarence Darrow, as well as Mother Jones, to Calumet. The National Guard was put on alert. These were tense times; fear of violence permeated the mining community. Because of these volatile conditions, theatrical producers canceled contracts and refused to send their casts to the dangerous village.

One of the greatest tragedies ever to occur in the Upper Peninsula happened in Calumet in 1913. In a strikebreaking attempt, 73 people, mostly children, lost their lives in the infamous Italian Hall Fire. The Calumet Theater served as a temporary morgue. Rows of small white coffins lined the dimly lit theater. The resident ghost quietly wept. Eventually the strike would end, but things would never be the same; the early years of optimism faded as the community fell on hard times.

From the 1920s to the 1960s, the grand old theater served largely as a movie house. Periodically, the aging structure had restoration work done, some of it inadvisable. In 1996 a major restoration was needed to restore the five proscenium archway panels that were painted over in 1934. This Works Progress Administration (WPA) art project redecorated the original panels with a Nordic art-deco look. This new appearance, with either nude or minimally dressed figures, disturbed the conservative townspeople. In righteous indignation, the powers demanded that the "inappropriate" figures be removed. With all the wisdom of censorship they were painted over. It was not until a 1996 restoration project that the five panels were brought back to their original splendor.

Another misguided restoration project occurred in 1945. This project slathered paint over the entire interior of the theater – woodwork and all. It was the cheap bid and they got what they paid for – bad restoration. It would take three grants and a quarter-of-a-million dollars in the 1980s to undo the damage and restore the woodwork to its original grandeur.

Today, the Calumet Theatre is back to providing quality theater for area residents. The local guild plays, along with another 60 to 80 events, draw 30,000 annual patrons, and are a credit to the municipally-operated theater.

Those who tirelessly gave of themselves to preserve and restore the historic building provided the community with a first-rate theater for future generations.

When the copper mines petered out, the population dwindled and the Calumet Theatre suffered. In the 1920s some stock companies were still touring, but each year the number decreased.

REMEMBERING
World War I

IRONWOOD MEMORIAL BUILDING

The Memorial Building honors those who died in the "war to end all wars."

In 1922, *Cloverland Magazine* admonished the city of Chicago for being unable to match the small town of Ironwood, Michigan, in its efforts to build a memorial to the soldiers of World War I. The article went on to state with bewilderment that the Windy City was 175 times larger then Ironwood, and at least a year behind Ironwood in the construction of a memorial to honor those valiant men who died in the Great War.

The gray terra cotta exterior of the Ironwood Memorial Building enhances the overall Greek design of the structure.

By 1922, Ironwood had raised more than a half-million dollars for the new WW I memorial. In November of that year the cornerstone was laid, and by August of 1923, the imposing building was dedicated during an American Legion Convention in the city.

The building of the Ironwood Municipal-Memorial Building was not an easy task. The site chosen for the Memorial building was occupied by an old tannery that was torn down – much to the delight of area citizens. The residents were delighted that the foul-smelling tannery was being removed from their neighborhood.

Because the structure sits on an irregular-shaped lot, the building took the shape of an irregular pentagon. Making the job even more difficult, bedrock discovered near the surface had to be excavated before construction could begin. When the impressive new building was completed, area residents were pleased and satisfied that they had chosen the site on McLeod and Marquette streets for the new building. The gray terra cotta exterior of the building enhances the overall Greek design of the structure. It has three entrances, making for easy access. One access, however, serves as the primary entrance. The main entrance lobby is eye-catching. Capturing your instant attention is a graceful and striking bronze lifelike statue of a "Doughboy" standing on a solid piece of granite. The larger-than-life statue dominates the spacious foyer and keeps a lonely sentry-like vigil in the center of the room.

This graceful and larger-than-life bronze statue of a World War I "Doughboy" dominates the spacious foyer in the Ironwood Memorial Building.

The walls of the lobby are impressive; a ten-foot high wainscot of Tennessee marble gives the foyer a rich appearance. Above the wainscot is a historic frieze of the local iron ore mines that were the life-blood of the community in 1922.

On the perimeter of the room are four large bronze tablets that bear the names of the 1,570 Ironwood men who marched off to the war that would "make the world safe for democracy." In addition, there are plaques honoring the 41 men from the Civil War and the 120 from the Spanish American War.

Halfway up the lobby staircase that leads to the second floor is an impressive stained glass window that pays tribute to the gallant men who served in the armed forces. The six-paneled masterpiece depicts scenes of military battles from the Civil War to World War I. Two of the nine-foot-high panels flanking the center panel (depicting the Battle of the Argonne) are of a Civil War scene at Fort Sumpter and Moro Castle from the Spanish American War.

The Memorial Building houses an auditorium, a swimming pool and a gymnasium. The auditorium is spacious with a seating capacity of 1,100. The popular, ceramic-lined swimming pool measures 20 feet by 60 feet; the gymnasium is small and outdated, but serves the community as an exercise room.

The entire left wing of the building serves as municipal offices for the Ironwood community, while the American Legion headquarters are located in the basement of the building.

The battle cry for World War I was "make the world safe for democracy." It never did make the world safe for democracy; the words rang hollow when Hitler's troops marched into Poland 25 years later. World War I was the first mechanized war and it brutally brought home the stark realization of the terrible carnage of combat. Prior to World War I, combat was often thought of as a glorious event. The "great war" turned the European earth red with blood and the romantic myth of war died forever.

Halfway up the staircase in the Ironwood Memorial Building is an impressive six-paneled, stained glass window that depicts battles from the Civil War to World War I.

The fervent patriotism that launched World War I was to end in corpse-filled, muddy trenches that saw no winner. Poison gas combined with new and terrible weapons of destruction resulted in the deaths of over 20 million men, women and children.

There are not many monuments or memorials in the Upper Peninsula that are dedicated to the veterans of World War I, and certainly none the size of the Ironwood Municipal Building. This structure represents the single largest memorial in the Upper Peninsula dedicated to the memories of those who fought in the "war to end all wars."

The brave and the adventurous marched off to war from Ironwood, in the hope of making the world a better place; instead they found themselves in a slaughter, where life was meaningless and the European soil became the world's largest killing field. They were not forgotten by the people of Ironwood, a community that cared enough about them to build a permanent memorial in their honor.

FABULOUS
Fayette

Fayette — a rich, historic site — a great camping site — an important part of what Upper Michigan is all about.

A view from inside a charcoal kiln of the limestone bluffs that surround Fayette Village.

FAYETTE HISTORIC STATE PARK

A jewel in Upper Michigan's state park system was once one of Upper Michigan's most productive iron-smelting operations.

The early morning sun streaks across Big Bay de Noc, penetrating Snail Harbor with fingers of light that quickly climb and illuminate the white limestone cliffs that wreath the small inlet. The apexes of the cliffs are crowned with emerald green bonnets that fittingly preside over the precipitous escarpment. Nearby, aging, baton sideboard houses, placed neatly on a dew-laden, rich green carpet, eagerly invite the warmth of the early morning sun.

Fayette awakens to another day.

Located on the Big Bay de Noc Peninsula, Fayette is perhaps the most picturesque of all the Michigan State Parks and the best-kept secret.

Fayette's origin in the 1860s came about as a result of an economic need by the Jackson Iron Company. The company, located in Negaunee, needed a cheaper way to get the pig iron to market in the lower Great Lakes. The traditional shipping route, east along Lake Superior through the Sault Ste. Marie locks and down to Cleveland and Detroit, was long and expensive. A shorter and cheaper route was needed.

In an effort to find a better way to market, the mining company searched for a port on Lake Michigan. After a brief exploration, Fayette became the site of choice. With its abundant supply of hardwood to make charcoal, and an available supply of limestone for flux, it was the ideal place to set up a smelting operation. The protected harbor added to the site's importance.

By the 1870s, Fayette became a prosperous peninsula town with a population of 500, and with all the amenities needed to sustain a work force and their families. A general store, a school

A view from one of the historic homes that's been renovated in the town site at Fayette Historic State Park.

This furnace complex constructed of native limestone is 42 feet high and lined with brick from Negaunee. The blast furnace produced 100-pound ingots that were stacked on the dock for shipment.

and community building, along with a barbershop and town doctor's office all thrived in the company town. It soon became the premiere iron-smelting operation in the Upper Peninsula. The furnace town prospered for 24 years and brought a boom to the whole Bay de Noc Peninsula. This was about to change. In late 1889, the charcoal iron market took a downward plunge. This resulted in the Jackson Iron Company ceasing operation at Fayette in 1891. It was the end of an era.

In 1905, the Jackson Iron Company sold the Fayette site to the Cleveland Cliffs Iron Company. Over the next 50 years the property ownership changed hands several times, finally being purchased by The Escanaba Paper Company in 1957. The parent company, Mead Corporation, deeded the property over to the State of Michigan in 1958. For years, the State of Michigan had coveted the Fayette property, but for various reasons was unable to obtain it. With the property becoming state-owned in 1958, the long awaited dream of creating a historic state park was about to unfold.

Over the next forty years, Fayette evolved into a premiere historic site, a jewel in the state park system. Today, the park has 61 modern campsites, five miles of hiking trails, a boat launch site, a picnic area and harbor for scuba diving. These amenities are notable, but still peripheral to the 14 historic buildings that have been restored or are in the process of restoration.

Walking through the historic site, one has a sense of being in another time or place. It is easy to imagine it's 1870 and you are there – a delightful walk back in time.

One of the busiest times at Fayette is the "Blessing of the Fleet" that takes place every summer. This ritual first began in 1948 and was one of the first of its kind held on the Great Lakes. The Catholic ritual first blessed only commercial ships, but as the event expanded, recreational ships also received the Bishop's blessing. Bands, floats, and a queen for the event make the day a festive one. In culmination, the Bishop tours the harbor and blesses each boat individually.

AN OJIBWA
Happy
HUNTING GROUND

PENTOGA PARK CEMETERY
AT CHICAUGON LAKE

*Over 5,000 attend the re-dedication
of the burial site in 1922.*

**The entry to the Ojibwa Indian
Burial Grounds as it is today.**

The most impressive Native American burial ground in the Upper Peninsula is located in Pentoga State Park on Chicaugon Lake. It is on County Road 492 near Stambaugh. Forty shelter houses stipple the peaceful cemetery, nestled in a grove of birch trees on the south end of the lake. The canopy houses on the graves are in varied condition, some needing repair, others have satisfactorily weathered decades of severe northern winters. A split rail fence, in need of reconstruction, wreathes the old cemetery.

Nature shingled the roofs of the unique shelter houses in a rich, deep, emerald green moss; the fibrous roofing was spawned by the umbrellac shade derived from the neighboring hardwood trees. The filtered light basks the cemetery with inviting warmth.

The old Indian burial ground almost perished at the turn of the century. In 1904, the site was in desperate shape, few of the houses that cover the graves were in decent condition, many were broken and randomly scattered throughout the burial grounds. A fence circling the hallowed ground was in need of repair. Nobody attended to the old burial ground: The aged cemetery appeared to be headed for extinction.

In the early 1900s, Herbert Larson, an Iron County engineer, was busy designing a road on the periphery of the south end of Chicaugon Lake. The road would be a connecting route between Iron River and the Mastodon Township Road. Larson heard about the old Indian burial ground, and decided to look at the site. He was appalled at the condition he found the cemetery in. Time, and lack of attention had decimated the sacred ground.

The surrounding forest, over the years, encroached the cemetery with a dense covering of vegetation. In addition, Larson learned that area land developers were platting the region for summer residences.

Larson objected strongly to any commercial development of the land, believing it would be sacrilegious to desecrate what once was an Indian village and now a historical cemetery.

The moss-covered houses on the graves in the Indian burial ground at Pentoga Park were used to place the deceased's personal items.

Determined to save the burial grounds, Larson recommended a plan to the local county commission. The proposal called for preservation of the site, and an access road to make the area tourist accessible.

The county board approved of Larson's recommendation and purchased the site. The commissioners then hired O.M. Brown to repair the shelter houses. At the same time, inmates from the local jail were used to clean up the site and retrieve and store any artifacts that were found. A considerable collection of historic pieces was unearthed in the clean-up. Sleigh bells, iron kettles, old axes, and tin pails were some of the Indian relics that were discovered. The shelter houses were restored and the historic relics were placed in the houses of the deceased. The artifacts didn't remain in the houses long. Tourists, eager to have an Indian memento, scavenged the houses and then added the valuable relics to their personal collections.

On September 23, 1922, a grand two-day rededication ceremony of the burial ground took place with over 40 Indian families and 5,000 county residents in attendance. The county declared a general holiday for the largest celebration in the region's history.

The body of the last Chicaugon Chief, Edward, and his wife Pentoga, were to be re-interred at the resurrected Pentoga Burial Ground. The Ojibwa chief at the time, ninety-year-old An-Ni-Wa-Ba, felt strongly that Edward and his wife should not be removed from their present burial site at the La Vieux Cemetery; to remove the bodies would be considered sacreligous to their religion.

The event was replete with a band from Caspian. It was a grand procession with the band leading the Indians down the Badwater Trail to the ceremonial site. Ojibwa tribal Chief An-Ni-Wa-Bi greeted the cortege arriving at the ceremonial platform with a speech. The chief recalled how the site they were on was once a tribal village, but the whites came in great numbers and the Indians were forced to move to La Vieux and Lac du Flambeau. The chief received a thunderous applause from the appreciative audience.

The second day of the re-dedication called for a mock battle that took place between the Menominee and Ojibwa tribes. The famed battle was called "Death's Door," and legend has it the "rocks ran red with blood."

The two affairs garnered $1,200; this, with a county donation, paid for the re-dedication.

The Pentoga burial ground reflects the traditional Ojibwa view of afterlife. The Ojibwa usually bury their dead with a blanket wrapped around their body, and a new pair of moccasins on their feet. Occasionally, the dead were buried on scaffolds.

The Ojibwa burial ground at Pentoga Park as it appeared in the early 1900s.

Upon the death of an Indian, the corpse was removed from its dwelling through a special exit, often out of a window, or a hole cut in the back wall. The Indians believed that a body taken out the normal exit would solicit others to follow.

After leaving the deceased's dwelling, the funeral procession advanced to the cemetery. Approaching the cemetery, the processioners began to chant. Once at the burial site, the chanting ceased and the medicine man delivered his eulogy to the departed. The deceased is told that he will be on his way to the "happy hunting ground."

After the body is lowered into the grave, mourners throw in handfuls of dirt. The corpse is always buried facing westward and with its earthly possessions. The shelter house was the final place for the deceased's personal items.

The Pentoga Indian Burial Ground has served Iron County well, not only as a tourist site, but also as a place of cultural preservation. Hopefully, the county will continue to allocate the necessary money to maintain this historic site.

THE LARGEST SPRING IN MICHIGAN

BIG SPRING (KITCH-ITI-KIPI)

Huge spring generates 16,000 gallons a minute.

The manually propelled pontoon boat glides slowly across the 200-foot crystal clear pond while overfed brown trout lazily swim below in its 45-foot depth, knowing full well that a fishing ban protects them from the human predators floating above.

This is Big Spring, Michigan's largest spring, located 13 miles west of Manistique. The small surface area of the spring would lead one to believe it had a limited water source: not so, 16,000 gallons of water a minute are propelled from the bottom, filling the spring crater to capacity. The overflow spills into an egress channel that meanders into Indian Lake. The sheer volume of bubbling spring water is astronomical; the quantity of water, if purchased by the average homeowner, would cost $85,000 a month.

Big Spring is also known by its Indian name "Kitch-iti-Kipi." Depending on whose interpretation you believe, it means any one of the following: Great Water; Blue Sky; Mirror of Heaven, plus a host of other names. Legend has it that the name is derived from a love gone wrong.

The story is told of a brave Indian chieftain who committed suicide by drowning himself in the spring, a futile attempt to satisfy the love of his life. There is no recent evidence of any unhappy lover taking his/her life in the spring as a final proclamation of unrequited devotion. Evidently, it was a one-time thing.

Big Spring was discovered (I'm sure the Indians were aware of it) in 1920 by the former Seney Postmaster, John Ira Bellaire. Prior to Bellaire's discovery, local lumberjacks used the spring as a garbage dump. Bellaire was an entrepreneur at heart and visualized the site becoming a tourist Mecca, from which he

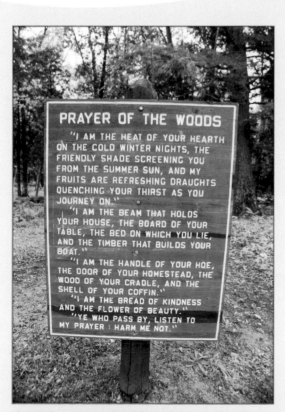

A park sign at Big Spring extolling the virtues of the woods.

PRAYER OF THE WOODS

"I AM THE HEAT OF YOUR HEARTH ON THE COLD WINTER NIGHTS, THE FRIENDLY SHADE SCREENING YOU FROM THE SUMMER SUN, AND MY FRUITS ARE REFRESHING DRAUGHTS QUENCHING YOUR THIRST AS YOU JOURNEY ON."

"I AM THE BEAM THAT HOLDS YOUR HOUSE, THE BOARD OF YOUR TABLE, THE BED ON WHICH YOU LIE, AND THE TIMBER THAT BUILDS YOUR BOAT."

"I AM THE HANDLE OF YOUR HOE, THE DOOR OF YOUR HOMESTEAD, THE WOOD OF YOUR CRADLE, AND THE SHELL OF YOUR COFFIN."

"I AM THE BREAD OF KINDNESS AND THE FLOWER OF BEAUTY."

"YE WHO PASS BY, LISTEN TO MY PRAYER : HARM ME NOT."

would handsomely profit.

With that in mind, he encouraged negotiations between the landowners, Palms Book Land Company and the State of Michigan. The property eventually was purchased by the state for one dollar, and in 1928 the area became a state park. Included in the contract between the state and the land owners was a stipulation that the 90-acres forever be used as a public park and bear the name, "Palms Book State Park."

Kitch-iti-Ki-pi Spring near Manistique Mich.

The old pontoon boat (1937) that plied Big Spring over 60 years ago.

The spring is a geological marvel. The basin of the fountainhead is composed of 400-year old dolomite and gray shale. Ancient lime-encrusted trees lie at the bottom of the spring but give the illusion of being suspended in the greenish water.

The water stays a constant, cool 45 degrees. This frigid temperature discourages any free-spirited tourist from jumping into the spring in a playful gesture. The rapid movement of the spring water prevents it from freezing in the winter.

The Department of Natural Resources plant brown trout every year in the cedar-lined spring. This is the trout's permanent home; they eventually die of old age after having served a life of providing tourists with delightful wonderment. In addition to trout, perch inhabit the spring before they migrate to Indian Head Lake.

Bellaire capitalized on his find. In the true sprit of the business-oriented 1920s, he sold trinkets and souvenirs in his Manistique store that extolled the virtues of the spring. Bottled water purported to be from the spring was sold to naive tourists, believing they just purchased a cure for all their infirmities. In addition, he sold leather pouches that the unwary public believed to be full of magic sand. A gullible sightseer, believing he just purchased a magical potion, would delightfully go on his way as Bellaire basked in the sound of his cash register ringing.

In the early years, poor road conditions made travel to the spring difficult. It was not until the 1930s that highway M-94 was built that afforded tourists easy access to the spring. The site originally had 90 acres but was expanded to over 300 acres, the state acquiring land as it became available.

The Civilian Conservation Corps in the 1930s assisted in the growth of the site by making an entrance road to the park and improving tourist amenities. Today, the spring boasts a ranger headquarters, a shaded picnic area, a large concession building, and modern toilets facilities. Nearby Indian Lake State Park has over 300 campsites that accommodate many of the 60,000 yearly visitors to the spring.

The raft that transports the visitors across the small pond was fitted with pontoons in the late 1950s; new decking was added in the early 1960s. A manual cable and pulley system is used to propel the raft across the small expanse. There is no attendant or ranger to provide the power to propel the raft – you do it! If you're not mechanically inclined, it may take a few minutes to figure out how it works.

The process is quite simple once you understand the principle of the cable pulley system. A three-foot handle is the propulsion lever. Pushing the lever into a lock position and walking forward the length of the raft will propel the raft to the opposite side. If you have a difficult time figuring out how it works, or lack the strength to propel it yourself, wait patiently for a more mechanically able and stronger tourist to come to your aid. In the meantime, look busy so no one is aware of your ineptitude.

To the thousands who annually visit the site, it is truly a Peninsula treasure. However, a word of caution: Don't go there expecting the spring waters to be sacred and not only cure your present ailments, but also provide you the ability predict the Super Bowl winner.

The spring may be a spiritual retreat, but it's not Lourdes.

A visitor propels the pontoon raft across the small pond via a lever and cable pulley system. No park ranger for this task – you do it.

THE FORT
That Was
Never Needed

FORT WILKINS

A fort built to protect early copper miners from an Ojibwa Indian uprising that never happened.

Alarmed at a possible Indian uprising, the United States Government in 1844 built a fort at the northernmost point of the Keweenaw Peninsula to protect copper miners from what the government perceived as angry Chippewa Indians upset at the intrusion of the copper explorers. As it turned out, the Native Americans were never a threat to the "copper prospectors" and the feared insurrection did not happen. Fortuitously, however, the contingent of soldiers assigned to the remote outpost did serve a purpose – they protected the copper-seeking prospectors and the speculators from each other; they became peacekeepers.

A transfer to military duty at Fort Wilkins had soldiers believing their last duty looked like a vacation paradise. Long winter months with boredom as a constant companion made the thought of a scrimmage with the local Indians something worth considering.

Fort Wilkins is nestled on the north shore of Lake Fanny Hoe and only a mile east of the deep-water harbor at Copper Harbor. This was a picturesque setting for the fort, though it is doubtful that any of the early soldiers stationed here in the years of 1844 – 1845 were delighted with this pleasant ambiance.

The federal government, shortly after stationing soldiers at Wilkins, realized there wasn't any need for an armed militia at Copper Harbor and abandoned the fort only two years later. The Indian revolt never occurred and the copper miners, realizing the fruitlessness in their mission to gain quick riches, left the area with dreams of wealth unfulfilled, abandoning the subterranean copper to large corporations who were now filling the vacuum left by the prospectors.

The 100 soldiers stationed at Fort Wilkins were more concerned about blackflies the size of horses and harsh winters that lasted for what seemed like decades than they were about minor peacekeeping chores.

For a short period of time after its decampment (1846-1855) the fort's buildings were used by the government as a storage facility and a residence for governmental survey parties. In 1855, the military, deciding it had little use for the fort, leased it to Dr. John Livermore. The entrepreneurial Livermore updated the old fort and opened it as a public resort and spa. Livermore died six years later in 1861, and the resort folded with his death.

Fort Wilkins in Copper Harbor as it appeared in the 1920s. The military had abandoned the fort decades earlier and it had fallen into a state of disrepair.

For the next six years, Civil War ravished the country and Fort Wilkins remained unoccupied. From 1867 to 1870, the military, for the second time, reoccupied the fort. When other posts had a surplus of troops, and there was nowhere else to send them, they were exiled to secluded Fort Wilkins. This outpost proved to be a disaster for the placement of troops; morale became a critical problem for the sequestered soldiers and desertion became a serious problem. In 1870 the military decided to close Fort Wilkins forever. It would never again be used as a military outpost.

From 1870 to 1921 the federal government retained ownership of the property, but did little to maintain it. Over this 50-year period, travelers, tourists and those needing a place for recreation, used the old fort site for leisure activities. Revelers, party seekers, and bicycle clubs all used the fort at their pleasure. They did nothing to maintain the old buildings, and more than likely contributed to its ruin. By the 1920s, the site was in a state of sad disrepair.

Locally, concerned citizens were upset about the continued desecration of Fort Wilkins and appealed to the government to deed the property over to the county for a public park. The government's need for the old fort was nonexistent and they were delighted to unload the buildings and property to Houghton and Keweenaw counties for the modest sum of $2,000. The counties kept the property for two short years, before turning it over to the State of Michigan in 1923.

The State of Michigan turned Fort Wilkins into a first-rate State Park that attracts visitors from across America. Sixteen of the original 21 buildings, including the kitchens, barracks, mess hall and officer quarters, were meticulously reconstructed using indigenous materials and methods of construction that were used in the mid-19th century.

Today, costumed interpreters greet the 10,000 annual visitors with a lively and rich narrative of what life was like 150 years ago in a remote military outpost. Seeing Michigan's northernmost state park is worth the journey up the forested Keweenaw Peninsula.

A restored Fort Wilkins as it appeared in the 1980s. The fort at the tip of the Keweenaw Peninsula is visited by thousands of tourists each summer.

THE PATRIARCHS OF PEQUAMING

CHARLES HEBARD AND HENRY FORD

Thomas Edison and Harvey Firestone visited Henry Ford at his famed bungalow in Pequaming.

Today a photograph of Ford, Firestone and Edison still hangs on a wall in the lodge.

Henry Ford and Charles Hebard were:
  (A) Men who determined the life-style of others.
  (B) "Czars" of the community of Pequaming.
  (C) Teetotalists, who thought alcohol was a nasty, evil drink.
  (D) Beneficent benefactors (in their judgment).
  (E) All of the above.

If you chose E, you were right, and probably had some inkling of how these early logging entrepreneurs operated. At different times, Hebard and Ford owned the small village of Pequaming, a diminutive lumbering mill community eight miles north of L'Anse.

Today, Pequaming is a half-abandoned community; but for 70 years it was a thriving logging village with a population of 300. Charles L. Hebard and Henry Ford were two powerful men who shaped Pequaming from 1870 to 1942. In 1870, Charles Hebard arrived in Pequaming. Wearing a distinguishing white goatee, he looked very much the part of a prospective patriarch. Hebard leased the land around Pequaming from King David, a local Chippewa chief. When King died, Hebard bought the land from his heirs. He wanted the site for a sawmill.

Within a short period of time Hebard built a prosperous sawmill and a unique village for his workers. It was not just any village, but a worker's paradise: a community of perfect physical and social order. The geographical layout was modeled after a rural English hamlet and the social blueprint was the world according to Hebard. He created what he thought was the ideal community.

Hebard viewed the crude life of a mill worker as despicable and felt he could change it. With a proper environment, he would make the mill workers' and the loggers' behavior more acceptable. Hebard hoped that by requiring the villagers live by a loftier set of principles, he could elevate their life-style.

The interior of the Ford bungalow is simple yet tasteful. The French doors provide entry into the well-appointed living area with its massive stone fireplace.

This was not a backwater lumber town. They had phone service in 1878 and electricity by 1881. Safety conscious Hebard even installed fire hydrants at every corner in the small but well-organized village.

If you lived in Pequaming there was one absolute standard: the drinking of alcohol was prohibited. To Hebard it was a nasty, evil habit and he would not tolerate it.

Hebard was the heart and soul of the community. Residents bought their groceries and clothing from his company store and sent their children to his company school. One dollar a year bought a year's medical coverage by the company doctor.

Hebard constructed houses for the mill workers that were sturdy and architecturally interesting. Tree-lined shady lanes with board sidewalks and shingled houses made for an attractive community. The immigrant occupants paid no rent and were allowed to keep cows and chickens on the premises.

There was an active social life in Pequaming. Recreational activities were numerous: a band, an orchestra and a hockey team were group activities that Hebard organized. Many who lived in Pequaming thought they were in a perfect community. A testimony by one of the villager's early residents, Mrs. Des Laurier, said, "We're all one big happy family."

In 1914, Hebard built the famous eight-bedroom bungalow on the north end of Pequaming. The fourteen-room bungalow is perched on a moderate bluff that gradually descends to Keweenaw Bay. The impressive seven-columned home was built on a spacious lot that embraced a grand wooded and lake vista.

The first floor of the bungalow is dominated by a large living room and elegant sandstone fireplace that faces a series of windows overlooking the bay. A large and nicely appointed dining room with French doors provides easy access to the living room and graciously complements the first floor. It also has a stunning view of the bay.

In 1923, after 53 years of ownership, Hebard sold his model village to Henry Ford. Ford needed the Pequaming mill for milled wood products for his cars.

Ford, like Hebard before, saw himself as a moral, spiritual

and civic leader, and not of an insensitive autocrat. He also had unyielding strict village rules. As his predecessor Hebard, Ford prohibited liquor. Some residents managed to circumvent Ford's dry stance by visiting the Bella Vista Bar just outside of the village limits. Saving a portion of wages was compulsory.

Ford said he was anti-paternal, but his polices were the opposite. He believed in orderliness and cleanliness, and it was evident throughout Pequaming. All residents had to cut their lawns and leave nothing unpainted. When Ford came to town the village would shut down for a day, just so the residents could paint anything that was not painted: all designed to please Henry Ford. After taking ownership, Ford increased the rent on the households from $1 to $12-$15 per month. He completely renovated the houses that began to deteriorate.

The spacious 14-room bungalow in Pequaming was the site of spirited fiddle dances when Henry Ford visited his remote cottage in the woods.

Ford demanded every resident give up their cows and chickens. He focused on cleanliness and thought the barn-yard animals were unsanitary. Following that edict, the white picket fences that enclosed the animals were removed. He also required every family to cultivate a garden. He built a new water tower with the Ford logo blazed conspicuously across the silver tank. You knew you were in Ford country.

Ford loved the Upper Peninsula and went there often, usually to oversee his holdings, Pequaming being one of them. Even though he frequently visited Pequaming, there is no evidence that he ever stayed in the stylish bungalow. Ford reportedly stayed on his yacht anchored just off-shore.

Ford entertained frequently and loved dancing. Frequently, he hired local fiddle and piano players who provided square dance music for a get-together on the impressively columned front porch. Both Henry and his wife loved dancing.

When Ford acquired Pequaming, the vast majority of the residents were Norwegian. That changed however, with Ford's control. He increased the wages of the mill workers, and as a result, other ethnic groups came to Pequaming. In time, the new workers were fused into a family town, not unlike the harmonious village that Hebard created 40 years earlier.

In 1942, Ford's need for hardwood significantly decreased. Ford cars were no longer using hardwood in construction. The famed "Woody," a Ford station wagon, was in its waning years.

As a result of the decline in the demand for wood, Ford abandoned Pequaming in 1942. The property sat idle for ten years and then was sold to attorney Lawrence Welsh and his business associates. Welsh inherited a ghost town; the 75 houses were empty and deteriorating badly. Rats and spiders were the primary residents of Pequaming from 1942 until 1952. The once thriving community had faded into an abandoned settlement; the lights went out in Utopia.

Welsh and his associates tried to revive the town, but all efforts failed. An art school sponsored by the University of Michigan set up shop for a short period of time, but it never caught on. Welsh then tried unsuccessfully to turn Pequaming into a treatment center for alcoholics; this also didn't work. Ironically, for 70 years the village was dry under Hebard and Ford, yet later efforts to turn it into an alcohol-free environment failed. So much for the concept of history repeating itself.

Did Hebard and Ford have an impact on the life of Pequaming villagers? No one knows for sure if their efforts resulted in desirable behavioral changes in the residents, and whether these new behaviors were passed on to future generations. Hebard and Ford, if alive today, would probably like to think that their efforts to reform man had met with some success.

Today, Pequaming is a mix of abandoned, deserted-looking structures and an increasing number of renovated buildings. The villager's houses are gone; they exist only in scrapbooks of descendants of the early mill pioneers. The rusty old water tower stands forlornly overlooking what once was a bustling mill town.

Scott and Lora Hartman purchased the Ford Bungalow in 1990. The couple is busy renovating the 14-room home – attempting to restore it to its previous grandeur. When the Hartmans bought the bungalow it had been stripped of much of its content. Light fixtures and furniture had been removed and little was left from the Ford era. The Hartmans have replaced much of the content and have made a considerable effort in restoring the bungalow.

The Hartmans live in St. Paul, Minnesota, and have no plans to live in Pequaming but they have restored the grand old bungalow into an attractive retreat. Groups as large as 14 can rent the historic bungalow for a week for $1,700.

Hebard and Ford would be pleased to know that their cottage on the bay has much the same look as it did a century ago, and that it's being used as a retreat for those in need of a quiet but elegant sanctuary.

The rusty, old water tower is one of the few remnants from the days when Pequaming was a thriving sawmill community. The "Ford" logo on the tower is barely readable.

WHERE THE WOODY
Got Its Wood

ALBERTA

The charming Ford village has a pleasant 50-acre lake.

On scenic Highway U.S. 41, eight miles east of L'Anse, the road bends down a moderate incline and into a gentle sweeping curve where a picturesque village lies at the end of the hill descent; a village straight out of a picture postcard with its white painted clapboard sawmill surrounded by neat rows of cottages. Across the road from the charming village is a small, 50-acre lake, nestled in a rich, green hardwood forest. There are no cabins on this serene pond, just a quiet solitude where light breezes send undisturbed ripples mutely to the uninhabited shore. Evenly laid letters on the lake perimeter boldly spell out the word F O R D. The lettering is easy to read by passing motorists.

The old Alberta sawmill is now a research and conference center. Students from neighboring public schools as well as Michigan Tech utilize the facility.

This is the quaint village of Alberta, the brainchild of Henry Ford, the industrial giant and inventor of the "Tin Lizzy," who created this model lumbering village in 1935. The village was named for Alberta Johnson, daughter of Henry Ford's superintendent. Alberta was one of Ford's five lumber mills in the Upper Peninsula.

Ford established the sawmill for the hardwood that he needed to build his station wagons. In the process, he attempted to create a

275

model village where his employees could live comfortably in an old-fashioned environment. Upon completion, the hamlet had 12 houses, a school, and a sawmill that employed 14 men.

It was a small mill by Ford standards, but still cut 15,000 board feet a day at peak production. The town and sawmill were never a great success; it was more of a public relations enterprise than a moneymaking operation.

The wood by-products were used to manufacture the famous Woody station wagons. With all-steel station wagons replacing the Woodys in the early 1950s, Ford would get out of the lumber business and close down his model village.

The mill was given to Michigan Technology University (MTU) located in Houghton, Michigan. MTU's School of Forestry and Wood Products turned the model town into a research and conference center. The facility was primarily a research center, but slowly evolved into an educational conference center. Grade school, high school and college students use the center as an educational site. The complex has dormitories and houses that are available for extended stays.

The sawmill and its adjacent pump house at the village entrance are part of the Alberta Village Museum which is coordinated by the Baraga County Historical Society. The pump house serves as a reception and gift area. A $100,000 grant from the Ford Motor Company helped make the museum possible.

Today, Ford's village and sawmill are open to the public. Volunteers from the Baraga County Historical Society provide tours of the facility; giving its participants a glimpse of how a company town looked and operated 60 years ago. Anyone who has an interest in either early lumbering mills or planned self-sustaining communities would enjoy a visit to Alberta. Its charm will not disappoint you.

Although not in use today, this sawmill cut 15,000 board feet a day when it was at peak production.

THE ASSAULT
ON MOUNT ARVON

All I could see from where I stood was three long mountains and the woods.

Edna St. Vincent Millay

Mounts Everest, McKinley, Kilimanjaro, move over. There's a new king of the mountain. It's Mt. Arvon, the highest point in the State of Michigan (1,979 ft.), located in the heart of the Huron Mountains in Baraga County. Now Arvon may not be as high as other mountains, or as awesome to look at, or as difficult to ascend, but believe me, it's the most difficult to find.

Being a typical male with Neanderthal genes, I felt the primal male impulse to search out and conquer Arvon – a centuries old exploratory drive imbedded in me by my Viking Nordic ancestors.

Adequate preparation was the key to having a successful climb. With this in mind I obtained topographical maps, a compass, sundial, an astrological chart, and an Ouija board. The Normandy invasion had fewer navigational tools – I would be ready to journey to the mountain. This was the way to navigate the hostile terrain, no sissy signs for me. Perry, Hillary, Byrd – they didn't need cute little blue markers, they gutted it with pure male drive and celestial knowledge – just the way it ought to be done. That's what I would do!

As an intrepid explorer, I arrived at the Huron Mountains fully prepared to take on all obstacles in my quest to climb the mountain. All obstacles but one – unmarked logging roads. I found a million – maybe two million logging roads, each road beckoning me, the fearless but neophyte explorer, to meander down its serpentine route – only to end up nowhere, or at times I thought, somewhere near Nepal. Of the million or so logging roads, I traveled 750,000 of them in search of the elusive summit. My travel time was 18.4 years – light years. My trusty maps were not doing the job.

My Jeep, after going through endless, bottomless mud holes and creeks that could swallow a Patton tank, looked as muddy as the Jeep in the television advertisement that shows a 4-wheeler miraculously driving out of a cavernous mud hole in some god-forsaken jungle, while making it all look like playful fun – the ad lies.

After many failed attempts and still no closer to the summit (and aging rapidly), I found it necessary to change tactics. It became apparent that if I were to reach the top of Arvon, I would have to resort to using the repugnant tourist markers. This humbling admission told me any thoughts of scaling Mt.Everest the following week should be delayed – indefinitely.

Taking the blue dot route to ascend the mountain was much easier, not as adventurous or as difficult, but definitely easier. However, it did cost me emotionally. I lost the feeling of being an adventurer – a conqueror of the deep impenetrable forest. Upon my return home I'd have to lie to my friends – tell them it was a death defying adventure; they'd believe anything – usually.

One of the many signs that guide you to the top of Mount Arvon. During the summer months, dense foliage makes many of the markers difficult to see.

I was very near the summit when I came to a small parking area; the climb from the parking lot to the top was now only twenty minutes away. Obviously, there was no need for the ample provisions that I had stored in the jeep in preparation for a much longer climb. I had enough water and food supplies on board to sustain the American troops in Afghanistan for six months.

Earlier, I envisioned myself lost in the dense forest and running out of food. For sustenance I would be forced to scavenge and eat wild berries, nightcrawlers and other slimy multi-legged things that squish in your mouth. My cunning woods skills would save my life – I would be a true wilderness survivor. But the blue markers dashed all the heroic and fanciful thought I had so dearly entertained. Now *National Geographic* magazine would never do a cover story on me, replete with pictures of a courageous, skilled explorer battling the elements in a duel to the death.

Near the end of this mini-hike to the top, I expected a grand vista to unfold before me, an unparalleled panorama of lakes and rivers imbedded in a green forest stretching to the infinity of a pale, blue sky.

This wasn't even close.

There were trees – lots of trees, trees everywhere – no panoramic view, no vista of unequaled beauty, no lofty heights to peer from – just trees. I could have been sitting in the midst of a swamp for all I knew. The only way I knew I achieved the summit was by a U.S. Geological Survey marker encased in cement at the precise point of the summit. This, and a mailbox-like container put there by a local Boy Scout troop. Inside the container was a small notepad and a pen for visitors to record their observations and the date they reached the summit. The noble vision I had of planting Old Glory on a remote mountain peak in testimony to my resoluteness and daring vanished in this mundane setting.

A Boy Scout mailbox at the top of Mount Arvon with a notepad and pen allows visitors to record their thoughts on climbing the mountain.

Perhaps the climb of Mt. Arvon was not what I expected, not the journey into the unknown where I pitted my wisdom and perseverance against the cunning forces of nature, but at least I was there. On the way home I hummed Roy Roger's tune: "Happy Trails."

By the way, in that Boy Scout notepad in the mailbox at the top? I carefully crafted a phrase that I'm sure will be remembered by historians. I wrote, "One small step for man, one big step for mankind."

THE JEWEL
IN THE LAKE

GRAND ISLAND

Lake Superior's second largest island.

A thick, emerald-green carpet of trees stretches over a 13,000 square mile island. Rimmed with sheer cliffs and sandy beaches, it sits on the south shore of Lake Superior, less than a mile from Munising. The forested island is eight miles long (north-south) and three miles across at its widest point. It is relatively uninhabited, with only 17 seasonal residents and the U.S. Forest Service summer presence. The remainder of the year, chilly Canadian winds blow over the deserted, rugged island. This is Grand Island, a jewel on the scenic shore of Lake Superior.

Archeological records indicate the island may have been inhabited as early as 1,000 years before the birth of Christ. A few artifacts indicate inhabitation in prehistoric times, but little else is known about the early years. The Ojibwa, a flourishing Indian tribe, were discovered living here in the mid 1600s by French Jesuit missionaries who were eager to convert the native population to Christianity.

The first European settler to live on the island was Abraham Williams from Decatur, Illinois. Williams moved to the Island in 1840 at the request of the Ojibwa Chief, Menomonee. Over time, more settlers came to the island, eventually establishing a lighthouse and fishery. The establishment of a permanent European population on the island created a need for a cemetery. As a result, a burial ground was created near Williams' Landing; it is the oldest white settler cemetery in Alger county.

The first burial in the cemetery may have been Williams's 16-year-old son, Isiah, who died in 1854. The overgrown burial ground is still used and has been an internment site on several

Grand Island's many trails offer tourists an opportunity for great wilderness biking. Visitors with bikes are transported to the island on a pontoon boat.

occasions in the past two decades; however, only Williams descendants and their spouses are buried in the cemetery.

William G. Mather, president of Cleveland Cliffs Iron Company (CCI), purchased Grand Island in 1900. Mather bought the island with the thought of turning it into a resort and game preserve. Along with the introduction of indigenous animals, he brought in species that were not native to the area: mule deer, antelope, and exotic birds. In 1906 Mather authorized a wolf hunt in an attempt to reduce the wolf population that was decimating his transplanted animals. It didn't work. When Mather's control of CCI ended in the early 1930s, the game preserve experiment was in decline. Today, there are no exotic species left on the island.

Deer Lake resident Gary McDonnell enjoys the beauty of Grand Island from one of the campsites on the island's pristine shore.

One lasting contribution that Mather did make to the island was the creation of a horse and carriage route that traced the perimeter of the island. Today, this serves as a trail for bikers, snowmobiles and hikers.

In the 1950s, CCI began to harvest the valuable timber on the island that included 500-year-old White Pine. The reaping of the timber was selectively done. As a result, over 98 percent of the land is still forested.

In 1998, CCI sold the island to The Trust for Public Land. The Trust held the land for one year with the purpose of selling it to the Federal Government when funds became available. In 1990, the Federal Government acquired the island from the Trust and named it the Grand Island National Recreation Area. The U.S. Forest Service became the island's manager and caretaker.

In the steep, 300-foot cliffs on the island, sea waves have eroded caves into the sandstone base, producing caverns very similar to the Pictured Rock caves. These caves are very difficult, if not impossible, to reach from the interior of the island, but easily accessible by boat.

Presently there are two unused lighthouses on the island; one is the North Island Lighthouse on the northern end of the island, and the other is the East Channel Lighthouse, located in the thumb or southeast corner of the island. The Channel Lighthouse is observable from the deck of cruise ships that ply the waters to Pictured Rocks during the summer months. Both lighthouses are on private property and the only way to adequately see them is from the water. The north end lighthouse has the distinct honor of being the lighthouse at the highest elevation in the United States.

Getting to Grand Island is quite easy. During the summer, a small pontoon boat that accommodates 4 to 6 people and their bikes makes hourly trips to the island. The boat is a private charter that contracts its service with the U.S. Forest Service. Cost for one person and a bike to be ferried to the island is $15.

A larger dock ramp and boat barge are only for Forest Service and island residents to use in transporting their cars or equipment. This barge is not for public use. Island residents are allowed to use the barge to transport their vehicles to and from the island twice a week; this is a gratis benefit the Forest Service provides for the island dwellers.

Animal life is in abundance on the island; fish, deer, bear, rabbit, ducks, beaver, otter and mink are the species that occupy the remote island. A license is required to either hunt or fish on the island. Echo Lake, a picturesque lake in the island's interior, is a rich source of bass, pike and pan fish, while Murray Bay has perch, pike and rock bass. In Trout Bay and the surrounding waters, lake trout and coho salmon are bountiful.

The home of Abraham Williams as it appeared in 1910. Williams was the first white settler to live on Grand Island.

There are two camp-sites on the island; one at Murray's Bay and the other at Trout Bay. Only low-impact camping is permitted on the island. When camping, it is recommended that you hang your food high in the trees, as black bears are known to snack on campers' left-out food. To avoid being a human hors d'oeuvre for a famished bear, it is advisable to follow a good camping practice by not storing food in your tent.

If you like unrivaled scenic day trips or solitude in overnight camping, Grand Island, with its granular sand beaches, awe inspiring sandstone cliffs, rich flora and fauna, is the place to re-energize your spirit.

A RETREAT FOR THE WEALTHY

HURON MOUNTAIN CLUB

One of the most exclusive clubs in America.

It may be the most exclusive club in Michigan – perhaps in the United States. Gaining membership in this private club is more difficult than getting an overnight invitation to the Lincoln bedroom at the White House. This is the preferential Huron Mountain Club, located just five miles north of Big Bay. With only 50 full-time members and 80 associate members, it has control of 24,000 acres of the most pristine land in the state of Michigan. The 60-mile perimeter of the club is large enough to declare sovereignty and apply for statehood. The immense estate has seven virginal lakes that are vast enough for navy military maneuvers.

The Huron Mountain Club, on the southern shore of Lake Superior in Marquette County, was established in 1899 as a shooting and fishing club by four Marquette men: John Longyear, Peter White, Horatio Seymour, Ephraim Allen, and eight Detroit businessmen. White, Longyear and their contemporaries looked at the land as a vast preserve to be protected; a valuable asset to be available for future generations. White liked to think of the property as a place where urban dwellers could come and experience the north woods as it had been when he was a youth.

White's vision was prophetic. Over a hundred years later the land has remained unsullied by man and is one of the few places of its size in America that has not been contaminated by the encroachment of humankind. Gaining access, however, to see this chaste beauty is very difficult – near impossible. Invitation by a club member is the only entry ticket to this nature haven. It has been a private sanctuary for over a hundred years and is likely to remain so for the next hundred. The members of the exclusive club guard its privacy with ferocity. A full-time deputized guard cruises the boundaries and 80 miles of walking trails in search of poachers and trespassers. A guardhouse and a steel barricade across the entry road present a stern denial to those uninvited.

Most of the current members are from either affluent Lake Forest, a wealthy Chicago suburb, or Grosse Pointe's upscale Detroit suburbs. The associate members (80) cannot own a home in the club. Associates can only become senior members when a vacancy occurs either by the death or resignation of a senior member.

The club is a small village of weather-bleached cottages that are on the bank of the mouth of the Pine River on Lake Superior. The cottages were constructed and maintained with indigenous lumber by a small lumber mill on the site. The mill is no longer at the club, but it did provide the residents with comfortable cottages. The use of treated lumber is forbidden. This makes cabin repairs more frequent, but says much about the Club's respect for the environment. The compound has a large log clubhouse with a cedar-shingled kitchen. Several adjacent outbuildings on the property are a carpentry shop, a generator plant building, garages for bush vehicles, a small grocery store, a dinning room, and several cottages for the permanent summer-time staff. The generator building no longer provides electricity for the club; the complex obtains its power from the Big Bay line.

The interior of the clubhouse at the Huron Mountain Club. The imposing stone fireplace is the centerpiece in the comfortable surroundings.

The automobile magnate, Henry Ford, had a two-story cottage built near the compound. The cabin was built with virgin white pine Ford obtained from his L'Anse sawmill at Keweenaw Bay. In keeping with the village ambiance, Ford built a sandstone fireplace on the west end of the home. So particular was the membership that even the illustrious Ford was not granted immediate membership; like everyone else he was put on a waiting list until an opening occurred. The exclusive club denied membership to wealthy Marquette entrepreneur and banker Louis Kaufman (See Granot Loma).

In 1997 the club created considerable controversy when they attempted to have part of its land exempted from property taxes. They sought the exemption under the Farmland and Open Space Act. In order to qualify for the tax break the club had to promise the land would be preserved. In addition, the Huron Mountain Club was contesting its taxes to the Michigan Tax Tribunal. The township residents were angered at what they saw as wealthy club owners attempting to weasel out of what the township felt was their fair share of support for the county. As a basis for re-structuring the taxes, the club contended the 20,000 acres was only worth $1 1/4 million. Assessment by the township placed the value of the land at close to $13 million.

The clubhouse at the Huron Mountain Club as it appeared in the 1890s. The log structure has cedar shingles on the second level. The use of treated lumber in repairing compound buildings is prohibited.

After 2 1/2 years of legal wrangling, the Huron Mountain Club dropped its tax assessment arguments and agreed to continue paying the $280,000 annual property tax. The club also discontinued the suit to have the land declared tax exempt and agreed to pay the township $7,000 of the $21,000 attorney fees the township incurred during the legal struggle. Many in Powell township were irritated over the township being needlessly stuck with a $14,000 legal fee that low-income township residents would now have to pay. Residents viewed the legal proceeding initiated by the club as nothing short of arrogant behavior by wealthy landowners.

There are a dozen or so private residences not related to Club members in the vast Huron Mountain Club property. Most of the private land ownership has passed down through generations. Private owners have access to their property but are not allowed to hunt or fish on club property unless they have a specific agreement with the club. Of the seven major lakes in the club holdings, only one, Conway Lake, has private residents' cottages. The club charter strictly regulates the interior lakes. Members prohibit fishing and any motorized boats on any of the lakes. Each private resident owner has his own key that allows access to their property when the gate guard is not on duty. The private landowners consider the Huron Mountain Club members as good neighbors and are pleased they have preserved the land in accordance with the founder's intentions.

If man feels closer to God when surrounded by his incredible handiwork, then those with access to the Huron Mountain Club's pristine beauty have an edge on those with a limited opportunity to walk in one of nature's gardens. Having the time and the resources to reflect on life in this serene sanctuary is not a guarantee of any special consideration in gaining entrance to paradisiacal afterlife, but one can't help wonder if being closer to the deity facilitates gaining a place in the heavenly kingdom.

A WILDERNESS Paradise

McCORMICK TRACT

Descendants of the famous Chicago inventor, Cyrus McCormick, gave 17,000 acres in Marquette County to the U.S. Forest Service.

It is truly unique, a pristine forested area of 17,000 acres imbedded in the heartland of the Upper Peninsula. This is the rugged McCormick Tract, a wilderness area bequeathed to the U.S. Forest Service by the descendants of reaper inventor, Cyrus McCormick. The Forest Service was deeded the property in 1963 after the death of Gordon McCormick, a third-generation descendent of the legendary Cyrus McCormick.

The valuable land, composed mostly of second-growth northern hardwood, is located in Marquette and Baraga counties, approximately 50 miles west of Marquette, with the bulk of the estate being in Michigamme Township. The land straddles the divide between Lake Superior and Lake Michigan watersheds. The headwaters of the Huron, Yellow Dog and Peshekee rivers are located in the vast tract. Eighteen small but stunning lakes dot the wild preserve and are the home of largemouth bass, northern pike and trout. The lakes however, are not abundant with fish, unlike most fish-rich Upper Michigan Lakes. The clear water lakes closely resemble lakes in the Canadian Shield that have smaller fish populations.

In the 1880s, Cyrus McCormick Jr., founder of the International Harvester Corporation, purchased a 160-acre parcel of land on southwest White Deer Lake; this is the heart of the McCormick Tract. Eventually, McCormick expanded his small development into a wilderness preserve that rivaled the famous Huron Mountain sanctuary just north of the McCormick Tract.

In 1902, Cyrus Bentley became a partner in McCormick's Upper Peninsula land holdings. Bentley, a wealthy International

The letters W.D.L. below the window sill on the main lodge represent the words White Deer Lake.

Harvester attorney and friend of McCormick, visited the remote wilderness retreat in the early years and was enamored with the natural beauty of the sanctuary. As a result, Bentley joined the neighboring Huron Mountain Club where he built his own log cabin.

The main lodge at the McCormick retreat had four bedrooms each with an adjoining bath. A massive granite fireplace dominated the lodge interior.

McCormick loved the wilds of the Upper Peninsula. He and Bentley decided to build a compound on an island in White Deer Lake, one of the many lakes in his vast estate. The lake is located ten miles north of Champion in the southern section of the immense acreage. Eventually, McCormick and Bentley constructed a small enclave of buildings on White Deer Lake Island, with each building having a name that described its function.

The Main Lodge was an impressive 2,888 square-foot, two-story, four-bedroom (each with an adjoining bath), log structure. The Lodge, dominated by a massive granite fireplace, was the central building in the small island development. In testimony to the lack of gender equality during the early years of the twentieth century, McCormick built a cabin that was specifically used by men and called the "Beaver." (It's unknown whether the women in the McCormick family protested the existence of this all-male commune building in their midst.) The Library cabin was used for reading, while the Living Room Cabin was used for guests. In addition, a rustic six-stall log boathouse and several docks were near the cabins on the shore of the small island. Five buildings on the island provided respite for McCormick's wealthy visitors from the Chicago area.

Bentley, however, desired a closer contact with the McCormick settlement 26 miles to the south. To achieve this he slashed a path through the rugged landscape that connected the two sites. It was not an easy task. Bentley wanted a state-of-the-art wilderness path, not a crude, difficult-to-travel route that would impede his wilderness journey. Swarms of black flies incessantly harassed laborers on hot, sweltering summer days as they slashed Bentley's path through near impassible swamps. Bentley, a fastidious man, wanted a trail that was "smooth enough to ride a bicycle down, wide enough to walk down with your arms outstretched and high enough to walk with an umbrella." Cyrus Bentley was unaware of it, but he created the first wilderness freeway.

On one occasion, Bentley became extremely upset when he encountered a stranger walking down his beloved trail. He was irate; someone daring to use his private path was unthinkable. To maintain his need for privacy, Bentley, again with considerable difficulty, built another path connecting the two remote cabin sites. He realized the 26-mile trek between the two points was excessively long for a single day's travel. To correct this he built a rest cabin at midway called the "Halfway Cabin," or the Arbutus Lodge. Eventually, the trail was converted to a dirt road where the family autos could conveniently and quickly travel between the lodges. After 1914 the path would be known as the Bentley Trail.

But all was not well in the fairyland forest. In 1927, the McCormicks and the Bentleys had a falling out and the families went their own ways. McCormick sold the Arbutus Lodge and the surrounding land to the Huron Mountain Club. The Club, in time, would sell the acreage to a logging company that would clear-cut one of the tallest jack pine stands in the world.

In 1947, the McCormicks and Bentleys stopped using the wilderness area. This neglect lead to the deterioration of the McCormick compound, the Arbutus Lodge and the Bentley path. Forest growth devoured the old Bentley trail leaving only an intermittent path that was difficult to follow. The once serviceable and stately wood walkways that Bentley constructed so carefully, dissipated into the swamps, leaving only decayed wood remnants.

By the 1980s, the U.S. Forest Service felt it was necessary to either renovate the old McCormick log buildings or remove them. The Forest service did not have the financial resources to restore the buildings; this resulted in the old buildings being put up for sale. The Forest Service considered burning the buildings if they could not find a buyer. Richard Hendricksen of Marquette came to the rescue and bought the old buildings for $50. Hendricksen planned to move the buildings to Marquette's Lower Harbor and reconstruct them in the White Deer Lake configuration. This plan fell through, as did his attempt to relocate the historic structures at the Tourist Park in Marquette. For now, the old buildings are stored in Marquette waiting patiently to be reconstructed in a grand setting where visitors can view how millionaires lived in the wilderness nearly a century ago.

In the year 2002, the McCormick Tract looks much the same as it did 100 years ago. The McCormick buildings are but a fleeting memory and the U.S. Forest Service continues to maintain the land as a wilderness preserve.

Access to the interior of the nature sanctuary is limited to a three-mile trail that connects County Road 607 (The Peshekee Grade) to White Deer Lake. Today, snowshoers, cross-country skiers, hikers, and fishermen enjoy the tract's rugged beauty, remote waterfalls, and unspoiled beauty; the essence of what Upper Michigan is all about.

Marquette Historian Fred Rydholm attempted to resurrect the old lodge in the late 1940s, but the extent of the lodge decomposition made recovery impossible. Rydholm was forced to abandon the project.

Library Acknowledgements

Bayliss Public Library – Sault Ste. Marie

Bessemer Public Library – Bessemer

Calumet Public Library – Calumet

Crystal Falls District Community Library – Crystal Falls

Dickinson County Library – Iron Mountain

Escanaba Public Library – Escanaba

Greenland Township Library – Mass City

Ironwood Carnegie Library – Ironwood

Ishpeming Carnegie Public Library – Ishpeming

John Longyear Research Library – Marquette

Manistique School and Public Library – Manistique

Menominee County Library – Stephenson

Munising School and Public Library – Munising

Negaunee Public Library – Negaunee

Ontonagon Township Library – Ontonagon

Peter White Public Library – Marquette

Portage Lake District Library – Houghton

St. Ignace Public Library – St. Ignace

Spies Public Library – Menominee

Tahquamenon Area Public Library – Newberry

Wakefield Public Library – Wakefield

West Iron District Library - Iron River